Israel Pocket Library

W9-CZD-410

HISTORY
until 1880

KETER BOOKS

This book is compiled from material originally published in the *Encyclopaedia Judaica*

CONTENTS

CONTRIBUTORS

Dr. Hanoch Reviv; Lecturer in Jewish History, the Hebrew University of Jerusalem

Dr. Bezalel Porten; Teaching Fellow in Jewish History, the Hebrew University of Jerusalem; Senior Lecturer in Biblical Studies, Haifa University

Prof. Menahem Stern; Professor of Jewish History, the Hebrew University of Jerusalem

Prof. Shmuel Safrai; Associate Professor of Jewish History, the Hebrew University of Jerusalem

Prof. Haïm Z'ew Hirschberg; Professor of Jewish History, Bar Ilan University, Ramat Gan

1 UNTIL THE MONARCHY

The Patriarchs of Israel. The beginning of the history of Israel, like that of many other nations, is obscure. The passage of time caused many features to fade from the memory of the people, while others were altered. Furthermore, the early period of Hebrew history, which was of decisive importance for Israel, did not leave any impressions on the environment in which the ancestors of Israel lived and functioned; and therefore, no external evidence concerning the beginning of the process of national consolidation has been found.

The Bible is the only source on the lives and activities of the Patriarchs, and the traditions it preserves about them are evaluated very differently by different scholars. There are some scholars who completely negate the historicity of the Patriarchs and their period, regarding the pertinent biblical data as myths or literary epics; while others discern in these stories cores of historical facts overgrown with later revision and editing. The difficulties that the biblical narratives raise for historical research relegate the dispute about the actual existence of the Patriarchs to a secondary place. At present, research is focusing on attempts to discover the period and the political, ethnic, and cultural background that was likely to have served as the setting for the emergence of the nation. The fixing of an exact period and background transforms figures such as the Patriarchs into real beings even if the question concerning the existence of the specific biblical personalities remains a matter of dispute. Because the Book of Genesis has been held to contain obscure chronological allusions, anachronistic descriptions (Philistines and Arameans; camels), and later adaptations, and redactions, no way has been found of utilizing it for

Tomb of the Middle Bronze Age (2000–1550 B.C.E.) at Jericho, containing household objects from the time of the Patriarchs. From K. M. Kenyon, *Excavation at Jericho,* Vol. I, London, 1960.

the purposes of chronology. Therefore, sources other than the Bible, such as epigraphical and archaeological finds from the Fertile Crescent, are employed as indirect proof of the reality reflected in the patriarchal narratives. Most scholars date the patriarchal period to the first half of the second millennium. It is during this period that West Semitic ("Amorite") elements began their migrations and movements in Mesopotamia. These West Semitic elements also increased their migrations west of the Euphrates, becoming nomads or settling in new, or already existing settlements. The Egyptian Execration Texts dating from the 19th–18th centuries B.C.E. provide clear evidence of the integration of these Western Semites in the city states of Syria and Palestine and of the existence of West Semitic rulers, especially in the plains and coastal areas which were then under Egyptian control. It can be seen that the mountain

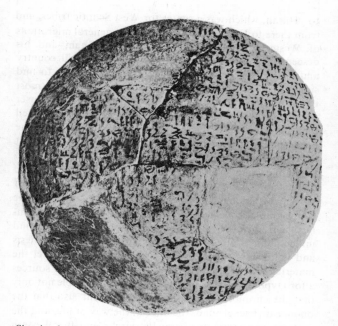

Shards of a pottery bowl found in Thebes, Upper Egypt, 19th–18th century B.C.E. inscribed with one of the Execration Texts. These contain maledictions on named enemies of Egypt, and mention cities and tribes under its control in the Palestine area. From K. Sethe, *Die Achtung Feindlicher Fursten, Voelker und Dinge auf Altaegyptischen Tongefaesscherben des mittleren Reiches,* Berlin, 1926.

regions, on the other hand, were underpopulated. Apparently the Western Semites reestablished the settlements in Transjordan and within a limited period (19th century B.C.E.) brought prosperity to the settlements in the Negev and Sinai along the routes to Egypt.

According to evidence provided in Genesis and in extra-biblical sources Abraham's family was of West Semitic origin. His migrations from Ur of the Chaldeans to Haran, which was a center for West Semitic tribes, and from there to Erez Israel, are part of the general migrations of Western Semites in that period. Abraham and his descendants traveled along the routes in the hill country and in the Negev. In these regions they were able to find subsistence and pasturage for their cattle and, most important, were able to avoid conflicts with the denser population in the plains and Egyptian garrisons stationed there. This description appears to be realistic in light of the urban picture that emerges from the Execration Texts. At the same time, the Patriarchs' sojourn in the Negev and their migration south to Egypt takes on a realistic dimension against the background of the existence of settlements along the trade routes in this period. The connection between the Patriarchs and the Western Semites, and their existence in the first half of the second millennium, is attested by a comparison between Genesis and written sources from Mesopotamia, which reflect the material and spiritual world of that period. Those sources afford typological parallels which make it probable not only that the chronological basis is the same but also that the onomastic background, the dialect, the way of life, and the customs are common to the Patriarchs and the Western Semites. Documents dating from about the 18th century B.C.E. found in the royal archives of Mari on the Middle Euphrates include useful evidence about organizations of West Semitic tribes, their patriarchal society, ways of life, leadership, and wanderings. Documents discovered at the Mesopotamian city of Nuzi shed light on various aspects of the family customs and laws that governed the households of Abraham, Isaac, and Jacob. The Nuzi documents illustrate the mixed Semitic and Hurrian society of Nuzi in the 15th–14th century B.C.E. It is generally assumed that those traditions preserved in these documents, which deal with family and judicial matters, were influenced by an ancient West Semitic tradition. According to another opinion, the connection between the Patriarchs and the way of life of Nuzi derives from another

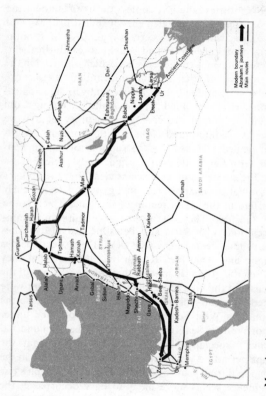

Map showing route of Abraham's wanderings and other main routes of the ancient East.

5

source, i.e., from the Hurrians who lived in the region of Haran in the 18th century B.C.E.

By the 19th century B.C.E. and perhaps even earlier, the first waves of Western Semites arrived in Egypt, at the southern edge of the Fertile Crescent. In the course of the following centuries these peoples declined under the pressure of foreign ethnical elements of Indo-European and Hurrian origin, who invaded certain regions of Mesopotamia, Syria, and Erez Israel and sought to establish themselves there. Allusions to these events, which occurred in the second quarter of the second millennium B.C.E., are preserved mainly in documents recovered by archaeological expeditions. However, an Egyptian tradition dating from the Hellenistic period preserved the memory of a wave of Western Semites and non-Semitic foreign groups which it called Hyksos, a corruption of an ancient Egyptian term for "rulers of foreign lands" referring to Asiatics. From later sources it seems clear that the Hyksos gained control over large areas in Egypt and set up their headquarters in the Delta region of the Nile, which is the biblical Goshen. They established an empire and maintained relations with Syria and Palestine. Royal dynasties were descended from them (XV–XVI Dynasties); names like Yaqob-har, Anat-har, Khyan, etc. indicate that they were of Semitic origin. It appears that the wanderings of the Patriarchs and the migration of Jacob's sons to Egypt were connected with the rule of the Hyksos there, because the migration of a West Semitic family to Egypt, then under control of Western Semites, could not have been an unusual occurrence, especially since it can be proved that the Egyptians permitted wandering shepherds to sojourn in the Delta region during years of famine. Further, Joseph's rise to prominence seems more likely to have occurred at the time of the Hyksos rule than during the native Egyptian rule, when cooperation with foreigners in many areas was avoided. The alien rule in Egypt ended in 1570 B.C.E., when the Hyksos were driven out by the natives. This date can serve as the *terminus ad quem* of the patriarchal period.

6

After the establishment of the New Kingdom in Egypt those political, ethnic, and social conditions which served as an ideal background for the activities of the ancient Hebrews no longer prevailed.

Another opinion places the patriarchal period at a later time, based on the accepted dating of the conquest of Canaan (13th century B.C.E., see below) and on genealogical and chronological data in the Bible, according to which Moses' generation is the fourth after Jacob. Thus, the 14th century was fixed as a suitable time for the patriarchal period. There are, however, gaps and inaccuracies in the chronological and genealogical data of the Bible, which are, moreover, mutually contradictory. Thus the number of years that the Hebrews sojourned in Egypt is given as 400 years (Gen. 15:13) or 430 years (Ex. 12:40), which is far more than four generations. In the light of the evidence it seems that the accepted dating of the patriarchal period is more accurate. The patriarchal narratives in Genesis describe the seminomadic way of life of the Patriarchs and their distinctive patriarchal society. The Patriarchs supported themselves by raising cattle, sheep, and goats (only Isaac engaged in seasonal agriculture in the western Negev, Gen. 26:12); they lived in tents in camps on the outskirts of the cities and were protected by the rulers of the sedentary population. They avoided mingling with the sedentary population, preserving their ethnic purity and their unique beliefs. Nevertheless, conflicts with the permanent elements sometimes could not be avoided (Gen. 34). Biblical accounts and non-biblical parallels do not strengthen the view accepted by other important scholars that the Patriarchs were caravan merchants active in the international trade conducted from north to south in the Fertile Crescent. Light is also shed on the sociological makeup of the Patriarchs by the connection between the biblical designation "Hebrew" and the appellation for the social class Ḫabiru (Ḫapiru) or 'Apiru, known from many sources, and current in the Ancient East over a long period. In the Bible non-Israelites called the Patriarchs and their descendants "Hebrews" (e.g., Gen. 39:17; 41:12) and the Israelites themselves used this name to identify themselves when dealing with foreigners (Gen. 40:15). Thus the name "Hebrew" came to designate Israel on the social level and did not refer to their obscure ethnic origin. If there is any comparison to be made between "Hebrew" and Ḥabiru, it is that the Hebrews belonged to this large class of people who were scattered over a wide area and consisted of nomads or vagabonds who lived on the margins and under the protection of societies whose laws did not apply to them. Their relation to their Canaanite hosts is that of *gerim* or metics (Gen. 23:4), and Canaan is the land of their *megurim* or sojourn as metics (Gen. 17:8; 28:4; 36:7; 37:1; 47:9; Ex. 6:4). From all that has been said thus far it may reasonably be assumed that the general term "Hebrew" (meaning the Ḥabiru) was applied only at a later stage to the tribes of Israel as a branch of this class and thus became an ethnic designation. It is possible that their non-Israelite neighbors, because they regarded the ancient Hebrews as a component of the general class of Ḥabiru, ignored those specific features which distinguished this small group from the other Ḥabiru and West Semitic elements.

The Exodus and Wanderings in Sinai. The Bible describes the Hebrews' migration to Egypt and their stay at Goshen as a favor bestowed upon them because of Joseph who had attained prominence in Egypt. There is no external evidence about their life and activities there. The Bible relates that after a certain period they were subjugated by the pharaohs. It is actually not unreasonable to suppose that after the expulsion of the Hyksos the Egyptians should have enslaved kindred Semitic elements still living in Egypt. Therefore the story of the slavery of the Israelites and their Exodus from Egypt should not be dismissed as unhistorical, especially since, as attested in an Egyptian papyrus, an occurrence such as the escape of the slaves from Goshen to the Sinai desert was not rare. It is of the utmost importance to fix accurately the date of the Exodus from Egypt, especially in light of the various traditions that are represented in the Bible. It should be noted in this connection that the enslaved Hebrews were exploited in order to build the cities of Pithom and Raamses (Ex. 1:11) and there is no doubt that these were built in the reign of Ramses II (c. 1290–24). This pharaoh built his new capital Per-Raʿmses (biblical Raamses) on the site of the ancient Hyksos capital. He also reconstructed Per-Atum (biblical Pithom). Also useful is the evidence found in an Egyptian papyrus, from the period of Ramses II, according to which the ʿApiru (Ḥabiru) participated in the building of Ramses' temple. From this it can be deduced that Pharaoh, the oppressor of the Israelites, "who knew not Joseph" (Ex. 1:8), is Ramses II. On the other hand a suitable background for the Exodus is the reign of just this pharaoh even if according to the biblical tradition it happened during the reign of the successor of pharaoh of the oppression (Ex. 2:23; cf. 15). It seems that the conflict of that period between the Hittites and Ramses II had an influence on the suppressed nomadic elements who took advantage of the events to escape from Egypt. Another possibility is that the Exodus from Egypt occurred during the reign of Merneptah, Ramses II's son. In a stele from the fifth year of his reign (c. 1220) celebrating Merneptah's defeat of his enemies in Ereẓ Israel, "Israel" is mentioned as a sedentary element, probably in the process of conquest. On the other hand, there are scholars who maintain that the mention of "Israel" in the stele refers to Israelite elements who never migrated to Egypt. Another opinion maintains that it hints at an earlier exodus from Egypt. The discussion of the Exodus is clearly connected with the Israelite Conquest of Canaan. As will be seen below, the main Conquest occurred in the 13th century B.C.E. This dating is also attested in the Bible (I Kings 6:1) which mentions 480 years between the Exodus from Egypt to the building of Solomon's Temple (c. 970 B.C.E.), a period of 12 generations according to the schematic biblical counting (cf. Ps.

95:10). A more realistic estimate of 12 generations as 300 years would place the Exodus in the 13th century (cf. Judg. 11:26).

The Exodus from Egypt left its imprint on the memory of the nation and became the symbol of the hope of liberation for all generations. Apparently many details about the Exodus and the journey in the desert were blurred, perhaps as a result of the special attitude of the Hebrews to these events. It is no wonder that legends and stories of miracles were combined with the account of these events. It is obvious that the main reason for the preservation of various traditions in the present form was the idea that the Exodus from Egypt was a divine act which preceded the revelation at Sinai, the dwelling place of the God of Israel where the Torah was given. According to tradition, the essence of Israel's uniqueness as the chosen people was expressed at the revelation at Sinai. Various analytical trends, especially those with fundamentalist inclinations, see in the revelation at Sinai those historic days when the tribes were consolidated into a nation and their monotheistic belief purified under the leadership of the outstanding personality—Moses.

No evidence has been found to support the miraculous biblical descriptions nor have the geographical aspects of the journey of the Hebrews in the Sinai desert been clarified yet. Even the location of the Red Sea, where Pharaoh and his soldiers died, and of Mt. Sinai, are unknown. These sites are usually established by reconstructions of the journeys. It would seem that there is no reason to doubt the reliability of the biblical account according to which the Hebrews did not choose the shortest way to Canaan "through the way of the land of the Philistines" (Ex. 13:17), i.e., the road along the seashore of the Mediterranean to Egypt. The reason they did not choose this route was that they wanted to avoid confrontation with the Egyptian forces stationed in the fortresses along "the way of the land of the Philistines" which defended the approaches to Egypt. The indirect journey was difficult and very long, and was dependent on

places with drinking water and oases. There is no doubt

Facsimile of stele of Seti I (c. 1313–1292 B.C.E.) found in Beth-Shean. The ninth and tenth lines mention "these Apiru [Ḥabiru] of the mountains of Jordan [Gilead]." The reference is to an attack by the Ḥabiru tribes. Jerusalem, Rockefeller Museum, Israel Department of Antiquities.

that the journey in the desert ended in Kadesh-Barnea, an oasis with abundant water in northwestern Sinai. From here the Israelites attempted to penetrate Canaan. On the basis of biblical descriptions and archaeological evidence it becomes obvious that those attempts to penetrate Canaan were actually part of a general phenomenon of invasion and settlement on the part of elements akin to the Hebrews that took place in this geographical area around this time, especially in Transjordan where permanent settlements were reestablished either at the end of the 14th century or in the 13th century B.C.E. by Ammon, Moab, Edom, and the Amorites. Egypt's inability to defend the border of the desert from nomadic tribes while she was involved in the war against the Hittites enabled those Western Semitic elements to consolidate in Transjordan, where settlements had ceased to exist a few centuries earlier.

The Conquest and Settlement of Canaan. There are grave difficulties in reconstructing the Conquest of Canaan by the tribes of Israel. The various biblical sources dealing with this subject are heterogeneous and there are many contradictory descriptions. Moreover, there are also inconsistencies in important details between these sources and archaeological finds. The biblical evidence, especially that which is found in Joshua, gives the impression that it had gone through a selective and unified editing. It is possible that the national memory, too, followed the same process, so that different traditions, which existed among various tribes or in different places, were reduced to a common denominator, until an "official" version of the history of the Conquest was formulated. This version represents the Conquest as a single campaign that was conducted according to an earlier plan which distributed the country in advance and was led by a sole leader, Moses, and later Joshua. Apart from this version there is other evidence that points to an entirely different situation. This evidence is to be found especially in Judges 1 and indirectly in the genealogical lists at the beginning of I Chronicles, in poetic compositions, and in other sources. The contradictory evidence points to a relatively long, heterogeneous process of conquest, which lacked advance planning, and in which individual tribes or tribal groups gradually conquered their territories, leaving Canaanite enclaves which had not been conquered at all (including towns which are mentioned in the Book of Joshua as having been conquered). It seems that contemporary reality necessitated a slow, continuous series of conquests and it is precisely this reality which emerges from the evidence that contradicts the "official" version.

Kadesh-Barnea, which marked the end of the journey of the tribes of Israel in the desert, was also the starting point of the Israelite attempts to enter Canaan. Probably at a certain stage they tried to go north straight to the Negev but they were deterred by a chain of Canaanite fortresses (Num. 14:40–45; 21:1–9; Deut. 1:43–46). This failure made them seek new solutions. The beginning of the process of conquest apparently occurred at the end of the 14th century B.C.E. and continued during the 13th century B.C.E. The biblical tradition about the Conquest of Transjordan places this event approximately at the beginning of the settlement of Ammon, Moab, and Edom (Num. 21:21), while Merneptah's stele from about 1220 indicates that during that year the Conquest was still in progress (see above). Two different traditions about the mode and journeys of the Conquest are found in the Bible. The best-known one is that which appears in Numbers 20:14ff., according to which the Israelites circumvented Edom because its ruler did not allow them to pass through his country. They therefore penetrated through a weak point in Transjordan, which was the Amorite kingdom of Heshbon, whose king Sihon had conquered the territory from the first Moabite king (Num. 21:21ff.). The Amorites' presence in eastern Transjordan is explained, according to one theory, as a southern migration of certain elements from the kingdom of Amurru in central Syria, in consequence of the battle between the Hittites and the Egyptians during Ramses II's reign. From here on, the tribes of Israel succeeded in 13 enlarging their holdings east of the Jordan as far as Bashan.

Another tradition was preserved in Numbers 33, which records the Israelites' march right through Edom and Moab and lists their stations on the way to Jericho. In the description of this route there is no mention of the kingdoms of Transjordan or of the bypassing of the populated areas on the desert's border as recorded in the previous tradition. In light of the contradiction between the two traditions, the following supposition arises. There were probably two waves of penetration into Canaan. The earlier one proceeded without difficulties along the plateau of Transjordan to Jericho, at a time when this area was still desolate, i.e., the end of the 14th century B.C.E. The second wave could not follow the same route because of the new kingdoms which had been established there in the meantime; it therefore had to bypass Edom and Moab and then force its way through the Amorite kingdom north of the Arnon. The time of this second wave was thus later, probably the 13th century. Although this supposition contradicts the spirit of the biblical texts whose aim is to produce a picture of a unified conquest, it offers a solution to the contradiction between the two traditions without negating either of them. It also supports and supplements the above-mentioned passages which suggest a complex and long drawn-out process of conquest. The two waves of migration to Canaan suggest that there may have been two waves of Exodus from Egypt, and perhaps also two wanderings in the wilderness of Sinai, especially when the abortive attempt to penetrate the Negev and the bypassing of Edom are attributed to the second wave. It is difficult to decide about the components of these waves. Although it is generally accepted that they consisted of the tribes of Leah, Rachel, and the concubines, scholars disagree as to the order in which these groups entered Canaan. Some assume that the Leah tribes migrated first, though according to the order of the earlier journey, which terminated at Jericho as mentioned in Numbers 33, it is more likely that the Rachel tribes (called also "The House of Joseph") were those who first invaded Canaan, the land west of the Jordan, without stopping on its east bank. Therefore, it would be a mistake to assume that the campaigns of these two waves were carried out according to the schematic description in Joshua. It seems more likely that these were "waves" in a very broad sense, and neither of them was necessarily a unified and planned undertaking. It seems that the waves of penetration were actually a pattern which points to frequent penetrations of individual tribes or groups of tribes.

The archaeological finds usually support the biblical evidence concerning the Conquest, except for a few instances of inconsistency. Research has not yet disclosed acceptable solutions to these inconsistencies: 1) The description of the conquest of Ai by Joshua is contradicted by the fact that this place was desolate during the period of the Israelite penetration of Canaan (Josh. 7–8). It is possible that it was confused with the neighboring Beth-El (cf. Judg. 1:22ff.). 2) The dramatic description of the conquest of Jericho (Josh. 5–6) is not proportionate to the archaeological evidence which shows that Jericho was a small unwalled and unimportant town. On the other hand, archaeological finds in various sites of Erez Israel and surveys clearly indicate that many towns (as Beth-El, Tell Beit Mirsim, Beth-Shemesh, Eglon, Hazor, etc.) were destroyed during the 13th century and at the beginning of the 12th century B.C.E. Small and impoverished settlements were established on the ruins of these towns by people whose standard of material culture was below that of the former population. Some were established in the same period in which the towns were destroyed, while others were established later. In addition, during this period new settlements were established on entirely new sites by the same impoverished elements. It should be noted that the destruction of the Canaanite towns did not occur during a short period; this also fits into the picture of a gradual Conquest by separate conquering units. From the archaeological finds it becomes clear that the Israelites failed to conquer the whole country, and that Canaanite enclaves remained (e.g., Shechem), 15 which were conquered later and not during the period which is described as the period of the Conquest. This fact, too, corroborates the testimony of the biblical texts which contradict the version of a single planned campaign.

DETAILS OF SETTLEMENT. The Conquest of Canaan and the settlement of the tribes of Israel in the land actually constituted one continuous process, with no intervening lapses. For this reason the account of the Conquest has to be accompanied by the description of the settlement in Canaan. The biblical sources make possible only a partial reconstruction, along general lines, of the conquest and the settlement. The tribes of Rachel proceded from Jericho through Gilgal to the central hill country northward to Shechem. Manasseh settled in the territory north of Shechem and later expanded to the plains and Transjordan. It is likely that the tribe of Manasseh became consolidated in the course of the settlement through the unification of strong sub-tribal units. Ephraim settled between Manasseh's territory and the region north of Beth-El. The small tribe of Benjamin was confined into a narrow strip of land between Ephraim and a chain of Canaanite cities in the south, and Hivite cities in the west (Chephirah, Kiriath-Jearim, Beeroth, Gibeon) which the Israelites did not conquer and with which they even made alliances (Josh. 9:3). It seems that the settlement of the "House of Joseph" tribes and their connection with the Hivite cities endangered the position and existence of the Canaanite kingdom of Jerusalem and its allies in the south. They waged war but were defeated (Josh. 10:1ff.). The Leah tribes constituted, as mentioned above, the second wave of conquerors and settlers. Some of them, Reuben and Gad, settled in Transjordan. Reuben maintained its seminomadic way of life on the eastern fringe of Gilead (I Chron. 5:9–10). Gad, on the other hand, settled south of the Jabbok and from there expanded to the north. The rest of the Leah tribes went west. Judah and Simeon together crossed the central Jordan and then went south through the territories of the "House of Joseph." At first, Judah succeeded in conquering

Jerusalem but failed to keep it for long. It was then conquered by the Jebusites, an ethnic element of northern (Anatolian?) origin. Judah came close to the seashore but there too failed to keep the conquered territory. Its original territory was between Hebron and Beth-Lehem. Judah absorbed, in a prolonged process of assimilation, kindred ethnic elements, which they conquered or which had settled in the south before Judah reached it. While Simeon settled in the Negev, it never became a permanently settled tribe, but continued to lead a seminomadic life. In the course of time part of its territory was absorbed into that of Judah. Other Leah tribes settled in the north. Less is known of their mode of conquest and settlement. Asher settled in western Galilee and expanded toward the seashore from the Carmel to Tyre. There is a special problem in connection with this tribe, because of the mention of the name "Asher" in Egyptian sources—an indication that the tribe had been in Canaan before the conquest. Some scholars deduce from this that this tribe was not among those who went to Egypt. Issachar settled in southeastern Galilee and in a small area of the Shephelah. There are some scholars who assume that this tribe too had been in Canaan before the Conquest, on the basis of the Beth-Shean stele of Seti I (beginning of the 13th century) which mentions alien ʿApiru (Ḥabiru) in terri-tory which is included in Issachar's lands. Naphtali settled in central and eastern Galilee, the Jordan Valley, and Chinneroth Valley. Zebulun settled mainly in southwest-ern Lower Galilee.

The location of the new Israelite territory and also the success of the Conquest raised many questions. Various political and geographic conditions aided the Israelites. Egypt's inability to deal with the specific problems of Canaan in that period left the population defenseless against invaders who employed special tactics appropriate to their social structure, fighting skill, and armament. However, it should not be forgotten that the Israelites' success in conquering Canaan was limited, insofar as they failed to occupy the plains, whose dense population was 17 defended by strong fortresses and chariots which the tribes could not overcome (e.g., Josh. 17:16–18). Moreover, it is not impossible that the Egyptians intentionally concentrated their defense on vital interests in those regions which seemed to them decisively important: the districts along the routes of communication which passed through the plains and along the coast. Actually the tribes of Israel occupied only the hill country where the Canaanites were not able to use their chariots and the southern regions that were underpopulated or not populated at all. The Israelites also had to face the resistance of the Canaanite settlements which were within the borders of their territories. They succeeded in conquering only part of them. In light of facts found in various passages of Joshua and in Judges 1, it becomes obvious that in a few places Israelites were subjugated by the Canaanites. The general picture of the settlement points to four Israelite regions, separated by narrow strips of fortified Canaanite cities. This picture, as is known, follows the topographic structure of Palestine and emphasizes the contrast between the population of the mountainous regions and the population of the plains. The northern region of settlement was bordered on the south by a strip of plains (Jezreel and Beth-Shean) with fortifications ranged from Beth-Shean to Megiddo. Further, even in the territories of the northern tribes there were numerous Canaanite enclaves which undermined the unity of the Israelites; the large block of central mountains was between the Canaanites of the valleys and the chain of Canaanite fortresses in the south, starting with Jerusalem and ending in Gezer. This chain separated the central tribes from the southern tribes. Between these three blocks and the Israelite settlements in the east there was a natural border—the Jordan. Thus, the Canaanite fortresses interrupted the continuity of the Israelite settlement and prevented close contact among the groups of tribes. This isolation created specific local developments in each group of tribes and weakened their attachments to one another. It is noteworthy that the break between the central and southern tribes

18

The limits of Israelite control in the time of the Judges (12th century B.C.E.). After Y. Aharoni, *Carta's Atlas of the Bible*.

Area of Israelite Control

was so absolute that even the most reliable biblical sources (including the "Song of Deborah") do not mention the tribe of Judah at all as a component of the tribal alliance during the period of settlement.

Within the framework of the limited Israelite territory there began, according to the archaeological finds and surveys, a process of transition from the nomadic way of life to a permanent agricultural mode of life in small, generally unwalled settlements. They were faced with grave difficulties, in particular a lack of fields suitable for cultivation and a shortage of water. As a consequence, the settlers had to cut down the forests within their territories (Josh. 17:14–18). Archaeological research shows that the settlement was, to a great extent, made possible by a special technique of waterproof lime-plastered cisterns. In this way the Israelites were not tied down to the few available sources of water but could settle in areas which had never been settled before, thus expanding their borders. The Israelite settlement in the mountains was also facilitated by the use of iron implements which began about this period. Implements made of hard metal enabled the settlers to cultivate their fields more efficiently.

The settlement of the Israelites was accompanied by shifts and movements of tribal and sub-tribal units both within and without the tribe's territory. A variety of reasons motivated these units to seek new territories, including lack or shortage of land suitable for cultivation, pressure from Israelite or alien neighbors, etc. Evidence for such events is found especially in the genealogical lists in the Bible and in particular in I Chronicles 1–11. In the genealogical lists are included fragments of information and various traditions about tribal and sub-tribal movements. These genealogies give information on their wanderings, their attachments with (and separations from) kindred or alien elements, and their elevation and decline. The tribal genealogy was constructed in a schematic way using familial terminology. This clarifies various phenomena such as the affiliation of clans and families to two tribes which obviously attests the transition of tribes from one territory to another. Such relations existed between Judah and Reuben (cf. e.g., Josh. 7:18 with Num. 26:6) and between Asher, Ephraim, and Benjamin (Josh. 16:3; I Sam. 9:4; 13:17), among others. It is also known that Manassite families in the west migrated to Transjordan and that families from Ephraim moved in the same direction (II Sam. 18:6). A good example of the migration of a family-tribal unit is Dan who, because it was compressed between the territories of its brother tribes and of alien inhabitants of the plains, moved to the northern border of the Israelite territory (Judg. 18). As mentioned above, echoes of the absorption of alien elements into Israelite tribal units or territories are preserved in genealogical lists, in the terminology of matrimonial relations and by tracing their lineage to the ancestor of the tribe. Most instructive are the genealogical lists of the tribe of Judah which are very complicated (I Chron. 2:4:1–23). These lists show Judah's affiliation with Canaanite, Edomite, Horite, and Gileadite groups.

Similar affiliations and assimilation can be found also in the tribe of Manasseh, whose genealogy reflects the absorption of Canaanite territories. One can assume that the changes in the status of the tribes, the description of their achievements, their territories, and occupations as they appear in the Blessing of Jacob (Gen. 49), the Blessing of Moses (Deut. 33), and the Song of Deborah (Judg. 5) reflect changes that took place within the tribes during the settlement period. It seems, however, that the territories of the tribes as consolidated and written down in Joshua reflect a later period.

SOME RESULTS OF SETTLEMENT. The settlement of the tribes of Israel in Canaan brought about an essential change in their economy: the wandering shepherds became settled farmers and craftsmen. An important question is how and to what extent the settlement influenced the social structure of the Israelites, their tribal and sub-tribal organizations, and the intertribal relations. The Israelite society was essentially patriarchal-tribal, a fact which is reflected in their customs. In essence the patriarchal order persisted among the Israelites throughout the biblical period. Biblical society, however, was deeply attached to the nomadic way of life and its characteristic traditions. It seems that it was in the nomadic period that the small Israelite units with ethnic family ties and common traditions united into tribal structures. There is no doubt that the tribe remained the largest and most important political and social unit in the period of the Conquest as well. However, the transition to permanent settlement left its impact on the tribe and its leadership. The confrontation with permanent culture and its needs brought about changes in the relationships between various components of the tribe. Likewise the concept of tribal leadership changed earlier. The new challenges in the period of the Conquest brought about changes in all levels of leadership insofar as the patriarchal leadership had to adapt itself to the conditions of permanent settlement. Although the patriarchal pattern survived, the criteria for electing this leadership underwent changes. Although there are not many references to social problems in biblical sources much can be learned by reading between the lines about the decline of the tribe and the emergence of the largest sub-tribal unit—the family, with the parallel rise of the power of the clan. It seems that intertribal relationships weakened as a result of the conditions of settlement. Israel in Canaan was a group of tribes with weak political attachments. It was not a firmly consolidated framework with distinct political aims and characteristics.

There is disagreement among scholars as to how the unification of the tribes into a nation took place. One trend in research regards the revelation at Sinai as the time when the tribes became a nation. Another trend is of the opinion that the settlement period was the formative stage in national consolidation. While the settlement period did, indeed, bring about changes, it is more likely that national consolidation took place in a later period, but in a literary-historical form was projected upon the settlement period and earlier. Nevertheless, it would be a mistake to assume that the tribes of Israel consisted of entirely separated and disconnected units. There were still common elements of vital importance: ethnic affinity, consanguinity, and a common religious-cultic tradition. This common tradition in its widest sense was able to take the place of the national consciousness that was lacking. These factors prompt a search for patterns of intertribal or supra-tribal organization that emphasizes the common elements among tribes without confronting the problem of political unity. Several possibilities have been advanced. One of the strongest propositions which has stimulated positive and negative responses maintained that there existed a supra-tribal organization, like the Amphictyony in ancient Greece and among the Etruscans in Italy. This organization with cultic-religious and political objectives united the tribes of Israel around a mobile sanctuary where the Ark of the Covenant was placed. The biblical sources do not offer much evidence in support of the existence of such an organization. There were, however, a number of tribal actions, as for example the narrative of the concubine in Gibeah (Judg. 19ff.), which give the impression that there actually existed some such supra-tribal organization. As is known, it illustrates an episode of internal conflict among the tribes and supra-tribal pressure on Benjamin. Moreover, the schematic pattern of 12 tribes, which always remains unchanged even if its components undergo changes—a fact which can be interpreted as the worship of the tribes around a sanctuary throughout the year—is a factor that cannot easily be ignored.

The Judges. The changes that Israel underwent are expressed in the characteristic features of its leadership. Most instructive is the fact that during the period of settlement there was no one leader of all the tribes or national leader—a clear indication that an overall national consciousness had not crystallized.

Nevertheless, the settlement period laid the foundation for a new type of leadership institution which had not   23 existed previously. As it was a product of the period it rose and declined with it. The Bible defines the new type of leader as "judge." To the judge and his period a whole biblical book was dedicated, i.e., the Book of Judges.

This book is the only source of information about characteristics of the judge as a leader—his qualities and activities. However, Judges is only a selection of stories concerning a few judges, and does not describe all the judges who lived and functioned nor all the events that occurred in this period. These stories were included in the book in a pragmatic pattern and were edited so as to stress the overall national character of the judges' activity. According to the available data, all these tendentious ingredients date from a later period. It is obvious that the judge was the answer to the problem of leadership which appeared at a particular stage of the settlement period, when the neighbors started to react to Israel's existence in Canaan, in the hope of taking advantage of the weakness and disunity of the tribes. The judge was first of all a prominent tribal leader who was elevated to this position in time of crisis when an external menace threatened his tribe's existence. His period of leadership was limited to the time that was needed to subjugate the enemy. Authority was given to the judge by the traditional leaders of the tribe. He was also impelled by the spirit of God so that he would succeed in his activities and that the faith of the people in his political and military skill would be strengthened. The divine favor that descended upon the judge increased his influence and authority over the tribe. Since the task of the judge was completed when the objective which made his leadership necessary had been attained, the principles of inheritance or pedigree which characterized the typical tribal leadership were not applied. This type of judging is not, as one might think, identical with the office of a judge in court. The Book of Judges presents two prototypes of the judges: 1) The charismatic leader, the "deliverer," who goes out to war against the enemies and defeats them (six: 24 Othniel, Ehud, Deborah, Gideon, Jephthah, Samson). 2) The "minor" judge who did not accomplish heroic deeds on the battlefield but who possessed tribal pedigree (Judg. 10:1-5; 12:8-15). It appears that these two types of judges were current during the period which is named after them. This period probably was at a later stage in the settlement period.

Insufficient chronological evidence makes it difficult for the historian to reconstruct the dates of the events recounted in Judges. The same applies to the order of the judges from the point of view of their time and activity. In only isolated cases is it possible to show that a certain event preceded another one. Anyway, it is obvious that the order in which the stories concerning the judges appear is not necessarily parallel to any chronological order.

The background of the activity of the first judge, Othniel son of Kenaz, who fought against Chushan-Rishathaim king of Aram-Naharaim, is not all clear (Judg. 3:8-10). According to one theory his deliverance was connected with the invasion of the territory of Judah by a northern ruler in the 12th century B.C.E. Another opinion is that the reference is to an Edomite ruler. No less vague is the background of the deliverance story of Ehud son of Gera and the period in which it took place. There was, apparently, a Moabite invasion of Cisjordan which subjugated the territory of Benjamin (Judg. 3:12ff.). Taking advantage of the weakness and disunity of the Israelites, the Moabites succeeded in occupying parts of their territories in the center of the country for some time.

The section dealing with Samson belongs to a comparatively early period (Judg. 13-16). The historical nucleus of this episode is obscure, as a result of the literary-legendary nature of the stories. One can recognize that the background of the traditions about Samson are connected with the period marking the beginning of Philistine settlement; in any case, it took place before the migration of the tribe of Dan to the north (see above).

Another episode that attained special notice is the conflict between the tribes of Israel and the Canaanite 25 element. It is possible that the battle of Deborah and Barak against the Canaanites illustrates a central event of the settlement period, a consequence of which was the liberation of the northern block of tribes from the increased pressure of the Canaanite chariotry. In the light of the parallel account in Joshua (Josh. 11:1ff.), this narrative presents many difficulties which have increased with the excavations at Hazor. According to one opinion Hazor and Jabin are a later addition to the story, and the Canaanite elements who took part in the battle were from the entrances to the valley of Jezreel. The Canaanite army was defeated in a battle at the foot of Mt. Tabor by Israelite troops, who took advantage of topographic and climatic advantages. Relatively many Israelite tribes participated in this battle (all the central and some of the northern tribes). In their victory they destroyed the Canaanite hegemony in the north including the valley of Jezreel. Moreover, for the first time territorial continuity was established between the northern tribes and the group of central tribes (Judg. 4–5).

The battle of Deborah and Barak should be dated, it seems, to the second half of the 12th century B.C.E. when the Philistines were in the country. This conclusion is based on the fact that the battle is recorded after mention is made of the judge Shamgar son of Anath who fought against the Philistines, and also on the fact that the tribe of Dan is mentioned as living in its northern territory. Another consideration is that Taanach in the Song of Deborah is mentioned as being "by the waters of Megiddo." This testifies to the latter's destruction which has been proved to have taken place in the last quarter of the 12th century B.C.E.

The Canaanite opposition was broken, and this destroyed the fragile balance of power in the north. There were no more Canaanite fortresses to stand in the way of peoples who looked enviously upon the fertile fields of the plains. The raiders of the border regions of the desert, being aware of the new situation, poured across the Jordan on their way west. The Midianites, and those accompanying them (Judg. 6:3-5; 7:12), plundered the Canaanite and Israelite settlements. The Israelites were the greater sufferers, since they lived in unwalled settlements until they were delivered by Gideon's troop which was supported by Gideon's tribe Manasseh and by the northern tribes. Gideon decisively defeated the Midianites and pursued them into Transjordan.

The Bible relates that after Gideon's victory he was offered the kingship, but he declined the royal honor (Judg. 8:22-23). However, there are many indications in the stories about Gideon that he still occupied a high position after his task was accomplished, some of which may be interpreted as signs of kingship: his receiving a portion of the spoil of the tribes, his marrying many women, and his making Ophrah, his hometown, into a religious center by erecting a sanctuary there in which he placed an ephod (Judg. 8:24-27). In addition, there are allusions to political and military control that he exercised over the Canaanite city of Shechem. After Gideon's death, his son Abimelech (Judg. 9) attempted to succeed to his position by utilizing the relations his father had with Shechem, his mother's native city. After disposing of all potential rivals to the succession, he attempted to exert his authority over Shechem by forming an alliance with the city's nobility. He also planned to maintain his authority among the Israelite tribes. However, Abimelech's efforts ended in failure with the destruction of Shechem (which is attested by the Bible and archaeological excavations at the site), shortly after which he died.

The Israelites' offer of kingship to Gideon has often been interpreted as the first sign of a change in the attitude of tribal leadership toward centralized rule—a change whose results were not felt until later. Scholars have seen in the Abimelech episode an experiment in imitating non-Israelite rule, and the creation of a transitional stage between a tribal order and a monarchy. However, these two stories concerning Gideon and Abimelech are actually only isolated episodes which had no sequel. Thus it is difficult to 27 deduce from them to what extent they were the precursors of the establishment of monarchy in Israel, although they are instructive in their own right.

At the end of the 12th century or the beginning of the 11th century B.C.E. Ammon in eastern Transjordan became stronger, thus endangering the existence of Israelite settlers there. The elders of Gilead turned to Jephthah and his troop for assistance against the Ammonites and in return they bestowed a special position upon him (Judg. 10:17ff.). At first Jephthah attempted to settle the dispute by means of diplomacy, but when that failed, he repelled the Ammonites, but did not defeat them completely. It seems that not long after, the Ammonites once again attacked the Israelite territory in the Gilead in the time of Samuel and Saul.

2 KINGDOMS OF JUDAH
   AND ISRAEL

Samuel and Saul: The Beginnings of Israelite Monarchy.
The heavy Philistine subjection of Israel provoked resistance among the two most oppressed tribes, Benjamin and
Ephraim. Given the nature of Israel's tribal organization, it
was natural that the centers of resistance were in the hill
country, where the influential spiritual leader Samuel, the
seer, was active and guided the spirit of rebellion. Among
Samuel's activities was the first active attempt to overthrow
Philistine rule—an Israelite rally at Mizpah attacked the
enemy and forced them to withdraw temporarily to the
Shephelah (I Sam. 7:7–12). Their oppression again brought
home to the tribes the advantages of centralized government, which they had already felt in dealing with the
neighboring Canaanite city-states. The division inherent in
the weak tribal organization that led to defeat in the
Israelites' confrontation with well-organized forces which
functioned on the principle of centralization encouraged a
disposition to exchange the traditional leadership of the
elders, and even the charismatic leadership of the judges,
for a stronger leadership which on the one hand would
embody the qualities of a leader who rallied the tribes, and
on the other convert his leadership into a permanent
institution. There appears to have been a desire among the
Israelites for leadership based first and foremost on military
capabilities, with authority succeeding by inheritance, in the
spirit of the suggestion made to Gideon. It is doubtful that
the intention was to establish a ruler modeled on the
example of the Canaanite king.

Samuel, to whom the leaders of the people turned to

anoint a king over them, opposed the concepts widespread among the Israelites, but finally agreed. It is not surprising that the first Israelite king, Saul, resembled the charismatic judges, at the same time clearly displaying the qualities of being a ruler like those of "all the other nations." His selection was no doubt related to his military leadership exhibited in the liberation of Jabesh-Gilead, a city with blood and family ties to Benjamin, Saul's own tribe. The biblical description of Saul's anointment as king is not sufficiently explicit, however, as to whether his anointment did, in fact, result from his war with the Ammonites in northern Gilead. Considering the fact that Benjamin was still subject to the rule of the Philistines of the Shephelah, it is surprising that there is no mention of intervention on their part in the activities of Saul. It seems that they considered them only a local matter. After a brief period of organization, however, Saul turned his power in their direction. Near Michmas, northeast of Jerusalem, the Philistine armies were routed and driven back to Philistia. Their control of the mountain areas was thus broken, although the Philistines remained a threat to Israel throughout Saul's life. The battles were renewed periodically, since the Philistines did not easily relinquish their hold on Israelite territories. In one attack the Philistine armies penetrated to the vale of Elah, where David, a young warrior from Bethlehem in Judah, defeated Goliath (I Sam. 17) while the soldiers from both sides watched the battle between them.

The expulsion of the Philistines marked the beginning of Saul's career. He then had to assert his authority over the Israelite population of the central mountain area and unite the tribes under his rule. It is in this context that his uprooting of the foreign enclaves in his tribe's portion—the Hivite cities which remained as a result of their covenant with Joshua and the elders—must be seen. From biblical accounts of his wars with Moab, Ammon, Edom, the kings of Zobah (I Sam. 14:47), and possibly the Hagrites (I Chron. 5:10) in Transjordan, it is possible to conclude that

Saul tried to attract the Israelite tribes in Transjordan by protecting them. He also fought the Amalekites who had penetrated into Judah, again to win this tribe over to him (I Sam. 15). The break between Saul and Samuel was exposed in this war, as the latter was dissatisfied with Saul's usurpation of authority, which he saw as offensive to sacred practices and to God's authority over Israel.

The Bible does not tell much about Saul's tactics in organizing his kingdom. It appears that he lacked sufficient time, or otherwise could not manage, to establish a truly central authority. He continued to rely upon the traditional tribal structures and institutions, raising members of his own family to important positions. There are, however, some signs of centralization during his rule, e.g., an indication of taxation and of royal landholdings from which Saul distributed property to his officers and others who were close to him. Of special significance is the establishment of a standing army, which was with him in his capital, Gibeath-Shaul (whose fortifications were rebuilt after its capture from the Philistines). Saul's concept of monarchy is also evidenced by his ambition to establish a dynasty of his descendants.

One of the most dramatic and moving sections of the Bible concerns Saul's relationship with David, who became a well-known military officer, the king's son-in-law, and friend of Jonathan, the heir apparent. David was forced to flee from Saul to the border regions of Judah and later as far as Gath, in Philistia. During his wanderings he gathered about him various elements which he fashioned into a band of warriors. They helped protect the border settlements, and lived off the contributions earned from those thus protected. During his stay in Gath, David received Ziklag as a landholding and fortress, ranging out from there against tribes that endangered the population. It was there that he began to develop relations with the elders of Judah, who followed Saul.

Achish, king of Gath, and the Philistine chiefs prevented David and his band from joining the battle near Jezreel, 31 where Saul and his sons died. In this war the Philistine armies penetrated the mountain area, with the Canaanite fortifications in the valley serving as their rear and support. This is yet another indication of how the Philistine hegemony extended far beyond the Shephelah base. Philistine rule over the central tribes was reestablished with the defeat of Saul. For this reason Eshbaal (Ish-Bosheth), the son of Saul, was able to reign only in Gilead—a region that kept faith with the line of their benefactor. The Bible lists the areas and tribes over which Eshbaal reigned, but these almost certainly reflect the kingdom of Saul, rather than of Eshbaal: Gilead, the Ashurites (=Asherites), Jezreel (the territory of Manasseh in the hills and that of the other tribes in the valley), Ephraim, Benjamin, and over "all Israel" (II Sam. 2:9).

The United Kingdom: David. After the death of Saul, David settled in Hebron, the center of his own tribe, Judah. He was crowned by the elders of Judah, who had not accepted the monarchy until then. Within a few years he ruled over the rest of the tribes of Israel (II Sam. 5:5), which accepted his authority especially after Eshbaal's failure to establish his kingdom in Transjordan. At about the same time he captured Jerusalem from the Jebusites, converting it into the capital of the kingdom and the estate of the Davidic dynasty. This conquest revealed David's far-reaching ambitions and statesmanship, for Jerusalem in Israelite hands served as the desired unifying bond between the southern tribes—Simeon and Judah—and their brothers in the north. The new capital stood at the very heart of the kingdom, yet because it was outside the Israelite territory it did not serve as a focal point of strife among the tribes or lead to charges of favoritism.

With this decisive step David's aims became clear to the Philistines. It appears that until then they had hoped to rule over Judah by means of a vassal in Hebron. Now, however, they brought their army to the very gates of Jerusalem and were defeated by David (II Sam. 5:17–21). Another attempt that threatened to cut off Ephraim and Benjamin from

David ended in failure; the Philistine force was broken and pursued to Gezer (II Sam. 5:22-25). The Philistines ceased to be a military power of any importance, and the route to the Shephelah was open to David. There is not much detailed evidence on how David exercised control over the Philistine cities. It appears that he did not actually conquer them, but maintained some type of loose control by means of which he received tributes and taxes, which served as a symbol of their subjugation. Even David's benefactor Achish, king of Gath, became an Israelite vassal (I Kings 2:39; I Chron. 18:1).

With the removal of this major military obstacle, David was able to take the first step toward converting his kingdom into a united national state—the creation of territorial continuity of all the tribes. In pursuing this goal David conquered foreign enclaves along the seacoast and in the fertile Jezreel and Beth-Shean valleys. A similar fate befell the non-Israelite population of Galilee. He also turned to eastern Transjordan in order to establish his rule over Ammon and Moab, which were endangering Israelite settlements there and controlled long stretches of the international "King's Highway." The Israelite threat also involved the Aramean kingdoms in Transjordan and Syria, which were summoned to the aid of Moab and Ammon. These allies were defeated by the Israelites, though not annihilated. After they recruited reinforcements from across the river they met David in battle and were routed this time (II Sam. 10:6-19). Vast territory fell to David—Transjordan and the Aramean kingdoms, including the valley of Lebanon. The Israelite borders now reached to Hamath, north of the valley and, judging by the borders at the beginning of Solomon's reign, David must have extended his rule as far as Tiphsah on the Euphrates (I Kings 5:4).

The Israelite empire established during David's reign became a major political and economic factor in Palestine and Syria. It bordered on two seas—the Mediterranean and the Red Sea—and two highways for international commerce, the "Via Maris" and the "King's Highway," traversed its length. It must be added that the existence and strengthening of David's kingdom was made possible not only by Israelite military initiative and the endeavors of its king, but also by a convenient international situation. During David's rule, the two traditional centers of power of the ancient Near East, Egypt and Mesopotamia, were on the decline. Thus, David was able to protect his achievements and conquests. David strengthened his rule by means other than military ones. He wisely established friendly relations that were reinforced by treaties with the kingdoms of Hamath and Tyre. The treaty with Hiram, king of Tyre, was particularly important because of the economic advantages flowing from connection with this maritime-commercial power to the Israelite position in international trade.

In the field of internal organization David concentrated his activities on the establishment of an administrative apparatus suitable for the needs of the kingdom and the conquered territories. He understood the necessity of uniting the tribes round his throne and the capital, Jerusalem. He had the requisite organizational and executive abilities necessary to create proper tools.

It is difficult to determine what model was used to lay the foundation for the Israelite administration at the beginning of David's reign. It seems that the administration inherited from Saul was not developed and was not on a much higher plane than the traditional tribal institutions. It is reasonable to assume that as a Philistine vassal, David studied means of government, but it is almost certain that he was also influenced by the organizational structure of the non-Israelite cities in Palestine, especially that of Jebusite Jerusalem which he had conquered. It appears that the traditional administrative institutions of these cities were well adapted to the needs of a national monarchy consisting of tribes. (It is difficult to suppose, as do some scholars, that David built his administration according to an Egyptian prototype.) It
is not surprising, therefore, that some of David's highest

officials came from among non-Israelite elements, as they were experienced experts in tasks that had not been practiced in Israel in the absence of a court (II Sam. 5:11-18; 20:23-26; II Chron. 2:15-17). Candidates for such positions and others in institutions that had not existed in Israel until then, such as the institution of levy (corvée), could not easily be found. It is instructive, however, that control of the military forces remained in the hands of a relative of David, Joab, and Israelites close to him.

The vast conquests and consequent incomes required placing the king's lands and properties on a firm base. A special staff, which also employed foreign experts (I Chron. 27:25-31), was formed to oversee royal properties throughout the land. Among David's outstanding achievements was the integration of levites in administrative affairs. They were located in key religious and administrative centers, especially in sensitive areas of the kingdom. There were 48 of these cities, known as "cities of the levites" (or Levitical Cities), four for each tribe. As defined in the Bible, the task of the levites was to be responsible "for all the work of the Lord and for the service of the king" and "for every matter pertaining to God and for the affairs of the king" (I Chron. 26:30, 32). There is no doubt that the literacy of the levites and their religious-moral authority could be of service to the kingdom and the monarchy if properly exploited or channeled, and it would seem that David succeeded in doing so.

It appears that the division of the kingdom into 12 administrative districts—known from Solomon's time (I Kings 4:7-9)—began to crystallize during David's reign. The framework of these administrative districts did not include territories beyond the areas covered in the census conducted by David. The connection between the capital and the subjugated and dependent territories was effected through vassal kings or Israelite appointees.

The task of unification which David set before himself succeeded substantially in placing Jerusalem and the monarchy at the center of national life. Toward this end,

David moved the Ark of the Covenant to Jerusalem and made preparations for the construction of a royal palace and a central temple. Still, he did not entirely succeed in preventing the resentment and dissatisfaction of a tribal spirit opposed to the interests of the centralized monarchy, which, by their nature, undermined tribal individualism and the authority of tribal institutions. It appears to have been difficult to maintain, at one and the same time, a kingdom based on a developed administration—with all the royal needs—and separatist tendencies widespread among the tribes, whose life-styles were based upon a large degree of independence from factors beyond the tribal framework or the weak intertribal organization. Certain difficulties arose during David's reign. The population census (II Sam. 24) carried out on royal initiative, almost certainly for the purposes of taxation and recruiting, met with open opposition. Furthermore, natural disasters, added to the many wars, aggravated the dissatisfaction. It appears that the widespread dissatisfaction within the king's own tribe of Judah found expression in the revolt of Absalom (II Sam. 15–19), which was joined by other tribal elements. Only because of the loyalty of certain followers and the mercenary army, his personal guard, was David able to overcome the rebellion and return to Jerusalem. At a later stage, the revolt of Sheba, son of Bichri of Benjamin, who attracted a following from among all the tribes except Judah, shook the throne. The source of the revolt may have been the widespread feeling of discrimination in favor of Judah, the king's tribe. In this incident David was able to extricate himself from the rebellion with the help of those loyal to him and supporters in his own tribe.

At the end of David's reign, a bitter struggle developed over the succession to the throne. It divided the court into the followers of Adonijah, who claimed the throne by reason of seniority, and the supporters of Solomon— the son of Bath-Sheba—who succeeded in eliciting the support of the aging king. Under their influence, David crowned
Solomon in his lifetime in order to preserve the continuity

of dynasty desired by him. This act did not pass without drastic opposition on the part of Adonijah and his followers.

Solomon. Biblical historiography represents Solomon, with considerable justification, as a wise sovereign who sought justice and peace. He had inherited an empire founded through warfare and unending crises and reigned over a people that had begun to become accustomed to a centralized framework. Most of his activities thus tended toward the strengthening and development of his father's achievements through political, economic, and administrative means. Through a series of treaties made with neighboring kings, which he reinforced by politically-motivated marriages, he sought to insure tranquillity within the borders of his kingdom. The Bible comments negatively on these marriages because they involved, for diplomatic reasons, the introduction of foreign cults into Jerusalem (I Kings 11:1–14). In particular, Solomon cultivated ties with Hiram, king of Tyre, and Sidon. Like his father, he benefited from these relations by receiving the support of Hiram's fleet to import essential raw materials, securing his technological assistance in building projects, and in exploiting natural resources and the development of his own fleet. Another treaty, also reinforced by marriage, was made with the pharaoh Siamun, who, according to one theory, had attempted to penetrate Judah during the second half of Solomon's reign. When he failed to achieve this, he gave his daughter to the king of Israel in marriage, along with the city of Gezer as a dowry (I Kings 9:16).

During Solomon's reign, which was for the most part peaceful, the natural geopolitical advantages of Palestine became apparent. By exploiting his control of the international roads and his hold on ports on two seas, he provided great impetus to the development of international trade. To this end he formed a cadre of royal merchants with a fleet that sailed great distances. Exotic products, precious metals, and rare fauna flowed into the kingdom by sea in exchange for copper mined and worked in plants estab-

Remains of part of the Solomonic gate at Megiddo, tenth century
B.C.E. Similar gates have been found at two more of Solomon's
"cities for his chariots," Hazor and Gezer (I Kings 9:15–19).
Courtesy Government Press Office, Tel Aviv.

lished specifically for this purpose (I Kings 9:26–28; 10:11,
22). Special attention was given to overland trade with the
Arabian peninsula. It appears that commercial connections
were the major reason for the well-known visit of the
Queen of Sheba to Jerusalem (I Kings 10:1–10). The corps
of royal traders was involved in international commerce,
purchasing horses from Anatolia and chariots from Egypt
for resale to other kings in the area (I Kings 10:28–30). The
monopolistic nature of Solomon's enterprises, the levying
of passage tolls on caravans, and taxation of his own
population enriched the royal treasury and served as a
stimulus to ramified and comprehensive building projects,
some of which it seems were planned during David's reign.
At the very center of his construction activity stood the
complex of royal buildings, consisting of the palace and the
38 Temple in Jerusalem, which was intended to serve as the

focal point of religious-cultic life on a national scale, in eclipsing the local cult centers scattered throughout the kingdom. In this fashion Solomon sought to strengthen the relationship of the tribes to Jerusalem and the reigning dynasty. He hoped that the Temple would unite Israel, overcoming the traditional and widespread separatist tendencies.

Many cities in the kingdom were developed and fortified. Some served as bases for the chariotry which was introduced into Israel for the first time (I Kings 10:26; II Chron. 9:25). It appears that economic development was not limited to royal circles. It must have had indirect influence on other elements of the population. There is no doubt that widespread literary developments, known from biblical sources and Jewish tradition, were related to the economic achievements of the monarchy.

For his many activities, royal administration, and the support of the royal household, Solomon relied upon a system of 12 districts, which took shape during his reign, and upon the use of corvée that was expanded to include laborers among the Israelite population, whereas David had relied solely on compulsory alien labor. It is apparent, however, that all these measures were insufficient to meet the great need; Solomon was forced to cede certain border cities to Hiram in order to cover his trade deficit (I Kings 9:10–13). For this reason the tax burden began to rise gradually, resulting in the impoverishment of the population and substantial agitation. Along with this, feelings of discrimination began to grow among the northern tribes, especially Ephraim, whose burden was exacerbated by the division of its territory into several administrative districts, while Judah, blatantly favored, remained outside this administrative system. Furthermore, the dissatisfaction of the priests and levites in outlying cultic centers about the treatment accorded to Jerusalem and the Temple contributed to the general malaise which began to make its mark toward the end of Solomon's reign. Against this background, the abortive rebellion inspired by Jeroboam son of Nebat, of Ephraim, who had been administrator of the forced Israelite labor, stood out (I Kings 11:26-40). Another rebellion was attempted in Edom. In addition it appears that toward the end of Solomon's reign the Arameans revolted against Solomon's subjugation of them and reestablished the kingdom of Aram-Damascus.

It is therefore evident that the prosperity during Solomon's reign had negative aspects, which were compounded by important factors that existed even before the establishment of the monarchy and rebelliousness whose roots were in the antagonism between the central monarchy and tribal separatist aspirations. These factors overcame the positive aspects of the monarchy until they destroyed the united kingdom.

Division of the Kingdom; The Earliest Kings. The internal dissension and rebelliousness did not shake Solomon's throne but broke out in full force after his death. Rehoboam, his son, did not enjoy his father's and grandfather's popularity with the people. He was faced with the difficult problem of perpetuating the monarchy in the face of a growing wave of strong demands from the tribes to ease the economic burdens. The leaders of the tribes saw the time as propitious for putting pressure on the new king. Rehoboam's rule was accepted without protest in Judah and Jerusalem, but the king required the assent of the rest of the tribes, which is a clear indication of the seriousness of the state of affairs. Rehoboam was unable to find a suitable way of complying with the demands of the tribes in Shechem to ease their burden, without risking his prestige, administrative dislocations, and loss of control. As a result of his refusal, the elders of Israel felt themselves free to sever their ties with Jerusalem, and crowned Jeroboam son of Nebat, who had returned from refuge in Egypt, with the support of certain prophetic circles .

The aims of those who wished to secede from Jerusalem and the Davidic dynasty were realized, but the recognition of the need for a monarchy remained in Israel. The crowning of Jeroboam proves that the elders wanted to perpetuate the monarchy, though separate from and without connection with the dynasty of David. The slogan circulated during the revolt of Sheba son of Bichri was used again: "What portion have we in David? We have no inheritance in the son of Jesse" (I Kings 12:16).

With the division, there arose two sister kingdoms, hostile to one another. In the south was established a small kingdom, including the territories of Judah, Simeon, and Benjamin, which appears to have broken its connection with the tribes of Israel even during the period of the united kingdom. Judah controlled Edom and the Shephelah. The kingdom of Israel in the north included all the territories of the remaining tribes, maintaining its rule over Moab and probably over Ammon. Its first capital was Shechem.

Scholars suppose that the division was a causal factor for a change in the nature of the monarchy itself. Judah maintained the continuity of the Davidic dynasty, which had its roots in the tribe of Judah, a factor of decisive importance in the kingdom. In Israel, however, the monarchy was established upon the agreement of a number of tribes and was dependent upon their continued support. It was predictable that intertribal rivalries would necessarily lead to an unstable monarchy, and certainly not to dynastic continuity.

The kingdom of Judah and the House of David did not accept the secession of the tribes. They regarded the move as illegal and sinful, in contradiction to national and religious imperatives. This viewpoint finds expression in biblical historiography. It was not, of course, shared by Jeroboam son of Nebat and the advisors who established the kingdom of Israel. Jeroboam's very first acts were directed toward the establishment of a separate framework, free of all spiritual and political dependence upon Judah and the Davidic dynasty and of any cultic relationship with the Temple in Jerusalem. To this end, he made use of the ancient cultic centers at the ends of his kingdom, Beth-El and Dan. Golden Calves, the base upon which the unseen God of Israel hovered, were placed in them; they were not, 41

The high place discovered at Tel Dan, probably the one built by Jeroboam II (I Kings 12:26–30). Courtesy A. Biran, Israel Department of Antiquities, Jerusalem.

as biblical tradition would have it, intended for idol worship. This tradition clearly reflects feelings in Judah toward Jeroboam (see I Kings 12:26–33); northern opposition to the Calves is not recorded before the prophet Hosea (eighth cent.; cf. Hos. 8:5f.; 10:5f.; 13:2). Jeroboam ordained a change in the times for festivals in order to discourage pilgrimages to the Jerusalem Temple (I Kings 12:33). In parallel fashion, he evicted the levites, who had been part of the administration of the united kingdom, to prevent the people's loyalty from turning toward Jerusalem, and appointed others. Despite the negative opinion displayed toward Jeroboam in the Bible, it is becoming increasingly clear that his actions were based on an earlier northern Israelite priestly tradition, not in any way connected with idolatry. His acts also brought about the collapse of the administrative system in Israel, which until that time had been based upon Davidic loyalists. Judah, for its part, refused to regard the division as a *fait accompli*.

This was the cause for the frequent wars between the two kingdoms. It appears that at first Judah was the more successful.

Five years after the division an Egyptian military expedition into Erez Israel was headed by Pharaoh Shishak, who had been Solomon's enemy and had given asylum to Jeroboam when he fled after the abortive revolt. The final aim of and pretext for this expedition are the subject of some controversy. According to the data in Shishak's topographical list, the largest Israelite cities were destroyed and razed and the most fertile areas of the Northern Kingdom were damaged. On the other hand, the amount of damage to Judah was much less, either because Shishak was not interested in Judah proper but rather in the Negev and the Aravah, or because Rehoboam had bribed the pharaoh with tributes. In any case, as a result of the Egyptian invasion, Rehoboam began to establish a chain of fortified cities (II Chron. 11:5–12). It is significant that Judah's northern boundaries were not fortified, perhaps because of the hope that continued control over the kingdom of Jeroboam would be possible. Rehoboam's expansionist aims were advanced by his son Abijah (911–908 B.C.E.), who had assumed some royal powers during his father's lifetime. He defeated Jeroboam's army and controlled the southern part of the hill country of Ephraim (II Chron. 13:13–19). There is reason to suppose that Abijah was in contact with Aram-Damascus, which had grown in strength since its liberation from Israelite rule at the end of Solomon's reign, and concluded a treaty with them directed against Jeroboam. From that point on, Aram-Damascus was a factor in the conflict between the two sister kingdoms and the chief beneficiary of their rivalry.

These frequent defeats undermined Jeroboam's rule, which apparently had not been sufficiently strong since the division. This may be seen from the short reign of his successor Nadab (907–906 B.C.E.). When fighting the Philistines—who sought to take from Israel its territory in the lowlands—he had also to deal with a rebellion led by 43

Baasha son of Ahijah of the tribe of Issachar. This rebellion brought to an end the dynasty of Jeroboam and the hegemony of the tribe of Ephraim over the northern kingdom. The new king (906–883 B.C.E.) insured himself against Aram-Damascus' intervention and succeeded in recapturing the territories lost during Jeroboam's time, from Judah, which was now ruled by Asa (908–867 B.C.E.). Baasha penetrated almost as far as Jerusalem, posing the serious danger of isolation to the capital of Judah. Asa was forced to turn to Ben-Hadad I, king of Damascus and succeeded in breaking off the treaty between Ben-Hadad and Baasha, and in provoking the penetration of the Arameans into the northern parts of the kingdom of Israel (I Kings 15:9–22; II Chron. 16:1–5). It is possible that at this time Israel also lost control of Moab. Baasha had to withdraw from Judah in order to protect his own kingdom from Aram. Asa utilized the lull in the fighting to fortify his northern boundary by means of the total conscription of the inhabitants of Judah. Some scholars see in this an abandonment of the hope of annexing Israel, which had been current in Judah since the division.

In Baasha's time, too, there was a diminution of earlier achievements as a result of his defeats. Baasha did succeed in preserving his throne, but with his death, civil war broke out in Israel and a few ministers struggled to obtain the throne. Elah (883–882 B.C.E.) was murdered in a plot instigated by Zimri, one of the officers of the army. Zimri was killed by Omri, with part of the nation backing Tibni son of Ginath. After several years of conflict, Omri succeeded to the throne of Israel.

Asa, King of Judah, and His Descendants. The Omride Dynasty in Israel. Whatever hopes there had been during Abijah's successes for reunification under the Davidic dynasty were destroyed by the military failures of Asa against Baasha. Asa was successful, however, in defending the south of Judah from Zerah, the Cushite (II Chron. 14:8–14). Though exact identification of Zerah is lacking, and there is no agreement on the exact nature of his forces, it appears that he was acting under Egyptian influence, trying to broaden the Egyptian holdings inside Judah's boundaries which had begun to be established with Shishak's campaign. With the defeat of Zerah and his forces, however, Judah regained the territories it had lost in Rehoboam's time, and even broadened them.

In internal policy Asa's name is connected with the purification of Judah of foreign cults. Idolatry had been current in Palestine as a result of Solomon's marital policy and the international connections of Solomon and Rehoboam. Although it did not strike deep roots among the populace, idolatry had political significance. Idolatrous tendencies seem to have been strengthened in Judah during the regency of Asa's mother (or grandmother), prior to his attaining majority. The purging of the foreign cults, which had become widespread, was connected with the removal of the queen mother from her high office and the reversal of her policies, which had almost certainly been responsible for the growth of idolatry in Jerusalem. Asa had the support of popular and prophetic circles for his purges. He appears to have lost this support, however, when he allied himself with the king of Aram-Damascus, and according to II Chronicles 16:7-10 he was even engaged in the oppression of his own people.

The accession of Omri to the throne put a halt to the collapse of the central government in Israel which began as a result of the riots after Elah's death. Omri took decisive steps to stabilize the kingdom, such as the construction of the new capital in Samaria. Like Jerusalem, this city became the king's personal landholding. It appears that Omri was subject to Aramean pressures, as is seen by the fact that Aramean commercial agencies (ḥuẓot) were located in Samaria and had special privileges (I Kings 20:34). At a later stage, Omri succeeded in establishing an independent foreign policy, concluding a treaty with Ethbaal, king of Sidon. This, like the treaties of David and Solomon, opened the Phoenician markets to Israel's agricultural products, and made it possible to import 45 essential goods and luxury products for Omri's kingdom. This treaty may have been intended as a stabilizing factor against the political aspirations of Aram-Damascus. The ties with Ethbaal were strengthened by the marriage of Israel's heir apparent to Ethbaal's daughter. Israel's main contribution to the alliance was control of the heights of Moab, in the territory north of the Arnon, whose conquest by Omri is attested by the Mesha stele[1]. The conquest enabled him to control and direct the products carried over the "King's Highway." It may be assumed that the efforts made by the king of Israel to improve relations with the kingdom of Judah were made out of his desire to establish an anti-Aramean alliance on the one hand, and to get Judah to join the Tyre-Samarian axis on the other. Judah's joining the axis was important, because of the Judahite control of the southern part of the "King's Highway," which passed through Edom, a land subject to it. In Omri's time Israel had become an important political factor. The stability and prosperity began to be felt when Ahab son of Omri started his reign; he added to the achievements of his father Despite this, Ahab is negatively evaluated in the biblical historiography due to his toleration of the expansion of Phoenician culture in his personal and royal affairs. The Tyrean cult began to gain popularity among Israel's upper classes—the officers and merchants—due to the close ties with Tyre, and especially because of the activities of Jezebel, the daughter of Ethbaal, and her followers (I Kings 16:32–33). The attitude of the biblical historiographer toward Ahab reflects that of circles close to Elijah. Elijah attacked the king, Jezebel, and the Baal prophets, who had attained a foothold in Israel (I Kings 18:18–45). Elijah enjoyed wide support among the populace, which bitterly resented the penetration of foreign cults and indeed suffered because of the innovations brought about by the Phoenician way of life.

The biblical view, however, does not negate the positive

---

[1] Account by Mesha king of Moab of his war with Israel (II Kings 3:4ff) discovered in 1868 and now in the Louvre.

aspects of Ahab as a ruler. During his time solidarity between Judah and Israel increased, strengthened by political marriages. There appears to have been a treaty between the two nations, which placed both on an equal footing. In addition, Ahab enjoyed considerable success in his battles against Assyria and Aram-Damascus; these battles had taken on considerable importance by the end of his reign. It appears that Aram's intention was to destroy the Israel-Judah alliance, which was directed against it. Furthermore, the rule of Jerusalem and Samaria in Transjordan bothered the ruler of Damascus, Ben-Hadad II. The unchanged economic interests of Aram made it necessary to hold the territory east of the Jordan as an economic hinterland for its caravan routes and agricultural products. At first the Aramean army tried to subjugate Israel by a quick campaign, which ended with its defeat at the gates of Samaria. The next battle took place at Aphek and also ended in a clear-cut victory for Israel. It is instructive that despite the Aramean defeat Ahab entered into a treaty with Ben-Hadad, whose terms were especially lenient: certain cities were returned to Israel and she received commercial concessions in Damascus. This desire to make peace with Aram without hurting her too much is criticized by the prophets. It is clear, however, that this desire resulted from political and military considerations connected with the events outside the borders of Aram and Israel, namely, the methodical penetration by Shalmaneser III, king of Assyria, into Syria, which posed a concrete danger for the states in that area. These states came to the realization that Assyria had to be fought by an alliance of powers, and Ahab was no doubt party to this feeling. For this reason Ahab did not want to harm Aram's power to fight against the common enemy. One of Shalmaneser's inscriptions, in which the Assyrian king claims a victory over the kings of Syria and Ereẓ Israel near Karkar (853 B.C.E.), prominently mentions "Ahab the Israelite" alongside the kings of Damascus and Hamath. Ahab came to the battle, according to this inscription, with a force of 2,000

Fragment of carved ivory panel depicting the Egyptian god
Hah, from King Ahab's "ivory house" in Samaria, first half
of ninth century B.C.E. Jerusalem, Rockefeller Museum, Israel
Department of Antiquities.

chariots—the largest contributed by any of the allies; be-
sides, he supplied 10,000 infantry. This is evidence not only
of his political-military standing but also of the economic
strength of the kingdom which could sustain such a force.
Especially instructive is the find of Ahab's stables at
Megiddo. To this may be added other archaeological
evidence which testifies to the great development of Israelite
cities, including the capital, in that period. The existence of
an "ivory house," which is known from the Bible (I Kings
22:39), is confirmed by ivory plaques found in Samaria.
Among the cities he refortified, according to the Bible, was
Jericho. The fortification of this city appears to be
connected with the increased control of Moab, north of the
Arnon, over which Israel ruled. There too, according to the
Mesha stele, widespread fortification activity took place.
During the battle with Assyria, or shortly thereafter, Mesha
revolted against Ahab, and began to eradicate Israel's rule
48 in Moab. He may have been encouraged by Aram-Damas-

cus, which resumed its thrusts against Israel after the battle at Karkar, at which the allies, at least temporarily, were able to stop the advance of Shalmaneser III into central Syria. (Another theory holds that Mesha revolted during the reign of Ahab's successor.) The renewed battle between Aram and Israel took place near Ramoth-Gilead, which appears to have been an area contested by the two sides. This time, Judah allied itself with Israel. The battle ended in the death of Ahab and the disengagement of forces following the king's death. It appears that the Arameans were unable to cross Israel's border in Transjordan, which means that the battle did not end in Israel's defeat.

Ahab's reign was a period in which Israel came to be a considerable force in the international affairs of the region; this resulted from her prudent policies and her highly developed military capabilities, which gave her an advantage over Aram. The great building and fortification activities reflect advanced economic development in the kingdom, as well as its stability which remained unbroken in Ahab's time despite the internal struggle against foreign religious and cultural influences. Attention should be drawn to the political, economic, and military ties that existed between Samaria and Jerusalem, which was ruled by Jehoshaphat son of Asa (c. 870–846 B.C.E.). As a result of this alliance, which was strengthened by a treaty, Judah enjoyed a relatively long period of peace. Jehoshaphat exploited these conditions by attempting a renewal of Red Sea commerce, which appears to have been interrupted after the death of Solomon. There is no doubt that Judah also received Phoenician technical support in this matter. The fleet which was built, however, sank before it could sail. The assertion of authority over Philistia and the Arabian tribes must be understood in the framework of the attempts to reestablish Judah as a commercial power (II Chron. 17:11). The rule of Edom was carried out by Jehoshaphat with the help of a governor, and at a later period by a vassal king. Because of Edom, Jehoshaphat feared a deep Aramean penetration into Transjordan which would have endangered his bases there. This is probably one of the reasons for the treaty with Ahab and the joining of the forces of Judah to those of Israel in the battle at Ramoth-Gilead. (One opinion holds that Judah also joined Israelite forces during the battle with Assyria at Karkar in 853 B.C.E. This would account for the high number of chariots of Ahab.)

Jehoshaphat devoted much attention to internal policy. He appears to have been the first king of Judah to establish firm foundations for the royal and administrative offices which had been undermined since the division of the kingdoms, because of the frequent warfare of his predecessors. During the earliest part of his reign he sent officers and levites into the Judean cities to teach the people the Law (II Chron. 17:7). This was probably connected with a reorganization of the judicial institutions in the provincial towns and the establishment of a supreme court in Jerusalem (II Chron. 17:7–9; 19:5ff.), run jointly by administrative personnel, the priesthood, and the national leadership. He divided Judah into administrative districts (II Chron. 17:2); one opinion holding that this division is preserved in Joshua 15. Jehoshaphat reorganized the regular army and the reserve forces and expanded the system of fortified cities and fortresses (II Chron. 17:13–19).

The cordial relations between Judah and Israel worsened during the short reign of Ahaziah son of Ahab (852/1–851/0 B.C.E.), who wished to be included in Judah's commercial sea enterprises but was refused (I Kings 22:49–50). With the accession of his brother Jehoram (851/0–842 B.C.E.) to Israel's throne, the friendly relations were resumed. Jehoshaphat even participated in an ill-fated campaign of Israel which was intended to reestablish Jehoram's authority over Mesha (II Kings 3:4–24). Following this, Edom broke free of Judah, whose borders were then breached by Moabite and Ammonite bands, and whose country was penetrated by nomadic tribes. Judah was saved as a result of quarrels among the invaders (II

Chron. 20:23–24).

The early part of the reign of Jehoshaphat's son Jehoram (c. 851–843 B.C.E.) was marred by internal upheavals, as attested by the murder of his brothers and certain high officials by Jehoram himself. It may be that the defeats at the end of Jehoshaphat's reign were responsible for the agitation which became even greater by the loss of Edom and the economic benefits Edom had provided (II Kings 8:20ff.; II Chron. 21:8). Added to all of this was no doubt dissatisfaction with the activities of the king's wife, Athaliah daughter of Ahab, who had been accustomed to Phoenician cultic practices in her home and worked at introducing into Judah these practices as well as the mode of life customary in the court of Israel. She may also have sought to increase Judah's dependence on Israel. There is reason to believe that the king of Israel and Jehoram son of Jehoshaphat combined their forces in a renewed treaty of the Syrian kings against Shalmaneser III. During the absence of Judah's army, the country was defenseless against an invasion by Philistines, Arabian tribes, and Cushites who reached Jerusalem, capturing all the royal family except for Ahaziah. The latter reigned after his father's death (843–842 B.C.E.), influenced by his mother Athaliah. He continued the policies set by his father, even joining Jehoram son of Ahab in a war against Aram at Ramoth-Gilead. During this period Ahab's son Jehoram reaped the fruits of dissatisfaction with the house of Omri. This opposition gathered strength as a result of Jehoram's failures on the field of battle. The king appears to have understood the dangers of popular opposition growing along religious lines and out of social tensions. The opposition pointed to royal circles as the source of evil. Jehoram tried to remove the stigma of Phoenician influence and attempted to appease the people, but he was too late to have any significant success. Perhaps he did not discern how widespread the dissatisfaction was. He was wounded during the renewal of the battle against Aram at Ramoth-Gilead. During his convalescence at Jezreel he was killed, when Jehu called for reprisals against the house of Omri. On this same dramatic occasion Ahaziah of Judah was wounded and died.

The Dynasty of Jehu in Israel. Athaliah and Joash, Amaziah, Uzziah, and Jotham, Kings of Judah. Jehu son of Jehoshaphat son of Nimshi (842–814 B.C.E.) was an army officer stationed in Gilead. He was swept aloft by the wave of popular rebellion, supported by the army, circles of prophets, and dissatisfied elements among the populace. With great cruelty, he killed the royal family and its courtiers, settling the long-standing debt against Jezebel. He decisively cut off every trace of the Baal worship, killing followers of the cult. Thus, he fulfilled the wishes of his supporters, but did not consider that in so doing he had also destroyed the political and economic bases of his kingdom by cutting, with one blow, the ties of Samaria with Phoenicia and Judah and upsetting the internal organization of his kingdom and its military capabilities. Jehu was thus open to the pressures of Aram-Damascus, which at this time was ruled by a new and powerful king, Hazael. In an effort to insure his own rule, Jehu quickly made himself submissive to the Assyrian Shalmaneser III, who reached Damascus in 841. Thus, for a short period of time Israel enjoyed a relaxation of pressures from the Arameans, who were busy defending themselves against Assyria. At a later stage, after Shalmaneser had failed to subjugate the capital of Aram, Hazael conquered the Israelite territories in eastern Transjordan. Toward the end of his reign, Jehu suffered another defeat when the Aramean army marched through Israel and reached the borders of Judah.

When Ahaziah died, his mother Athaliah grasped the reins of leadership in Judah by killing the royal family (II Kings 11:1; II Chron. 22:10). It is evident that she did not enjoy much popular support, since even before murdering the king's family she had been resented. There is no doubt that the revolution of Jehu in Samaria had its reverberations in Jerusalem, where the very way of life and practices which had been rooted out of Israel continued to be

52

observed. It is of little wonder that a minor revolt took place in the Judahite capital, led by the Temple staff and supported by the army and leaders of the people. Athaliah paid with her life and Joash son of Ahaziah (836–798 B.C.E.), the only one to have escaped death at the hands of his grandmother, was made king of Judah. His coronation was accompanied by a covenant made between God and the king and the nation, and between the king and the people. These covenants stressed loyalty to the God of Israel and the renewed continuity of the Davidic dynasty in Jerusalem. The Jerusalem priesthood gained significant influence in political affairs thanks to Jehoiada the priest, who had been the instigator of the rebellion. The Temple was restored to its former glory; it was repaired by means of contributions solicited from the nation. That same year Hazael, king of Aram, reached Judah after having defeated Jehu. Joash was forced to pay a heavy tribute, which was taken from the Temple treasury (II Kings 12:18–19; II Chron. 24:23) in order to put off the destruction threatening his country. It may be that this act was interpreted as a blow to the Temple, thereby opening a wedge for activities against the king. With the death of Jehoiada the priest a struggle broke out between the priesthood and the secular administration, which aspired to positions of power in the court. The secular administration won in this struggle, though it appears that the priesthood did not accept the loss of its special status, which had been gained after the revolt that put Joash on the throne. Against the king, who now supported the newly-risen secular power, a conspiracy arose which resulted in Joash's assassination. This lack of stability continued during the reign of Amaziah son of Joash. The new king sought to allay tensions by not touching the descendants of his father's murderers, though he did revenge himself against the murderers themselves. It appears that he was able to quiet the circles which had formed the conspiracy, because the biblical sources speak of the conscription and organization of the army in Judah (II Chron. 25:5) to fight in Edom. 53

This would have been impossible during a period of internal disturbances. For this purpose he engaged a troop of mercenaries from Israel, but not wanting to arouse new internal resistance, Amaziah gave up the mercenary force from Israel and fought Edom by his own means. It appears that he was unable to conquer the whole of Edom. At a later date, for reasons not sufficiently clear, he turned against Israel. Amaziah was defeated by Jehoash son of Jehoahaz, the king of Israel, who entered Jerusalem, destroyed parts of her walls, looted the Temple and palace treasures, imposed economic sanctions, and took hostages away with him (II Kings 14:8–14; II Chron. 25:17–24). Amaziah became a vassal of Israel. This appears to have led to rebellion against his rule and his eventual assassination.

The defeats of Jehu led to the loss of territory and power by the kingdom of Israel. The period of decline continued during the reign of Jehoahaz son of Jehu (817–800 B.C.E.). Echoes of this appear in the cycle of narratives about Elisha (II Kings 5–7). At the same time, Aramean pressures reached their peak, as a result of which the kingdom of Israel was forced to contract into the nearby environs of Samaria. Some slight relief from Aramean bondage was provided when Adad-nirari III, king of Assyria, conducted a campaign into Syria against Aram and Damascus its capital, failing however to defeat her. He appears to be the *moshiᶜa*, "deliverer," who, according to the biblical sources, saved Israel from Aram (II Kings 13:5). It is possible that Jehoahaz was subjugated by the Assyrian king, paying him, like Jehu before him, a levy during the time he was in the vicinity of Damascus. An Assyrian inscription mentions "the land of Omri" (an appellation for the kingdom of Israel even after the end of the Omri dynasty), among the lands subject to Adad-nirari III. It appears that during the latter years of Jehoahaz, Israel began to break free of the firm hand of Damascus, which was busy defending itself against Assyria. A recently discovered stele mentions Jehoash (Joash) son of Jehoahaz, king of Israel (800–784 B.C.E.), among those subjugated by Adad-nirari

III. It may be that this subjugation was a continuation of the tactics of his father (if indeed the sources mentioned above refer to the time of his father and not to Jehoash's period), or he may have surrendered after the campaign of the king of Assyria into the valley of Lebanon in 796 B.C.E. In any case Jehoash utilized the decline of Aram to recapture territories taken from Israel during the reigns of his predecessors (II Kings 13:9–14). He also stopped incursions by Moabite marauders (13:20). This is yet another indication of Israel's renewed military capability, which also displayed itself in Jehoash's war against Amaziah, king of Judah, in which he defeated Amaziah's armies and reached Jerusalem.

A protracted period of nonintervention on the part of Assyria in Syrian affairs, which occurred after Jehoash's time, had a positive influence upon the policies of the region's countries, including Israel and Judah. Furthermore, these two countries began to assume prime importance in filling the political vacuum left in the wake of Aram's decline following her war with Assyria. Thus, the period of Jeroboam son of Jehoash (789–748 B.C.E.) was one of ascendancy for Israel. Some of his political and military achievements are briefly described in II Kings 14:23–29. These sources indicate that Jeroboam held widespread territories, including Aram-Damascus and eastern Transjordan. His northern boundary reached the kingdom of Hamath, as in the days of David. The political and military activities were accompanied by economic expansion and building and fortification work in Samaria and its environs. Hints in the Books of Chronicles and Amos lead one to believe that Jeroboam initiated and strove to establish broader settlement areas in Transjordan and gave large pieces of land to his officers and followers. These individuals eventually developed into large and wealthy owners of estates of commanding influence, playing substantial roles in the final days of the kingdom of Israel. There were good relations at this time between Israel and Judah, as evidenced by a mention of a joint census in 55

Transjordan (I Chron. 5:16–17).

Judah, too, enjoyed a stability which flowed from the convenient international situation. From the time of Joash the rule of Judah's kings was disturbed by incessant internal struggles and an inability to gather sufficient support to overcome the opposition to their rule. The reign of Jeroboam's contemporary, Uzziah (Azariah) son of Amaziah (785–733 B.C.E.), was one of the most flourishing in the history of the kingdom of Judah. In the absence of external disturbances Uzziah completed the conquest of Edom, including the important bay of Elath and its harbor (II Kings 14:22; II Chron. 26:2). He subjugated the Arabian tribes who lived at the borders of his kingdom, and asserted his authority over Philistia, including Gath, Jabneh, and Ashdod (II Chron. 26:6–7). He strengthened his sovereignty over these areas by means of a far-flung building campaign and expanded agriculture and pasturing operations in eastern Transjordan to meet the needs of the royal economy. A similar development was accomplished in the Negev and the Arabah, including operations to insure water supply, settlements, and a chain of fortifications for communications and defense (26:10ff.). The army of Judah was reorganized and supplied with new weapons (26:11–15); special attention was given to the fortification of Jerusalem. These biblical data are probably connected with the anti-Assyrian war preparations which occupied the region due to the penetration of Tiglath-Pileser III into Syria. It is likely that the "Azriau from the land of Yaūdi," mentioned in Assyrian inscriptions as the leader of a group of allies who fought the armies of Assyria in northern Syria and were defeated in 738, is in fact Uzziah, the king of Judah. The question of how Uzziah became head of the alliance which fought in northern Syria is a difficult one. It is almost certain that Judah replaced Israel in importance in the area after Israel's precipitous decline following the death of Jeroboam son of Jehoash.

The Bible attributes Uzziah's leprosy to his attempts to secure special privileges for himself in the Temple service (II

Chron. 26:16–21). The incident is not sufficiently explicit, but it is clear that the king's cultic activities were rejected by the priesthood. There may even be in the conflict between Uzziah and the priests a continuation of the struggles that existed between the Temple staff and his father and grandfather. Both calculations from biblical sources and chronological calculations lead to the conclusion that as a result of Uzziah's infirmity his son Jotham (758–743 B.C.E.) took part in the administration of the kingdom. Furthermore, Jotham's regency, though counted in the Bible as a separate rule, is included in the years attributed to Uzziah, who was still alive. It even appears that the years given as Uzziah's period of rule include a few years from the reign of Ahaz, his grandson. Jotham son of Uzziah acted according to the guidance and direction of his father. It is not unreasonable to assume that a good portion of the building and other activities ascribed to the father was actually accomplished by the son. In the light of what has been said above, it is difficult to distinguish between their reigns. In any case, he appears to have appeased the priesthood. He, too, is credited with the fortification of Jerusalem and cities of Judah and with the building of fortresses. In his time Ammon was brought under Judah's rule (II Chron. 27:5). It appears that as a result of this victory he was able to enlist the aid of Jeroboam son of Jehoash in the campaign into Transjordan (see above). After the defeat of 738, in which Judah was not directly affected, Jotham attempted accommodation with Assyria, thus arousing the ire of Rezin, king of Damascus. The latter had restored independence to Aram with the help of his ally the king of Israel. These two kings attempted to involve Judah in a new anti-Assyrian campaign.

The Last Days of Samaria. The Kingdom of Judah Until its Destruction. With the death of Jeroboam son of Jehoash chaos broke out in Israel. Influential in the upheavals characteristic of this period were the great landowners and prominent parties from the eastern side of the Jordan. The short reign of Zechariah son of Jeroboam (748/7 B.C.E.)

ended in his assassination at the hands of Shallum son of Jabesh (i.e., from Jabesh-Gilead). Shallum was deposed, before he could ascend the throne, by Menahem son of Gadi (747/6–737/6 B.C.E.), who also appears to have been from Transjordan. He seems to have attempted to expand his territories and establish a firm rule (II Kings 15:16), but the iron hand of Tiglath-Pileser III prevented him from achieving his aims. There is no doubt that Menahem son of Gadi is "Menahem of Samaria," who is referred to in an Assyrian inscription of 738 B.C.E. as one of those who paid taxes to the king of Assyria. It may be assumed that after the defeat of Azariah-Uzziah in northern Syria, Menahem was quick to be counted among those loyal to Tiglath-Pileser III. Biblical sources describe Menahem as having been forced to pay a heavy tax to Pul (i.e., Tiglath-Pileser), the king of Assyria. This money was exacted from the wealthy landowners of Menahem's kingdom (II Kings 15:19–20). One theory based on the Samaria ostraca holds that the tax was collected in the form of agricultural products. After the death of Menahem, Pekahiah, his son, lost control of affairs and soon fell in a conspiracy led by Pekah son of Remaliah (735/4–733/2 B.C.E.), one of the nobles of Gilead. The cause of the conspiracy seems to have been dissatisfaction on the part of Transjordanian Israelites with Assyrian domination of Israel; these parties cultivated their own connections with Aram. Thus, when Pekah began his reign, he entered into a treaty with Rezin, king of Damascus, which was aimed against Tiglath-Pileser III. In order to create a secure flank these two attempted to compel Jotham, and later his son Ahaz (743–727 B.C.E.), to abandon Judah's policy of submitting to Assyria. They attempted this by fomenting rebellion in Edom and inciting Philistia (II Kings 16:6; II Chron. 28:17–18), and by a military campaign toward Jerusalem which was intended to upset the Davidic dynasty. Ahaz therefore turned to Tiglath-Pileser III for aid, and, according to the biblical sources, submitted to the king of Assyria. He is blamed too for introducing alien cult usages into Jerusalem, a sign of the growing foreign influences upon Judah (II Kings 16:3-4, 10-18; II Chron. 28:3-4, 21-25). It is not clear whether the appearance of Tiglath-Pileser in Damascus resulted from Ahaz's request, since it is highly unlikely that the king of Assyria would have responded to such a call if he had not already decided to attack Damascus anyway. What appears more likely is that Ahaz turned to Tiglath-Pileser in 734, while the Assyrian army was already engaged in campaign along the Phoenician coastline, reaching as far as the "brook of Egypt" (Wādi El-Arish). This Assyrian venture was intended to strengthen control over the Philistinian coastal cities, and especially over Gaza. Thus Ahaz's request must have fallen upon receptive ears, since it suited Tiglath-Pileser's political-military plans. In 733-732 the Assyrians besieged Damascus and captured it, making it a center of an Assyrian province. During the siege Tiglath-Pileser also conquered portions of eastern Transjordan and penetrated Galilee and the Valley of Beth-Netuphah. As it appears from Assyrian sources and biblical references (II Kings 15:29), he may have reached as far as Ashkelon. Immediately following these events another revolt took place in Samaria. In place of the cruel and destructive Pekah son of Remaliah, who brought disaster to the kingdom, Hoshea son of Elah (733/2-724/3 B.C.E.) became king, his position being confirmed by the Assyrian ruler.

Throughout this period Judah maintained its vassal status, thus being saved. Assyrian records tell about Ahaz (called Jehoahaz in the inscription) who paid a tax in 728 B.C.E.

With the death of Tiglath-Pileser III widespread revolt broke out in Syria and Palestine. Even the kingdom of Israel, encouraged by Egypt (II Kings 17:4), joined in the revolt. The new Assyrian king, Shalmaneser V, punished the rebels by means of a military campaign. Upon reaching Palestine, he besieged Samaria for three years, and the capital fell in 722 B.C.E. The exile of its inhabitants and the turning of Samaria into an Assyrian province was completed by the next Assyrian king, Sargon II (II Kings 17:6; cf. 18:9–11). It appears that Sargon II must have rushed his army westward in 720 to suppress rebellion in many parts of the area. Judah refrained from participation in this uprising. Assyrian inscriptions from Sargon's time mention Judah's submission. Still, there are hints about the involvement of Hezekiah son of Ahaz (727–698 B.C.E.) in support of Ashdod, which was in rebellion against Assyria. As a result of this, sections of Judah's western border were attacked. In any case, Judah enjoyed a period of relative quiet, possibly because of its submission to Assyria. However, as soon as the Assyrian danger had passed, Hezekiah adopted a series of measures which may be interpreted as a shift in policy. The purification of the cult from foreign and popular elements (II Chron. 28:24; 29:3) was intended to raise national morale and unite the people around the House of David and the Temple. Even the literary activity (Prov. 25:1) was an expression of a new nationalistic spirit which, like the purification of the cult, expressed aspirations of political independence. There were even attempts to bring closer to Judah those residents of the former Israel, living in nearby Assyrian provinces which had been established on the territories of the former kingdom of Israel. To this end, Hezekiah sent envoys to invite these people to participate in the Passover festival in Jerusalem, the date of which was made to conform to the calendar kept in the north (II Chron. 30:1–21). It is clear that these aspirations were bound to become involved with anti-Assyrian activities which were growing from Egypt to Babylonia. The mission of the Assyrian Merodach-Baladan (II Kings 20:12; Isa. 39) to Jerusalem was intended to clarify Judah's stand in these activities. With the death of Sargon II the balance seems to have been tipped in favor of Hezekiah's participation in the anti-Assyrian front. Jerusalem prepared for revolt. The capital was fortified, and the Siloam tunnel was built to bring the water of the Gihon within her walls in time of emergency. The army was reorganized in preparation for the revolt. It appears from

Part of the Siloam tunnel constructed by King Hezekiah c. 701 B.C.E. to bring water from the Gihon stream into Jerusalem in case of siege. Photo Werner Braun, Jerusalem.

Assyrian inscriptions that at this time the pro-Assyrian king of Ekron was imprisoned in Jerusalem, and Philistia was attacked (II Kings 18:8). This was done by Judah to create territorial continuity with Ashkelon, also a participant in the revolt.

Sennacherib, who succeeded Sargon II, successfully fought Babylonia, and attempted to conquer the cities along the Phoenician coast, afterward making his way toward Erez Israel. During this campaign, according to sources describing his acts in Erez Israel, Sennacherib conquered Beth-Dagon, Jaffa, Bene-Berak, and cities of the kingdom of Ashkelon. At Eltekeh, at the approaches to Judah, he defeated the Egyptian relief force which had been sent to help Hezekiah. The Assyrian army entered Judah, destroyed its cities, distributing them among the Philistine kings, and exiled many of the people. A siege was laid upon Jerusalem. Hezekiah, encouraged by Isaiah the prophet who had high standing in the king's court, did not open the gates of the city to Sennacherib, though he did send him a heavy tribute. The subsequent activities of Sennacherib are not clear. He left Judah, though opinions are divided as to his reasons. He may have returned to Palestine at a later date. In any case, Hezekiah remained on his throne as an Assyrian vassal.

This subjugation to Assyria continued during the reign of Manasseh son of Hezekiah (698–642 B.C.E.), who reigned during the rule of the last great Assyrian kings. He introduced a host of pagan cults into Jerusalem and Judah (II Kings 21:1–9; II Chron. 33:2–9), continuing a policy established by his father toward the end of his reign. He also paid taxes to Assyria. A late source (II Chron. 33:11–13) relates that Manasseh was taken captive in chains to Babylonia, though he later returned to reign over Judah. The implication is that Manasseh must have taken part in an anti-Assyrian rebellion in another area of the Fertile Crescent. Evidently for political reasons involving imperial interests the Assyrians returned him to the throne. It is said that when he returned to

Judah, he rooted out idolatrous practices and fortified Jerusalem and other cities' (II Chron. 33:14–16). Again, these acts should be seen in the context of rebellion against Assyria, which resulted from upheavals in the empire at this time.

The reign of Amon son of Manasseh was short-lived, ending in his assassination. One theory holds that the murder was connected with an internal struggle over the political orientation of Judah. Amon was killed because of his pro-Assyrian stance, just at a time when the Mesopotamian power was beginning to display signs of weakness. Josiah son of Amon (639–609 B.C.E.) was brought to the throne by forces loyal to the House of David. They had before them the example of Hezekiah who had tried to unite the nation and deepen its national and religious awareness by purifying the cult and repairing the Temple. As in former times, the usual political motivation behind these acts existed. In this case the motivation was the decline of Assyria during the time of Josiah. While in earlier times Assyrian declines may have been temporary, however, it was clear during Josiah's reign that the fall of Assyria was not just a passing phenomenon. The Books of Kings and II Chronicles are at odds over the order of events and their times. It appears that II Chronicles is the more dependable, since its chronology and time fit in with the stages of the decline of the Assyrian empire (II Chron. 34–35).

Josiah began by showing his faith in the God of David; he then cleansed his capital and cities and some of the former Israel territories of idolatry; and he finally arranged repairs of the Temple. This last deed is connected with other actions whose purpose was religious reform and the raising of national morale. These included the finding of a Torah scroll, the forming of a new covenant between the nation and its God, and the celebration of the Passover in the capital. The biblical sources indicate that along with the national and spiritual activities of Josiah, there was also a territorial expansion into those Assyrian provinces which were on the soil of the former kingdom of Israel. This explains the appearance of Josiah in Megiddo, where he tried to stop the forces of the pharaoh Neco. The latter had attempted to help the tottering Assyrian forces which had fortified themselves along the Euphrates against the advances of Nabopolassar, the Chaldean, who was the founder of the neo-Babylonian empire. Neco wanted to exploit the decline of Assyria to acquire its territories west of the Euphrates. At the battle of Megiddo the army of Judah was defeated and Josiah was mortally wounded. His attempt to stop Egypt before it reached the Euphrates made Josiah a potential ally of Babylonia. Josiah's political judgment was farseeing, flowing as it did from the hope that Babylonia would be the key rising power in the Fertile Crescent. With the death of Josiah, Judah's last period of national prosperity came to an end. After him came a period of decline, wars, bloodshed, and destruction. Jehoahaz, his son, reigned in his stead, but was shortly removed by Neco, who made the areas west of the Euphrates his sphere of influence. Jehoahaz was replaced by Jehoiakim (608–598 B.C.E.), Josiah's eldest son, who almost certainly must have displayed more loyalty to Egypt than his deposed brother. Judah became an Egyptian satellite, and was forced to pay heavy tributes (II Kings 24:33).

Beginning with Jehoiakim, Judah was buffeted by the severe conflict between Babylonia and Egypt on the one hand, and the proliferation of conflicting political views among its own ruling classes and people on the other. With Nebuchadnezzar's defeat of Neco (605 B.C.E.) and penetration into Philistia, some of Judah's population was exiled to Babylonia. It is even possible that a Babylonian army reached Jerusalem in 603. As a result, Jehoiakim was subject to Babylonian rule for a few years, though at the same time he tried to maintain his connections with Egypt, which encouraged him and promised aid. When Egypt enjoyed some temporary success in stopping Nebuchadnezzar, Jehoiakim's connections with Egypt turned into full-scale rebellion against Babylonia. Throughout this

64

period the prophet Jeremiah counseled against a Judah-Egypt alliance, advising that the only way to save Judah from destruction was surrender to Babylonia. Promised Egyptian aid never reached Judah, when Nebuchadnezzar attacked using his forces and soldiers from countries he had conquered (II Kings 24:2), Jerusalem was placed under siege at around that time and Jehoiakim died during the attack. His son Jehoiachin was exiled to Babylonia (597), along with his court, army officers, and craftsmen. Babylonian and other documents make it clear that he was well treated in exile, even retaining his royal title.

Nebuchadnezzar appointed as king of Judah Zedekiah son of Josiah (596–586 B.C.E.), who was at first loyal to Babylonia. At a later period he made connections with anti-Babylonian elements and joined a rebellion which encompassed Palestine, the Phoenician coast, and Trans-jordan. This revolt had the active support of Egypt, now ruled by Pharaoh Hophra. Zedekiah remained loyal to the rebellion even after some of the rebels surrendered to Nebuchadnezzar. He even resisted the pressures of prophets led by Jeremiah, as well as of some of his courtiers, who feared the fate Judah might suffer because of its rebellious activities against Babylonia. The Lachish ostraca testify to the events of those days, when the Babylonian army stood at the gateway to the country. These ostraca reflect the internal confusion among the administrators, army, and courtiers, and illustrate the emergency situation within Judah. The Babylonian army penetrated the land and began to destroy its fortifications (589). It appears that an Egyptian force was rushed to Judah at that time, providing some temporary relief from the siege of Jerusalem, but the force was defeated. The capital then came under protracted siege until it was conquered and destroyed, along with the Temple. Zedekiah was captured while trying to escape and was severely punished. Judah was depopulated by the exile of her populace and by the flight of refugees to neighboring countries. Nor was she able to stop the Philistines, Edomites, and Arabian tribes from taking parts of her territories. The remnants of the population of Jerusalem and Judah concentrated themselves about Mizpeh. There Gedaliah son of Ahikam was appointed by the Babylonians to govern the remaining inhabitants of Judah. He was murdered, however, by conspirators from among Judah's former officialdom, who were encouraged by outside forces. With his death, the end came for the last vestige of independence that yet remained. The territory of Judah became an administrative unit of Babylon, with no Jewish representatives, and was no longer a Jewish center.

It appears that in 582 an additional exile of Judahite population took place, further evidence that the Judahites had been part of the rebellion which encompassed the area at that time. The destruction of Jerusalem and the end of the kingdom of Judah brought to an end the long period of independence and sovereignty which the people of Israel had enjoyed. There remained only the deep impress of this period upon the history of the nation and the hopes it gave to future generations.

The Prophets. A unique role in Jewish history was played by the prophets, religious thinkers who in some instances were regarded by the rulers as their advisers. Their advice related to religion, ethical, and even political matters viewed under the primacy of the obligations of the people to God. The early prophets greatly influenced the political destiny of Israel. Samuel chose both Saul (I Sam. 9) and David (I Sam. 16) to be kings over Israel; Elijah opposed the policy of Jezebel and did not hesitate to rebuke the king Ahab; Elisha had one of his colleagues anoint Jehu king of Israel, and inspired the latter's rebellion against Jehoram (II Kings 9). Several kings had their own court prophets. Both Nathan and Gad served with David, and duly reproved him as occasion demanded.

The classical prophets, whose sayings are incorporated in the biblical books called after them (in the Latter Prophets section), stressed ethical monotheism more than ritual, though demanding both sets of values. Simultaneously, they were generally universalistic rather than narrowly

nationalistic, reproved rather than foretold, and spoke as individuals rather than in groups. They appeared in the course of some three centuries, from a few decades before the fall of Northern Israel (722 B.C.E.), until a century after the destruction of Jerusalem (586 B.C.E.). They addressed their message to the contemporary situation, and saw the changing fortunes of three major empires—Assyria, Babylonia and Persia—as significant steps in a divine world-plan involving the destiny of Israel.

Their writings are characterized by the insistent denunciation of corruption in the ethical and social fields. Even kings, priests and judges were warned fearlessly that unrighteousness would spell the end of Israel.

3 SOCIAL STRUCTURE OF ANCIENT ISRAEL

The Source. The only source of information on Israelite society in ancient times is the Bible. Archaeological excavations have so far produced no significant additional material on this subject; nor have the few epigraphical sources of that period which have been discovered in Palestine added to our knowledge in this field. The information gleaned from the Bible is fragmentary, discontinuous, and sketchy. Moreover, it is difficult to obtain a general picture on the basis of biblical material, since this material was mostly written at a much later date than the period it describes, even though it may have contained ancient traditions. The realistic aspects of society and social problems were of incidental interest to the authors and editors, who were preoccupied with questions of morality and social justice. Thus it is only indirectly that the Bible permits us to view the social structure and its component parts, the social concepts and customs, of the ancient era.

Methods. Owing to the nature of the unique source, the student of ancient Israelite society must rely chiefly upon typological comparisons with other societies bearing a chronological, ethnic, geographic, and linguistic relationship to ancient Israelite society, as well as with later societies having the same social structure. Such a study will range from the tribal organization of pre-Islamic Arabia to that of Bedouin tribes in the 19th century. The analysis of ancient or recent parallels is guided by the fragmentary information provided in the Bible, which reflects a very well defined social system and way of life.

Hebrew Society Prior to the Conquest of Canaan. The

information derived from the Bible and by analogy from relevant examples (most particularly from the archive tablets found in the Mesopotamian city of Mari, which contain important details about Western Semitic tribal organization), indicates that in the pre-Canaanite period the structure of the Hebrew tribes was patriarchal and their way of life nomadic or seminomadic. Tribal structure was made up of variously sized units which were related to one another by blood, claimed descent from the same patriarchal ancestor, and shared a religious-cultic tradition. During that period it appears that the Patriarchs were a minor element amid the various West Semitic groups which dominated the Fertile Crescent from the second half of the third millennium B.C.E.—especially during the first half of the second millennium B.C.E.—which saw them spread into the Syrian-Israelite region.

The Period of Settlement in the Land of Israel. Most of the evidence concerning the tribal structure of Israel relates to the period of the settlement in the Promised Land and thereafter. There is no unequivocal material concerning the time and nature of the formation of the tribes. The 12 tribes, as we know them from the Bible, are merely a schematic device, a fixed number whose components apparently changed in the course of time, as may be concluded from certain sparse but unmistakable references. Some of these component parts probably dated from pre-settlement days, whereas others were apparently the product of the conquest and the settlement itself. According to one theory, the duodecimal scheme was based upon an actual supra-tribal organization similar to the Greek and Etruscan amphictyonies. Another theory emphasises the "democratic" rather than ritualistic nature of the organization. Other scholars question the existence of any supra-tribal organization. It seems obvious, however, that whatever its nature, such an organization undoubtedly did exist.

Tribal and Sub-Tribal Units. The tribal framework contained two kinds of sub-tribal units (Josh. 7:13–14). **69**

This subdivision may also be schematic to some extent, as may be deduced from the variety of terms used to designate these subunits. It is, however, evident that the smallest unit was the household *(bet ha-'av)*, consisting of the sons of one father, with their wives and offspring. Several households made up a clan (*mishpahah;* Num. 2:34), which produced the military unit called *"elef"* (Judg. 6:15; I Sam. 17:18 and 22:7 et al.). The tribe consisted of several such clans. One tribe, Dan, supposedly consisted of a single clan. The "nuclear family," with which we are familiar nowadays, had no independent existence in those days, but was only a component of the larger household. The individual male enjoyed equality under the law and by tradition, but not within the family structure. The individual could participate in the large gatherings of his unit, which in turn gave him a voice in tribal and clan decisions, including the selection of tribal institution leaders.

Institutions. Tribal leadership and institutions arose from among the elders, as the heads of clans and households were known. They wielded political and judicial authority. This was a leadership elected by the units on the basis of lineage, experience, and wisdom, as well as the size of the bloc which supported the person in question. It is difficult to determine to what extent this representative and governing body known as the elders had a consistent nature and whether it had exclusive power in the spheres of its authority. Apparently it was not a rigidly consistent institution. There were temporary leaders who emerged in times of crisis to save the tribe from its enemies, and their authority was charismatic and outside the traditional leadership. It is, nonetheless, apparent that the term judge was frequently applied to important individuals whose authority derived from their lineage and property, and who were thus similar to the traditional elders. The so-called "minor judges" (Judg. 10:1–4 and 12:8–15) belonged to this category. It is not entirely clear what was the highest rank in the tribal hierarchy. Certain biblical texts suggest that the term *nasi* designated this highest authority. It seems likely that the *nasi* was elected from among the elders (Num. 1:44 and 2:7).

Social Changes among the Settlers. The transition from a nomadic or seminomadic existence to a settled way of life affected the tribal society. While the tribal structure with its subunits remained unaltered, it was adapted to the new circumstances and needs, so that institutions and functions acquired new meanings. The primary cause of the gradual breakup of the ancient tribal equality was the new bond with the land. Permanent settlement on the land strengthened the power of private property and enhanced proprietary awareness. The social distinctions between sub-tribal units also increased, as did the differences between the tribes, resulting from the varied geographic and geopolitical conditions they encountered in their settlements. All this in turn served to weaken the intertribal association and the supra-tribal organization. The economic basis of the clans and households also changed. Sheep and cattle raising, previously the exclusive resource of the tribe, was being replaced by the cultivation of fruit and grain crops. At the same time, crafts necessary to the settled way of life and to agriculture were also on the increase. One side effect of the Israelite settlement was the appearance of a marginal society of unintegrated, nonproductive elements without property, who became mercenaries and followers of revolutionary leaders (Judg. 9:14, "worthless and reckless fellows"; and 11:3, "worthless fellows").

Urbanization. Urbanization accelerated social and economic processes. Although Israelite elements had existed in townships prior to the settlement, they had never constituted an integral part of an urban system. It seems that insofar as the patriarchal ancestors did maintain contact with cities, it was always under the specific protection of the rulers of the territory through which they passed or in which they dwelt temporarily. This class of alien transients was known in the ancient East as "Ḥabiru," from which, according to some authorities, the word Hebrew derives.

After the conquest of Canaan, Israelites became permanent dwellers in settlements of various sizes. The qualitative changes which took place among the Israelites who became urbanized is clearly seen in various biblical texts. Such texts deal largely with the institutions of leadership, although there were no doubt corresponding changes in the personal and judicial spheres as well, as evidenced by the laws in Deuteronomy, which are clearly associated with an urban existence (Deut. 19, 21, etc.). Tribal traditions and customs began to weaken, although they did not entirely disappear. The elders, an institution with tribal-patriarchal roots, became the established authority in the Israelite city (I Sam. 11:3). At the same time, the congregation of all free citizens emerged as a broader-based institution (*ibid.* v. 1). It becomes evident that urban life produced new criteria for the selection of elders, economic power replacing hereditary status. Thus of the ancient tribal institution only the title and framework remained, while the content underwent complete change. Urban life also affected the status of the sub-tribal units—the clan and the household grew in importance while the status of the tribe declined. This must have been so, despite the biblical emphasis on the tribe as the chief organization of Israelite society.

Changes in the Tribal System. The most basic changes were those which affected the tribal system. This large entity did not disappear entirely during the period under discussion. The tribe and its leadership remained very powerful. The Bible gives us a picture of a tribal framework which did not disintegrate even while it changed from being a group related by blood to a typical territory-based unit. There have been theories that the tribe originated with the settlement. Be that as it may, the criteria which determine membership in a nomadic tribe, i.e., blood ties and a common patriarchal ancestor, were obviously unsuited to the new way of life, in which geographic consideration took precedence over genealogy. In other words, membership of a tribe became predicated upon residence within its territory. In this way the tribes were able to absorb alien ethnic elements, as well as migrant groups from other tribes, who either became absorbed in the tribe or retained a form of dual-tribal affiliation. Thus the city with its inhabitants became a new component of the tribal system, to which a person could be related in the same way that he was related to a clan or household, and which appeared in genealogical lists as a descendant of the ancient ancestor of the tribe. There are numerous examples of this concept in the early chapters of I Chronicles. The picture which emerges is, no doubt, highly simplified, but it must have had its basis in reality, since in many cases an entire clan must have settled together in one city and formed the bulk of its population.

This is not to suggest that the urban citizen was subject to the authority of the tribal elders, for the city was a fairly independent entity. Rather, the city as an autonomous whole participated in the overall tribal organization which, by then, had some of the characteristics of a political alliance, where previously it had been an association of clans. All these changes took place over a long period of time and in a complicated manner. The process of settlement varied in its phases from tribe to tribe and from clan to clan. The story of the migration of the tribe of Dan from the south to the north (Judg. 17, 18) illustrates this fact, as does the evidence that certain tribes, e.g., Reuben and to some extent Simeon, continued to live a seminomadic, or even purely nomadic, existence until fairly late in the monarchic period (I Chron. 5:6–10), i.e., the latter half of the eighth century B.C.E. Other tribes evolved a totally different way of life in the course of the settlement (Judg. 5:17).

The Monarchy and the Tribal System. The monarchy in Israel emerged as an antithesis to the ancient tribal system. By its very nature, and in this specific instance, the monarchy acted as a catalyst upon certain social processes, of which some were ancient and others new. It is hardly surprising that the advent of the monarchy in Israel became the decisive factor in the disintegration of the tribal system. 73

In the beginning the monarchy apparently attempted to coexist with the tribal authority, and probably strove to incorporate it into the administration of the kingdom. However, the growing strength of the centralized royal authority inevitably led to clashes with the separatist interests of the tribal leaders, who naturally struggled to preserve their autonomy, even though they had previously concurred with the creation of the monarchy in order to meet certain exigencies. The activities of the monarchy, especially the division of the land into administrative regions (I Kings 4), also served to weaken and restrict the traditional, tribal-rooted authority. Thus, in the course of the monarchical era, tribal membership became largely a traditional symbol lacking any real function. The monarchy also undermined the tribal leadership by creating a whole new class of functionaries—"royal employees" dependent on the king, from the highest ministers (I Sam. 8:18–26); I Chron. 18:15–17; II Sam. 20:23–26; etc.), to officials, professional soldiers (I Kings 9:22 et al.), and managers, and laborers on the royal estates (I Sam. 8:12). Concurrently, the appointed priesthood and the Levite administration, as well as an emergent mercantile community, thrived under the influence of the monarchy. The monarchical economy encouraged the rapid development of specialized skills and enhanced crafts and the status of artisans. The elders were rapidly losing power in the urban centers, and authority became increasingly vested in the ministers who governed the affairs of the city. Nevertheless, these changes did not seriously affect the customs and the way of life within the framework of the clan and the household, which continued to derive their inspiration from the patriarchal tradition and the ancient social institutions. The kings took care not to destroy the accepted way of life. In any event, the clan was still a vital and effective factor during the period of the Return to Zion (Ezra 2; Neh. 4:7).

National Class Structure. The decline of the tribal system and the reorganization of the population, first in terms of territory and then as a kingdom, led to the emergence and crystallization of a nationwide class structure. The main stratum consisted of landowners, large and small. A class of artisans arose beside it. Additional strata emerged in the course of the monarchical period: royal functionaries, merchants, and government officials. It remains, however, impossible to reconstruct a satisfactory picture of the overall social stratification of ancient Israel. The Bible refers to various social classes whenever the narrative requires it, and apparently recognizes the existence of social stratification, although it emphasizes chiefly the division between the free and the enslaved, the poor and the rich. It would, therefore, be a mistake to attempt to reconstruct a complete model of the stratification of that society. A broad outline which includes an upper, a middle, and a lower class, together with the marginal elements and the slaves, will have to suffice. The priesthood and the Levites are not included in the aforementioned division, because of their special status and ritualistic functions, although in part they may have been considered as officers of the government (II Sam. 8:17 et al.).

Landowning Class. The broad base of the kingdom—and later of the separate kingdoms of Israel and Judah—were the landowners and the peasantry, who together comprised the bulk of the population. The sources frequently mention the landowners ("the great men," II Sam. 19:33), both on account of their political activities, and in connection with the bitter denunciations hurled at them by the prophets. Large estates had begun to appear even before the monarchy, as may be seen in the case of prominent individuals like Barzillai the Gileadite (II Sam. 19:32) and Nabal the Carmelite (I Sam. 25:2), in David's time. However, on the whole, great estates were a product of the political-economic policies of the kings, who rewarded their supporters and followers with land grants of conquered, annexed, or purchased territories (II Sam. 9:7–10; 19:30). There seems to have been a concentration of such *latifundia* in Transjordan. The economic power wielded by the estate owners soon turned into a massive political weapon in times of crisis and royal weakness, such as toward the end of the Kingdom of Israel—a period during which the Transjordanian nobles apparently exercised a decisive influence in the affairs of the capital, Samaria. In the Kingdom of Judah the landowing class does not seem to have played such a major role, perhaps because it was a small class—in view of the territorial limitations and the topography of the kingdom—and perhaps also because the Davidic dynasty was a strong one. From about the middle of the ninth century B.C.E., a section of the population described as "the people of the land" *(am ha-arez)* became increasingly prominent. There has been a great deal of speculation and research concerning this group, whose nature is not entirely clear. "The people of the land" played an active role in events of the highest political significance, such as the crowning of a new king, especially following revolutions and regicides (II Kings 11:14; II Chron. 33:25, et al.). From these sparse references it may be deduced that "the people of the land" was a broadly representative class in Judah and that its power rested in its ownership of the land, although it seems unlikely that this class included the major landowners. Apparently "the people of the land" succeeded the ancient "democratic" concept of the "congregation," which had more or less vanished shortly after the establishment of the monarchy. It has been suggested that the Northern Kingdom's equivalent of "the people of the land" were the "mighty men of wealth" *(gibbore ha-hayil)* mentioned in II Kings 15:20 and Ruth 2:1, upon whom the Israelite king Menahem imposed a special levy in order to pay the tribute to King Tiglath Pileser III of Assyria. There were 60,000 of them at that time. Some scholars have suggested that the term designated a landowning warrior who supplied his own as well as his men's military equipment.

Lower on the social scale stood the class of the small landowners, the tenant farmers of the great estates and of the royal estates. The origins of this group may have been in peasantry which had lost its own land through poverty or expropriation (Isa. 5:8). Some may have been settled on the land by the kings who wanted to strengthen the border regions or prevent social unrest. Thus the kings were able to enjoy larger revenues from the land than if it had been cultivated by slave labor.

Merchant Class. The mercantile community was of great social and economic importance. As we have seen, this class emerged and grew thanks to the royal initiative in international commerce, which was begun by King Solomon (I Kings 9:26–28; 10:14–15; II Chron. 20:35–36), and reached its peak in the golden age of the two kingdoms, i.e., the ninth century B.C.E., under Ahab and Jehoshaphat. While there is little data on this matter also, it would seem that there was a broad spectrum of mercantile activity, both on the international level and within the realm, both as part of the royal administration and as private enterprise. The Bible is not explicit in these matters, but it seems that the higher echelons of the merchant class exercised a considerable influence in the royal court, even in political affairs. There are indications that the Israelite merchants, like others in the Ancient Near East, invested in areas which did not have a direct bearing upon their main trade—finance, real estate, the slave trade, etc. (cf. Ex. 22:24; Lev. 25:36–37; Isa. 24:2; Jer. 15:10; et al.). It is not inconceivable that the merchants, through their commerce with neighboring and distant lands, served as the channel through which outside cultural and material influence penetrated Palestine. Moreover, it is likely that this class, together with the great landlords, intensified the class distinctions among the free population of Israel.

Artisan Class. The development of crafts was also accelerated by the advent of the monarchy. Archaeological finds in Israel have shown that the monarchical age brought about an expansion of crafts and increased productivity to sustain the economy and commerce of the realm (I Chron. 4:23). Throughout that age, crafts remained within the family and were not open to all comers. Skills were passed on from father to son (I Chron. 2:55 and 4:21). Though there may have been some pressure upon the artisans to.

widen their ranks in order to provide for the expanding economy of the kingdom, the familial pattern remained in effect. This is not to suggest that there were proper guilds, or guild-like organizations, as one scholar proposed. Craft guilds are based upon different principles and have different organizational structure. Certain texts superficially seem to suggest the existence of guilds—the mention of streets devoted to a certain craft (Jer. 37:21), artisan quarters (Neh. 3:32), industrial centers (Neh. 11:35 and compare Isa. 44:13, et al.), as well as craft nomenclature for families (Neh. 3:8, 12, 15, 31). However, this conclusion is misleading; there were no commercial guilds in existence. It appears that only at a relatively late date did the artisans entirely sever their ties with the land and it may be assumed that in small communities artisans owned land. It is not possible to determine the exact relationship of the artisan class to the other strata of society, but it is most likely that it represented one of the chief components of the middle stratum and the marginal elements.

Marginal Elements. Lower still on the social scale were the laborers without property or skill, who were hired by the day or by the season (Lev. 19:13; Deut. 24:14–15; Isa. 16:14). They were employed on the great estates, by the craftsmen, and in the service of the king or private individuals. In addition to these there were the remnants of the autochthonous elements which for some reason had failed or been unable to assimilate among the Israelites (Deut. 29:10). Called "aliens" or "resident aliens," they existed on the fringes of Israelite society. Their status determined the nature of their relationship to society. Legally and socially their status fell between that of the wholly disfranchised slaves and the free populace (II Chron. 2:16). It is likely that later on other alien elements were added to the authochthonous group. Their status apparently improved with time, and this may account for the apparent contradictions concerning their way of life and privileges in biblical texts. The aliens generally enjoyed the status of protected dependents (Deut. 1:16; 5:14; 29:10), and were more than once cited together with the poor and the helpless (Lev. 19:10 and 25:6), who were entitled to partake of a special tithe and other poor dues (Deut. 14:28–29 and 24:19, et al). Conversely, mention is also made of propertied aliens (Lev. 25:47; Deut. 28:43). A distinction must be made between the marginal, indigenous alien residents and a certain limited group of autochthonous families who allied themselves with royal families and the highest officialdom and kept their ancient exalted status. This was the outcome of moves made by the early kings, who had to establish a new administration at a time when there were no Israelites with the necessary qualifications.

Slaves. Lowliest of all were the slaves, who were deprived of all rights. They were of various origins—some had been captives taken in battle (cf. Deut. 21:10–14, II Chron. 28:8ff., et al.), and some were descendents of the aboriginal inhabitants of the land (I Kings 9:21; cf. Ezra 2:43–54; Neh. 7:46ff.). Finally, there were Israelites who were so improverished as to submit, voluntarily or under duress, to bondage to their creditors (II Kings 4:1–17; Isa. 50:1; Neh. 5:1–5). Biblical law endows the Israelite slave with certain rights (though these may fall within the bounds of a social-legal utopia), entitling them to their freedom after a limited time in bondage (Ex. 21:2–11; Lev. 25:40; Deut. 15:12–18). However, there is little evidence that slaves were in reality granted their freedom on a regular basis. There does appear to have been some distinction between the status of a purchased slave and one who was born in the household (Gen. 17:12; Lev. 25:41). Private persons as well as the king owned slaves (II Sam. 12:31). There are also some hints suggesting the existence of temple slaves, the "Nethinim" (Ezra 8:20, cf. Ezek. 44:7; Neh. 3:31 and 11:21), who were drawn from among the alien elements. There is no available data concerning the number and economic importance of slaves in ancient Israel. By analogy with other ancient societies in the Near East it may be assumed that during periods of expansion and conquest they were numerous and of some economic importance. 79

4 FROM THE DESTRUCTION TO ALEXANDER

The Restoration. The destruction of the Temple constituted a double crisis. Not only was the people cast off the land but the Divine Presence departed from Jerusalem (Ezek. 10:19; 11:23). Once the city was bereft of the God of Israel, its Canaanite origins came to the fore (Ezek. 16). The process of restoration from Babylonian exile would be a lengthy one that would carry the people along the same route traversed by their ancestors who emerged from Egypt. Like the Exodus from Egypt, the one from Babylonia was depicted in miraculous terms. The Sinaitic theophany was paralleled by the reconstruction of the Temple, which restored the Divine Presence to Jerusalem (cf. Ezra 6:12; 7:15), while the revelation of the laws to Moses had its counterpart in the reading of the Torah and the legislative activity of Ezra. The sanctity of the newly occupied land could only be preserved if the Sabbath was observed, if each member of the nation cared for his brother, and if the men did not take wives from among the pagan peoples. The Restoration was depicted in the terms outlined above in Deutero-Isaiah, Ezra, and Nehemiah. As the Lord revealed Himself by preparing a passage through the Red Sea, so would He reveal Himself by clearing a road through the desert separating Babylon from Jerusalem (Isa. 40:3ff.). Israel would be redeemed from its present as from its former bondage and gathered in from the four corners of the earth (Isa. 43:1ff.). As Israel took spoil from the Egyptians upon its earlier Exodus (Ex. 3:21-22; 11:2-3; 12:35-36), so would it now receive the tribute of all the nations (Isa. 60). The miraculous and munificent return described by the prophet is echoed in the historical books. The neighbors of the repatriates from Babylonia "strengthened their hands" with silver and gold vessels, cattle and goods of all sorts (Ezra 1:6). The Persian king Darius contributed toward the construction and sacrificial cult of the Temple (Ezra 5:8ff.) and this policy of support was continued by Artaxerxes I, who together with his seven advisers, also sent contributions (Ezra 7:15ff.). Though nothing is told of the journey of the repatriates who returned shortly after Cyrus' decree, the return of Ezra and his small band was carried out under divine guidance. In his memoirs Ezra writes "I was ashamed to ask the king for a band of soldiers and horsemen to protect us against the enemy on our way; since we had told the king 'The hand of our God is for good upon all that seek Him'..." Fasting and prayer thus secured safe passage (Ezra 8:22ff.). Since the historical books of Ezra and Nehemiah are structured so as to base the account of the Restoration on the model of the early stages of Israel's nationhood there is no "complete" account of the history of the period. The source is silent on the 30 years of the reign of Darius after the dedication of the Temple (515–486). A single sentence states that "at the beginning of the reign" of King Ahasuerus (Xerxes) i.e., in his accession year, an accusation was written against the inhabitants of Judah and Jerusalem (Ezra 4:6). Egypt had rebelled against Persia on the eve of Darius's death and the rebellion was subdued by Xerxes. It had traditionally been the case that Judah could sustain her rebellion against an imperial power, be it Assyria (Isa. 30–31) or Babylon (Jer. 37:6ff.), only by reliance upon Egypt. Thus it may be that Judah was involved or suspected of being involved in the Egyptian rebellion. The historical source is silent for another period of almost 30 years. In the seventh year of Artaxerxes I (458) Ezra was officially authorized by the king to "investigate" the situation in Judah and in Jerusalem in accordance with the law of God which was in his possession. He was entitled to appoint judges for the Jews beyond the confines of Judah, that is throughout the satrapy of the Trans-Euphrates ("Beyond the River"). Jews ignorant of the divine law were to be instructed, while those who violated either that law or the law of the king were to be suitably punished whether by death, banishment, fine, or imprisonment (Ezra 7:25–26).

Ezra. Who was this Ezra and why should Artaxerxes grant him such broad authority in the year 458? In a genealogically conscious era, Ezra's genealogy is one of the most elaborate. He is a priest who traces his line directly back to Aaron through the latter's son and grandson Phinehas son of Eleazar. His immediate ancestor is given as Seraiah whose name is identical with that of the chief priest slain by Nebuchadnezzar at Riblah (2 Kings 25:18ff.). With the exception of two lacunae, the genealogy is identical with that in I Chronicles 5:29–40. As recorded in the Book of Ezra (7:1–5) it gives the appearance of schematic arrangement (seven names between Aaron and Azariah (absent in Chron.) and seven names between Azariah and Ezra (hypocoristic of Azariah). While the genealogy is silent, perhaps deliberately so, about Ezra's relationship to the executed Seraiah's grandson, Jeshua son of Jehozadak, its schematic selectivity suggests divine determination: "For Ezra had set his mind on investigating the Torah of the Lord in order to teach effectively its statutes and judgments in Israel" (Ezra 7:10). The Hebrew term for "set" is identical with that used to describe the erection of the altar (Ezra 3:3), indicating that Ezra was fulfilling the second major task in the complete restoration of Israel. What were his qualifications for this undertaking? He was a "scribe skilled in the Torah of Moses given by the Lord God of Israel" (Ezra 7:6; cf. 7:11). In its Aramaic formulation his title was "scribe of the Law of the God of Heaven" (Ezra 7:12, 21). The scribe was not only one versed in writing (cf. Ps. 45:2), he was also learned, "a wise man" who transmitted his wisdom (cf. Jer. 8:8). The divine law in which Ezra was proficient was "the Wisdom of his God in his possession" (Ezra 7:25). In their wisdom, scribes were also called upon to advise kings and fill other governmental posts so that scribe, "secretary," also appears as an official title (II Sam. 8:17, et al.; Ezra 4:8 et al., Neh. 13:13). Whether in his capacity as scribe Ezra held a post in the Persian government, as some scholars have maintained, is uncertain.

Whatever his status in the Persian Empire, Ezra "the priest and scribe" (Ezra 7:11) claimed that divine favor was responsible for Artaxerxes' giving him everything he requested (Ezra 7:6). The historical reason for the fame Ezra enjoyed may have been the revolt which broke out in Egypt ca. 463/2. It was in the interest of the Persian king at just this juncture to strengthen his hold on the territory bordering on Egypt. The Jewish garrison at Elephantine in Egypt having remained loyal to Artaxerxes throughout the decade of rebellion in lower Egypt, the king must have felt that he could rely on the Jews in the Trans-Euphrates as well. Their loyalty would be assured if the internal law which they observed received the same absolute sanction as did imperial law (Persian *dātā;* cf. Esth. 1:19; 8:8; Dan. 6:9) and if the enforcement of both laws was entrusted to a respected Jewish personality such as Ezra. It should be mentioned that scholars are not in agreement as to the date of Ezra's mission, some preferring to see it in the reign of Artaxerxes, the second king of that name, who reigned from 404–359. The seventh year of his reign would accordingly have been 398, and Ezra's mission would likewise have coincided with a rebellion in Egypt. This later revolt included all of Egypt and the garrison at Elephantine acknowledged the ruling Egyptian king Amyrtaeus by June 19, 400. The motive for the privileges granted Ezra are thus the same whether the king is hypothesized as Artaxerxes II or Artaxerxes I. Were the king in fact Artaxerxes II Ezra would have followed Nehemiah, whose arrival in Jerusalem, because of a correlation with a date in the Elephantine papyrus (cf. Cowley, *Aramaic Papyri* 30:18, 30 with Neh. 12:22–23) is fixed to 444 (cf. Neh. 2:1). Some scholars, rather than

Aramaic papyrus of the Jewish garrison at Elephantine in Egypt, fifth century B.C.E. New York, Brooklyn Museum.

shifting Ezra to year seven of the reign of Artaxerxes II, maintain that the king was Artaxerxes I and emend the year date to 27, 32, (33), or 37, thus placing Ezra's arrival either in 438 (during Nehemiah's first mission), 432 (433) (after Nehemiah's first mission), or 428 (during Nehemiah's second mission). The arguments for the shifting of the king and the emendation of the date are numerous but most rest on specious considerations and dubious textual interpretation. The return under Ezra was a replica in miniature of that under Zerubbabel. Stress was laid on the unity of Israel. Ezra's caravan contained members of the major groups of society. Included were two priestly families, Hattush of the Davidic line and 12 lay families numbering together with Ezra, 1,500. Special efforts were taken to enlist Levites, of whom 38 were recruited, and Temple servants, who numbered 220 (Ezra 8:1–20). Concern for Temple cult and personnel played a primary role. Contributions of gold, silver, and vessels from the king and his advisers and from Jews remaining in Babylonia were duly recorded, carefully transported, and officially deposited in the Temple (Ezra 7:15–16; 8:24–34). All the Temple officials from priest to lowly servant were to be exempt from taxation by the Persian government (Ezra 7:24). Just as the Temple dedication was celebrated by the sacrifice of 12 he-goats as sin offerings, to atone for the whole house of Israel (Ezra 6:17), so the arrival of Ezra in Jerusalem was marked by the sacrifice of 12 bulls as burnt offerings and 12 he-goats as sin offerings (Ezra 8:35–36). The numbers of the other sacrifices were typological multiples—96 rams, a multiple of 12 (cf. Num. 7:87–88), and 77 lambs, a multiple of seven, the number offered on all the festivals, the New Moon, the New Year, and the Day of Atonement (Num. 28–29).

DISSOLUTION OF MIXED MARRIAGES. Ezra set out from Babylon on the first of Nisan (Ezra 7:9), departed from a place called Ahava on the 12th of Nisan (Ezra 8:31), and arrived in Jerusalem on the first of Av some five months later (Ezra 7:8). On the 20th of Kislev, in the middle of the winter and in pouring rain, Ezra convened an assembly in Jerusalem (Ezra 10:9ff.) with the express purpose of dissolving the many mixed marriages, prevalent in all levels of society, which were called to his attention shortly after his arrival.

Interestingly there is no mention of Jewish women married to foreign men. The whole situation revolves around foreign wives. There is not even any effort made to convert them to Judaism. Israel is the "holy seed" and must not become contaminated by the "abominations" of the Canaanites, Ammonites, Moabites, and Egyptians. Mixed marriages would be "sacrilege" against the holy. At the core of this view of the situation lies not only a midrashic interpretation of the various laws in the Torah regarding intermarriage (Ex. 34:11ff.; Deut. 7:1ff.; 23:4ff.) but the notion that the land, being resettled as in the days of the conquest, was once more susceptible to the taint of its aboriginal impurity (cf. Ezra 9–10 with Deut. 7–9). The procedure which culminated in that fateful assembly on 20 Kislev, 458, bore distinct resemblance to the ceremonies surrounding the condemnation of Achan, who committed sacrilege through misappropriation of the devoted things (cf. Ezra 9:1–10:8 with Josh. 7; Deut. 7:2, 26).

The mourning and confession of Ezra upon learning of the mixed marriages and the subsequent ceremony on that rainy day established the mood appropriate to the dissolution of the mixed marriages. However, the act itself was preceded by three months of work, from the first of Tevet to the first of Nisan, which consisted of investigating and recording the names, according to their families, of each male who had married a foreign wife. The list is headed by four members of the high-priestly family who agreed to put away their foreign wives and offered a ram as a guilt offering (Ezra 10:9–19), the sacrifice prescribed for one who unknowingly committed sacrilege against a sacred object (Lev. 5:14ff.). The number of lay families as recorded in the Masoretic Text was ten but a Septuagint reading in Ezra (10:38) yields the traditional 12. The latter figure indicates that although the recorded instances (111 or 113) were few, relative to the size of the population, the desecration affected "all Israel." Strangely, the outcome of this enterprise is uncertain. The concluding verse to the whole account in the Masoretic Text is obscure and noncommittal, but the apocryphal Book of Esdras is decisive in asserting that the men all sent away their foreign wives together with their children (I Esd. 9:36).

FORTIFICATION OF JERUSALEM. Similarly uncertain are the circumstances surrounding the next step attempted in the Restoration of the people to its land. The source for the event is an Aramaic correspondence between officials in Samaria and Artaxerxes (Ezra 4:8–23). The letters are not dated and the account is incorporated into Ezra according to a topical arrangement—setbacks first (Ezra 4), successes, last (Ezra 5–6)—rather than a chronological one (i.e., Ezra 4:6–23 preceding Neh. 1). The Samarian officials were the chancellor Rehum and the scribe Shimshai. They write in the name of the local bureaucracy as well as of the settlers from Erech, Babylon, Susa, and elsewhere, introduced into the area by the Assyrian king Ashurbanipal (669–27), possibly around 642. The letter informs Artaxerxes I that the Jews who recently arrived (along with Ezra?) were busily fortifying Jerusalem. It goes on to say that the city was notoriously rebellious and that if the fortifications were to be completed, the people would merely not pay royal taxes. The king reported back to his officials that he had duly investigated the reputation of Jerusalem and discovered that it had been a rebellious city as charged. He therefore ordered the Samarian officials to proceed to Jerusalem and put a halt to the fortifications. They acted with dispatch and by force of arms.

The desire of the Jews to refortify Jerusalem was natural. Jeremiah had prophesied that "the city would be rebuilt upon its mound" (Jer. 30:18), and according to Deutero-Isaiah, Cyrus himself would carry out the task (Isa. 44:28). Cyrus apparently never issued such orders and hopes for an early Davidic restoration ceased with Zerubbabel's inexplicable disappearance from the scene. The broad powers given to Ezra may have encouraged the Jews to believe that the time was ripe to rebuild Jerusalem. Perhaps, too, the struggle for independence pursued by Egypt, now in alliance with Athens, spurred on Judah. Whatever the reason, the plan miscarried. The northern rival Samaria prevailed and Judah was put to shame. Word of the situation eventually reached Nehemiah, the king's cupbearer in Susa. His immediate reaction was similar to that of Ezra upon learning of the mixed marriages—fasting and confession of guilt (Neh. 1). However, Nehemiah was a decisive man of action. Praying to God for assistance, he sought an appropriate moment to ask leave of the king to travel to Judah and rebuild Jerusalem. Leave was granted, 87 and preparations for the journey and the task to be undertaken were carefully laid. Nehemiah requested, and received, letters of safe conduct and a military escort—unlike Ezra, who relied on divine assistance alone—along with an authorization to the keeper of the king's forest for timber for a Temple citadel, his own residence, as well as for the wall of the city (Neh. 2:1–9).

Nehemiah. The account of Nehemiah's activity is reported in his own memoirs. Like Ezra, Nehemiah ascribed his success with the king to the hand of God (Neh. 2:8). Historically it is not clear what prompted Artaxerxes I to contradict himself in 445 and allow the reconstruction of the walls he had earlier ordered destroyed. Perhaps the high position and forceful personality of Nehemiah were responsible. Nehemiah noted that the queen was present when he put forth his request. Certainly he showed skill in formulating his petition. Like Haman who sought from Ahasuerus destruction of "a certain people" who "do not keep the king's laws" (Esth. 3:8), without mentioning the Jews by name, so Nehemiah sought permission from Artaxerxes to rebuild "the city of the graves of my fathers" (Neh. 2:5), not specifying Jerusalem. Even if the king were fully aware that the permission being granted Nehemiah reversed an earlier decision of his, he may have felt that if his trusted servant were in charge of the project, fear of rebellion was minimal. Accordingly, Nehemiah was appointed governor of Judah, a post he held from 445 until 433 (Neh. 5:14) and then again for an unspecified period after returning to the court at Susa (Neh. 13:6–7). This appointment may also have been an attempt to strengthen Persian control in the area in the wake of the recent rebellion of Megabyzus, satrap of the Trans-Euphrates.

REBUILDING OF THE WALL OF JERUSALEM. In his memoirs, Nehemiah described his task of building the wall as having gone through seven stages, each one punctuated by opposition on the part of Judah's neighbors. These were Sanballat (I) the Horonite, governor of Samaria (cf. Cowley, *Aramaic Papyri* 30:29), Tobiah of Transjordan, and Geshem (Gashmu) king of Kedar (cf. Tell el-Maskhuteh inscription). Both Sanballat and Tobiah were "Jewish," i.e., worshipers of the God of Israel, as attested either by their own names or those of their descendants (cf. Cowley, *Aramaic Papyri* 30:29; Aramaic papyri from Wadi Daliyeh), who inherited their official posts. Both were allied by marriage to prominent families in Judah (Neh. 6:17ff.; 13:28). For a time Tobiah enjoyed a chamber in the Jerusalem Temple (Neh. 13:4ff.). The factors that allowed the high priest Eliashib to join Nehemiah in reconstructing the wall in the teeth of Sanballat's opposition yet permitted Eliashib's grandson to marry a daughter of Sanballat to Nehemiah's great annoyance (Neh. 13:28) are unknown. Suffice it to say that all three foreigners viewed Nehemiah as a personal enemy. The feeling was reciprocated. He never referred to Sanballat as "governor," denigrated Tobiah by referring to him as the "Ammonite servant" (Neh. 2:10), and called Geshem simply "the Arabian."

The first stage of Nehemiah's activity was his journey to Jerusalem. His arrival greatly displeased Sanballat and Tobiah because "someone had come to seek the welfare of the Israelites" (Neh. 2:10). In stealth and with circumspection Nehemiah conducted a nocturnal inspection of the wall and then inspired the leaders to agree to reconstruction by informing them of the divine and royal favor he enjoyed. Sanballat, Tobiah, and Geshem mocked and derided the decision of this second stage of Nehemiah's activity, but he replied with an affirmation of divine assistance and told them decisively, and apparently not gratuitously, "you have no share, right, or memorial in Jerusalem" (Neh. 2:11–20). The policy of exclusion initiated by Zerubbabel (Ezra 4:2–3) and carried through by Ezra (Ezra 9–10) was now being vigorously pursued by Nehemiah.

The third stage in Nehemiah's activity constituted the actual building (Neh. 3). Jeremiah had prophesied, "Behold, the days are coming, says the Lord, when the city shall be rebuilt for the Lord from the Tower of Hananel . . . to the Horse Gate . . . sacred to the Lord" (Jer. 31:38ff.). The wall was divided into some 40 sections, and groups from all classes of the people were assigned to work on each section. The first section extended from the Sheep Gate to the Tower of Hananel and was restored by the high priest Eliashib (Neh. 3:1). One of the last sections constructed was the Horse Gate where, too, priests were at work (Neh. 3:28). In addition to providing a detailed description of the wall, the list is valuable for some of the random information it supplies, e.g., it indicates the presence of guilds in Jerusalem such as the goldsmiths', the ointment mixers', and the merchants' guild (Neh. 3:8, 31). When Sanballat and Tobiah learned that construction had begun in earnest they became angry and mockingly exclaimed, "Can they revive the stones from the dust heap? From burned stones? Should a fox jump up, he would demolish their stone wall." Nehemiah cursed them for their taunts as the work proceeded apace until the wall reached half its intended height (Neh. 3:33–38). The reaction of Sanballat and Tobiah, the Arabs, Ammonites, and Ashdodites to this fourth stage of the reconstruction was to prepare armed intervention. Word of the plan reached Nehemiah through the Jews dwelling in those districts, and he not only placed guards at vulnerable spots along the wall but armed the builders. He encouraged the workers by assuring them that should attack come, "our God will fight for us" (Neh. 4).

This fifth stage of activity almost brought the work to its completion. It was now threatened, however, by internal discontent. Jews were not behaving like "brothers." Short of food to eat and money for taxes, many were forced to take costly loans, mortgage their fields, and sell their children into slavery. Even Nehemiah and his servants were guilty of extorting heavy interest and taking pledges. Demanding interest from a brother in need was incompatible with fear of the Lord (Neh. 5:9; cf. Lev. 25:36) and would not be conducive to God's blessing on the newly occupied land (cf. Deut. 23:20–21). If the building of the wall were to be brought to successful completion, all debts had to be canceled and pledges returned. Nehemiah convened an assembly of the people and forced his reform through (Neh. 5).

Unable to thwart the building itself, Sanballat and Geshem sought to lure Nehemiah into a private conference where presumably his life would be threatened. They circulated the rumor that he was planning a rebellion and appointing prophets to acclaim him king of Judah. They themselves hired Noadiah the prophetess to frighten him and the prophet Shemaiah son of Delaiah to entice him into seeking refuge in the Temple. Tobiah's allies in Judah likewise spoke to Nehemiah on behalf of Tobiah. The reaction of Nehemiah's enemies to this stage availed as little as the earlier ones. After 52 days of strenuous labor, the wall was finished on 25 Elul, 445. Josephus maintained that the labor took two years and four months (Ant. 11: 179). There remained nothing for the "enemies" to do but appear downcast and acknowledge God's contribution to the project (Neh. 6), and so the seventh and final stage of Nehemiah's building activity was brought to a successful conclusion. Guards of the city were appointed and Nehemiah's God-fearing brother, Hanani(ah), was put in charge of the citadel (Neh. 7: 1–3).

RELIGIOUS INSTRUCTION AND DEDICATION OF THE TEMPLE. It was now the 14th year since the arrival of Ezra in Jerusalem and nothing had yet been said of his having implemented the instruction to teach the Torah (Ezra 7: 25). No doubt he had been engaged in this project over the years, gathering around himself a band of teachers, primarily levites, able to expound the Torah and render it into the Aramaic vernacular. The timing was now right for a grand ceremony patterned on that of Zerubbabel and the first repatriates. To emphasize the imitation of the earlier period the editor of the historical source (Ezra-Nehemiah) even reproduced verbatim the original list of repatriates (Ezra 2; Neh. 7: 6–72). Although fortification of Jerusalem enhanced the status of Judah and removed its shame, Davidic kingship had not been restored. Foreign rulers still occupied the land. The gains already achieved could only be 91 maintained if the people observed the Torah.

On the first of Tishri after their return, Zerubbabel and the Jews with him had reestablished the Temple altar to offer burnt offerings "as written in the Torah of Moses the man of God" (Ezra 3:1–7). Now on the first of Tishri after the completion of the wall the people called upon Ezra to publicly read from the "book of the Torah of Moses which the Lord prescribed for Israel" (Neh. 8:1). The description of the ceremony, which began at sunrise, makes it clear that Ezra was prepared for the occasion. A special wooden podium was prepared, and six men stood on his right and seven on his left, altogether 14. Upon opening the Torah, Ezra blessed God and the people responded with "Amen," and prostrated themselves. Ezra then read until noon and 13 levites expounded the significance of the text and perhaps translated it into Aramaic. The people interrupted the reading with crying, and Ezra and Nehemiah informed them that the day was holy, one of rejoicing, feasting, and giving gifts to the poor. Similarly, when the Temple foundations had been laid, the elders who remembered the original Temple broke out in tears, while others rejoiced (Ezra 3:12).

After the original repatriates had dedicated the altar on the first of Tishri, they celebrated the seven days of Sukkot by offering the sacrifices, "according to number and prescription." This would bring the number of bulls to 70 (Num. 29:12–32), suggesting the 70 members of Jacob's family (Gen. 46:27; Ex. 1:5) and indicating the unity of Israel. The Jews under Ezra and Nehemiah gathered on the second of Tishri to continue studying the Torah and they discovered "written in the Torah which the Lord prescribed through Moses that the Israelites should dwell in booths on the festival of the seventh month" (Neh. 8:14). And so "the whole congregation which had returned from the captivity" constructed booths on their roofs, in their courtyards, in the Temple courtyards, and in public squares. Such an observance had not been held since the days of Joshua, i.e., the time of the conquest. The Torah was read daily throughout the festival (Neh. 8:13–18). Is it coincidental that these reading ceremonies fell in the 14th year? (Ezra arrived in the seventh year of Artaxerxes I and Nehemiah in the 20th year.) Might this have been related to the Deuteronomic injunction to publicly read the Torah every seventh year, the year of release, at Sukkot time with the idea of instructing future generations "as long as they live in the land which you are about . . . to occupy" (Deut. 31:10ff.)?

The imagery of the booth *(sukkah)* recurs in the Bible with overtones of redemption and providence. The levitical injunction to dwell in booths is explained by the notion that God settled the Israelites in booths *(sukkot:* cf. also Ex. 12:37) when He delivered them from Egypt (Lev. 23:43). Subsequently God's own booth or dwelling was in Jerusalem. There He protected His people (Ps. 76). After God's judgment of the wicked city the purified remnant will again be protected by a booth (Isa. 4). The activity of Nehemiah in rebuilding Jerusalem's walls and repairing its breaches (cf. Neh. 1:3; 2:5, 17; 3:35) was doubtless believed to fulfill the prophecy of Amos that God would "raise up the fallen booth of David" (Amos 9:11). The final deliverance—complete independence—would be celebrated annually when the nations came to Jerusalem to worship the Lord on the occasion of Sukkot (Zech. 14:16).

To hasten that day the Jews now reconstituted on their soil, their Temple reconstructed, and the city fortified, concluded on the 24th of Tishri a solemn agreement to "follow the law of God which had been transmitted through Moses the servant of God." The covenant ceremony was preceded by purification, i.e., separation from the foreigners, fasting, sackcloth, and confession, and concluded with the signature of a written document by Nehemiah, 21 priestly families, 17 Levites and 44 lay families (Neh. 9:1–10:30). In addition to having sworn to observe the written Torah, the people undertook to observe some 18 decrees not explicitly mentioned in the Torah but derived from it through the procedure of *midrash halakhah,* 93 "legal interpretation," developed by Ezra and his associates. The earlier celebration of Sukkot, building booths out of the various species "as written" (Neh. 8:15; cf. Lev. 23:40) is an example of such interpretation and of one subsequently abandoned. The decrees, now recorded, centered around the prohibition of mixed marriage, the observance of the Sabbath and the seventh year, and provisions designed to show that the people would "not neglect the House of ... God" (Neh. 10:31-40).

Nehemiah had raised up Jerusalem's stones from the dust (Neh. 3:34) in answer to the call of Deutero-Isaiah (Isa. 52:2). The agreement not to intermarry (Neh. 9:2, 10, 29, 31) was necessary toward fulfillment of the promise that "the uncircumcised and the unclean" shall no more come into the "holy city" (Isa. 52:1). Jeremiah had promised that once more people would proclaim, "the Lord bless you ... O holy hill" and that "Judah and all its cities shall dwell there together" (Jer. 31:22-23). The penultimate task of Nehemiah was thus the populating of the now secure and spacious "holy city." The leaders already lived there and the rest of the people cast lots to bring 10% of Judah's population into the capital. The partial list of towns in which the rest of the people were settled indicates that the southernmost town was Beer-Sheba and the northernmost Bethel. The western border extended to Ono, while the list of the first repatriates and the list of builders indicated that to the east the province of Judah included Jericho (Ezra 2:34; Neh. 7:36, 3:2, 7:4; 11:1-36).

The final ceremony in which Nehemiah participated was the dedication of the walls. The people, the gates, and the wall were purified. Two musical processions were organized to march around the city in opposite directions on the top of the wall and meet in the Temple for the sacrificial service. The procession going to the right was led by Ezra; the one to the left included Nehemiah. The circumambulation is reminiscent of certain Psalms: "His holy mountain ... is the joy of all the earth ... walk about Zion; go round about her" (Ps. 48:2, 13).

Nehemiah remained in Jerusalem for another dozen years before returning to Susa. Virtually nothing is known of his rule during this period other than his own statement that he ruled with a lighter hand than his predecessors and did not claim the governor's food allowance from the local populace. This in spite of the fact that he supported a retinue of 150 and regularly entertained foreign visitors. The refrain in Nehemiah's memoirs runs "Remember to my credit, O my God, all that I did on behalf of this people" (Neh. 5:19; 13:14, 22, 31). God's attention is similarly drawn to his opponents (Ezra 6:14), and these did not disappear after his main task was completed. During Nehemiah's absence, Tobiah was assigned a chamber in the Temple by Eliashib the priest, and the people failed to pay the Levites their allotments, so that they left Jerusalem and retired to their fields. Upon his return, Nehemiah expelled Tobiah and enforced payment of the tithe (Neh. 13:4–14).

Even more serious than neglect of the levitical dues were the outright violations of the first two decrees in the solemn agreement sworn to earlier—work and commerce on the Sabbath and marriage to Ashdodite, Ammonite, and Moabite women. Nehemiah rebuked the leaders for the Sabbath desecration in terms reminiscent of Jeremiah who had said, "If . . . you keep the Sabbath day holy . . . this city shall be inhabited forever. . . . If you did not listen . . . fire . . . shall devour . . . Jerusalem" (Jer. 17:24–27). He then ordained that the gates of the city be shut for the Sabbath and the levites stand guard against local and foreign traders. The fate of Solomon's kingdom was cited against the men who took foreign wives, and Nehemiah cursed all, struck some and pulled out their hair. The grandson of the high priest Eliashib, who was married to a daughter of Sanballat, was "chased away." Successful implementation of the other cultic decrees was assured (Neh. 13:14–28).

Since kingship was not to be restored until the advent of the Hasmoneans 300 years later, Judah continued to exist as a theocracy—a province ruled by God's law with a civil head in the person of the governor appointed by the Persian king and a religious head in the person of the high priest of the line of Zadok. In the fourth century there appear coins and seal impressions bearing the Aramaic inscription *YHD* = Judea. With one or two notable exceptions, our information for the remaining 100 years of Persian rule dries up. It is possible that Nehemiah's brother Hananiah succeeded him as governor (cf. Cowley, *Aramaic Papyri* 21). In the last decade of the fifth century the governor was one who bore the Persian name Bagohi (Cowley, 30/31). The high priest Johanan was challenged by his brother Jeshua and Johanan murdered him. A stiff penalty was thereupon placed on the community by the strategos of Artaxerxes II who also bore the name Bagohi (Jos., Ant., 11:298–301). One incident that has come down through the Aramaic papyri relates that Bagohi joined the sons of Sanballat, Delaiah, and Shelemiah, in responding favorably to the request of the Elephantine Jewish community for intercession with the Persian ruler in Egypt toward the reconstruction of their temple (Cowley, *Aramaic Papyri* 30–32). The attraction–repulsion between Samaria and Judah of the days of Nehemiah repeated itself on the eve of Alexander's conquest. Nikaso, daughter of Sanballat III, was married to Manasseh, brother of the high priest Jaddua. Jerusalem authorities objected to the marriage and asked Manasseh to choose between his wife and the priesthood. He thereupon accepted the offer of Sanballat to be high priest in the temple to be errected on Mt. Gerizim and "governor of all the places" under Sanballat's control. Many Jewish priests followed him to Samaria (Jos., Ant., 11:306–12). The Samaritan schism thereupon became final.

5 SECOND TEMPLE (HELLENISTIC-ROMAN PERIOD)

In the last third of the fourth century B.C.E. decisive changes and developments took place in Ereẓ Israel. Prior to that time the country had been under the rule and influence of the great oriental powers and civilizations. Thereafter, and until the Arab conquests in the seventh century C.E., Ereẓ Israel and all its neighbors fell under the influence of kingdoms and cultures whose main source of inspiration derived from the Greek and later also from the successor Roman world. Alexander the Great's subjection of Ereẓ Israel in 332 B.C.E. encountered no serious opposition; only in Gaza did the Persian garrison defend itself heroically against the conqueror. Jerusalem and Judea reached a settlement with Alexander according to which they continued to enjoy the rights granted to them under Persian rule. However, relations between the Samaritans and the Macedonian conquerors soon deteriorated. Alexander the Great did not remain long in Ereẓ Israel, and its conquest was completed by his commanders who laid the foundations of the Hellenistic regime in the country.

Ptolemaic Rule. After Alexander's death (323) Ereẓ Israel was caught up in the vortex of wars fought among themselves by his successors, the Diadochi, among whom control of the country changed hands several times, in consequence of which the population suffered greatly. In 301 the country was finally conquered by Ptolemy I, the ruler of Egypt, and included in the Ptolemaic kingdom until 200, its history during this period being bound up with that of the Ptolemaic state. In the third century Ptolemaic rule in Ereẓ Israel was on the defensive against the Seleucid kingdom which governed Syria and which also laid claim to Erez Israel. For most of that century the Ptolemies generally had the upper hand and only with the accession of Antiochus III (223–187) to the throne of the Seleucid kingdom did the initiative pass to the rival dynasty. Already at the beginning of his reign Antiochus succeeded in conquering the greater part of Erez Israel but was defeated by the Ptolemaic army at Rafa in 217. After an interval he renewed the war and in 200 his forces gained a notable victory near the sources of the Jordan, as a result of which, despite repeated efforts by the Ptolemies to regain control of Erez Israel by war or political means, its rule passed to the Seleucid dynasty. Nevertheless, in point of its duration the Ptolemaic sway over Erez Israel lasted longer than that of any other foreign power in the period between the downfall of Persia and the rise of Rome. Moreover, the administrative patterns as well as the social and economic institutions and influences which appeared under the Ptolemies persisted in the country until the Roman period. In the days of Ptolemaic rule, Erez Israel did not constitute a distinct administrative region, its territory being an inseparable part of the region known officially as Syria and Phoenicia. The borders of this district were not permanent but liable to changes resulting from the ascendancy now of the Ptolemaic, now of the Seleucid kingdom. In any event, it is clear that Ptolemaic Syria and Phoenicia included the whole of Erez Israel and Transjordan. Among the most conspicuous results of Greek rule in Erez Israel was the transformation that took place in the ethnic composition and organizational forms of its population. An extensive Greek settlement took place, Greek military colonies were established, and the character of the ancient cities underwent a change. In fact the vast majority of the Hellenistic cities were ancient ones which were now organized according to the politico-social pattern of the Greek cities. Within a short time the members of the upper classes among the local population joined the ranks of the settlers 98 who had come from Greece, particularly prominent in this

Silver coin of the Persian period, fourth century B.C.E., bearing a falcon and the Aramaic inscription *YHD [Yahud]* (Judah). Jerusalem, Israel Museum, H. Bessin Collection. Photo D. Harris, Jerusalem.

respect being the Phoenicians who became the standard bearers in Erez Israel of Hellenism. Among its most notable centers were Gaza and Ashkelon on the southern coast and Ptolemais (Acre) to the north. Cities bearing a Hellenistic stamp were also established in the vicinity of the Sea of Galilee and in Transjordan. The process of Hellenization was extremely slow in the interior of Erez Israel. There the original Semitic character was preserved—except for Samaria, where Macedonians settled already at the beginning of the period. Hellenism also made deep inroads in the

Coin of the Hasmonean king, Alexander Yannai (103–76 B.C.E.), bearing a lily encircled by the Hebrew inscription, "Jonathan the king." Jerusalem, Israel Museum, Israel Department of Antiquities Collection.

Idumean city of Marisa, the Ptolemaic administrative center in southern Erez Israel. Under the Ptolemies and later under the Seleucids, Judea was one of their many administrative units. The Hellenistic period witnessed the continuation of the state of *Yahud* which dated from the days of Persian rule. To the Hellenistic rulers Judea represented a nation—an ethnos—whose center was in Jerusalem and whose autonomous leadership was entrusted to the high priest and the Gerousia, the council of elders. In this way there were preserved in Hellenistic Judea the patterns of Jewish administration in the form it had assumed under Persian rule. The high priests belonged to the house of Zadok and the division of Jedaiah, and were descendants of Joshua son of Jehozadak, the high priest at the time of the Return. The high priesthood passed by inheritance from father to son. To the Jews and non-Jews alike the high priest was the head of the nation, its religious as well as its political leader. He presided over the council of elders and was charged with the supreme supervision of the Temple, with the security of Jerusalem and the provision of its regular water supply. Supporting the high priest was the Gerousia, which was, it seems, officially even superior to him. The Hellenistic kingdom confirmed the Jewish "ancestral laws" as the constitution binding on the entire territory of semiautonomous Judea. This constitution was identical with the Pentateuch as interpreted and shaped by Jewish tradition throughout the generations. Recognized as they were by the ruling kingdom, the Jewish authorities were permitted to impose the commandments of the Torah on all the inhabitants of Judea and to eradicate idolatry from its soil.

Judea's religious and social life centered round the Temple. The Greek historian Polybius even described the Jews as a nation that dwells around its famed Temple in Jerusalem. Associated with the Temple were the priests who represented the aristocratic class in Judea which included not only the high priest, the recognized head of the nation, but also many members of the Gerousia and those in leading positions. To the non-Jews, Judea was a land governed by a hierarchy. In addition to the dynasty of the high priests there were several notable priestly houses who fulfilled important functions in Jewish society and in its political life. Among these were, for example, the sons of Hakkoz (Accos). Johanan son of Hakkoz conducted negotiations with Antiochus III in order to obtain privileges for Jerusalem after its conquest by the Seleucids; his son Eupolemus led the delegation to Rome on behalf of Judah Maccabee. Conspicuous among the lay houses which attained positions of great influence in Judea in the third century B.C.E. was that of the Tobiads, whose roots went back to First Temple times and the basis of whose power was in southern Gilead where the family estates, famous as "the land of Tobiah," were situated. The influence of the Tobiads increased under Persian rule. The Tobiah who lived in the days of Nehemiah was connected by marriage with important personages in Jerusalem and was among those who organized the opposition to the policy and decrees of Ezra and Nehemiah. One of his descendants, Tobiah who lived in the days of Ptolemy Philadelphus, was the head of the military colony in the "province of Ammon" which was composed both of Jews and non-Jews. Joseph b. Tobiah, following in the ways of his father, established close ties with the royal court and transferred the center of his activities from Transjordan to Erez Israel. A temporary deterioration in the relations between the high priest and the Ptolemaic kingdom presented Joseph with new opportunities. Appointed tax-collector by that kingdom, he collected the taxes on an unprecedented scale and felt at home in Samaria no less than in Judea, to which his operations brought great wealth. With him there entered into Jewish life ways and customs alien to the Jewish tradition. His path was followed by his sons, and the Tobiads and their circle became the chief disseminators of Hellenism in Jewish Erez Israel. In their way of life the upper Jewish classes, both priestly and lay, drew increasingly closer to the non-Jewish sections of the population, and there was a revival of tendencies which had not entirely ceased even in earlier generations: opposition to the emphasis on the uniqueness of the Jews, and a desire to merge with the upper strata of the general society of Erez Israel. Hellenistic influence in Judea was chiefly evident in the sphere of material civilization. As early as in the Persian period the coins of *Yahud* had imitated those of Athens, and the Hellenistic financial system gradually conquered Jerusalem too. In the spheres of building and of art, the influence of Hellenism also made itself felt. A notable outward indication of the Hellenization of Judea was the widespread use of Greek names, of which Jews, and not only those estranged from Jewish tradition, felt a need. Yet it must be emphasized that shortly before 200 B.C.E. Greek culture had in general not succeeded in striking deep roots in Judea. Due to the practical requirements of life Jews learnt to speak Greek, but it is doubtful whether there were as yet many Jews in Erez Israel who learnt the language in order to study Greek classical works and thought.

Seleucid Rule. Antiochus III's conquest of the country did not greatly change the pattern of the administration and the habits prevalent in Ptolemaic Judea. The Seleucid king confirmed the existing regime there and even gave its inhabitants additional privileges: the Judean population was exempted from all taxation for three years and thereafter granted a reduction of a third in its taxes. The priests, the freedmen, and the members of the Gerousia were given complete exemption from taxes. Similar relations continued also under Antiochus' son, Seleucus IV (187–175). However, the political and financial crisis which came upon the Seleucid kingdom led to changed relations between it and the Jews. As a result of Antiochus III's defeat by the Romans and the peace treaty of Apamea (188) a heavy financial burden was imposed on the Seleucid kingdom which was obliged to pay an indemnity to the victorious Roman republic. The kings of the Seleucid dynasty now found themselves compelled to raise money from every source. Nor did they overlook the treasures kept in the wealthy temples throughout their kingdom. This explains the attempt of Seleucus IV to plunder the Temple treasuries, an act which, though not directly aimed at the Jewish religion, must be regarded as the first stage in the conflict between the Jews and the Seleucid kingdom.

The reign of his brother Antiochus IV Epiphanes (175–164) proved to be a turning point in the history of the Jewish nation. During the first seven years after his accession his military and political activities centered on his kingdom's southern border—on Ptolemaic Egypt—and hence the importance he attached to Judea. Already at the beginning of his reign he intervened in the internal affairs of Jerusalem, deposed the high priest Onias III and replaced him by the latter's brother Jason who had Hellenizing tendencies and had promised the king to raise more taxes than his predecessor. With the Seleucid kingdom's approval Jason introduced far-reaching changes in the administration of Jerusalem, whose purpose was to transform that city into a *polis*, named Antiochia, by establishing in it institutions characteristic of the Hellenistic *polis*. Notable among these was the gymnasium, which soon superseded the Temple as the focus of social life, to the deep dismay of those loyal to the Jewish tradition. After a few years Antiochus also deposed Jason and appointed Menelaus in his stead (171). Henceforward a new chapter opened in the relations between the Seleucid kingdom and Judea. Against the background of Antiochus' Egyptian wars significant events took place in Judea. Already in 169 B.C.E., on his return from his first invasion of Egypt, the king with the help of Menelaus plundered the Temple treasuries, and a year later, during his last expedition to the Nile Valley, rumors of Antiochus' death spread in Judea. Returning to Jerusalem, Jason seized power in the city. But when Antiochus was on his way back from Egypt after Roman intervention against him, he captured the city and punished its inhabitants. To ensure his future control of Jerusalem he stationed in its citadel, the Acra, non-Jewish settlers who were joined by extreme Hellenists from Menelaus' party. By their domination of the capital of Judea, the Jewish character of the city became obscured. Antiochus went a step further. He totally prohibited the fulfillment of the *mitzvot* of the Jewish religion and any Jew found observing the Sabbath or circumcising his son was put to death. He likewise forced upon the Jewish population idolatrous rites and prohibited food, chiefly the eating of swine's flesh. The Temple was desecrated and henceforward called after Olympian Zeus (167). Contrary to Antiochus' expectations the majority of the nation remained faithful to its religion and members of its various classes showed a readiness to undergo martyrdom. The unlimited devotion of the Jewish masses to their religion was in any event deep-rooted but on this occasion there unfolded, for the first time in the history of mankind, an epic chapter of martyrdom on a large scale, to bequeath, in the resistance of the martyrs and the Hassideans [2] during the religious persecutions, a symbol and an example throughout all succeeding generations to both Jews and non-Jews. Associated with this martyrdom was an eschatological expectation. There was a growing belief that a period of unprecedented suffering was approaching, heralding the downfall of the evil kingdom and the fulfillment of the visions of the end of days.

The Hasmonean Revolt. Against Antiochus' policy there arose a large movement of rebellion which was speedily forged into a powerful fighting force by the Hasmonean dynasty, a priestly house from Modi'in in the district of Lydda. Henceforward, for a period of about 130 years, the Hasmonean dynasty was at the center of Jewish life. The revolt was led first by Mattathias. Under him the rebels refrained from fighting pitched battles against the Seleucid army, contenting themselves with guerrilla warfare, Mattathias' activities being directed at consolidating the organization of the rebel groups and at ending Seleucid rule in the villages and country towns of Judea. His strategy gradually reduced the area in Judea under Seleucid control and in effect isolated Jerusalem from the other military bases of the enemy. After Mattathias' death the leadership passed to his sons, of whom Judah, known as Maccabee, was distinguished for his military talents. Gaining four decisive victories over the Seleucid armies, Judah used his military superiority to liberate Jerusalem, except for the Acra, in Kislev 164. The Temple was purified of idolatry and the sacred service in it entrusted to priests from among the ranks of the rebels. To commemorate the purification of the Temple a festival, that of Ḥanukkah, was instituted to be

[2] Pietist sect originating c. 3rd century B.C.E.

observed for all generations. The Seleucid kingdom could not long remain indifferent to the operations of the Hasmoneans. There was also a growing fear that Judah would take the Acra. Lysias, who acted as regent on behalf of the youthful king Antiochus V, attempted once more to invade Judea and subdue the rebels. The invasion ended in a settlement. The Seleucid kingdom unequivocally revoked Antiochus Epiphanes' policy of religious persecution, and with the aim of appeasing the Jews, Menelaus, now made the scapegoat for the failure of that policy, was executed, and Alcimus, a moderate Hellenist, appointed high priest. The Seleucid kingdom did not recognize Judah Maccabee as the head of the Jewish nation, although he continued to be the leader of troops of Jewish fighters loyal to him. The principal achievement of the Jews was the Seleucid kingdom's recognition of their complete religious freedom, although militarily and politically the treaty bore the character of an armistice only. Tension increased in Judea with the appearance in Syria of a new king, Demetrius I (162), who supported Alcimus and sought to put an end to Hasmonean supremacy in Judea. In the encounter between Judah Maccabee and the Seleucid commander Nicanor, the former gained his last victory (the Day of Nicanor, Adar 13, 161). Henceforward political independence became Judah's ardent purpose, and to this end, ties with Rome seemed an important step. The treaty concluded between them marked the Roman republic's official recognition of Judea. While it is not clear whether the treaty had any immediate results, since it did not deter Demetrius from again sending his forces against the Jews, the Hasmoneans nevertheless set great store by it since it admitted Judea into the ambit of international relations. Judah Maccabee did not long enjoy the results of his victory over Nicanor, for Demetrius' defeat of his enemies in the east enabled him to send large forces to Judea, and Judah fell in battle (160 B.C.E.). Jonathan and Simeon, Judah's brothers, gathered around themselves the remnants of the fighters but failed to regain Jerusalem, and were compelled to adopt the earlier tactics of guerrilla warfare. Rallying after several years, the Hasmoneans took up their residence at Michmas (Mukhmās). When a rival to Demetrius I arose in the person of Alexander Balas, new opportunities presented themselves to Jonathan the Hasmonean. Appointed high priest by Alexander, he first served in that capacity on Tabernacles 152, and during the next 115 years the high priesthood continued to be held by the Hasmonean dynasty. Jonathan went from strength to strength and was able to take advantage of the Seleucid kingdom's internal difficulties for the advancement of Judea. The country now filled a role of prime importance throughout southern Syria. Among the territorial achievements under Jonathan was the annexation of southern Samaria and the region of Ekron; the southern coastal cities, too, came under Jewish influence.

Independent Judea. Jonathan was treacherously murdered by Tryphon, the Syrian commander. His successor and brother, Simeon, followed in his footsteps and even obtained recognition of the freedom of Judea from the Seleucid king Demetrius II who agreed to exempt the country from paying taxes to the kingdom (142 B.C.E). This official recognition was regarded by the Jews as the beginning of the freedom of Ereẓ Israel ("Then the people of Israel began to write in their instruments and contracts: 'In the first year of Simeon the high priest, the commander and leader of the Jews'"—I Macc. 13:42). Simeon continued in various ways the work of Jonathan. In foreign affairs he adopted a hostile attitude toward those forces in the Seleucid kingdom that were inimical to the independence of Judea. To make Judea militarily secure he eradicated the last cells of opposition from its soil, and obtained for it access to the sea. As early as at the beginning of his rule he dispatched an armed force to Jaffa, and, driving out the non-Jews, secured the harbor for Judea. He also took Gezer which dominated the road leading from Judea to the coastal plain and captured the Acra, the conquest of these places having been made possible by the speedy progress of the Jewish army in the 107 technique of subjugating cities. The inhabitants of Gezer were expelled, the city was cleansed of idolatry, and Jews loyal to their religion were settled in it. There Simeon built a palace for himself, and the city, of which Simeon's son, John Hyrcanus was appointed governor, became one of Judea's administrative centers. The capture of the Acra (Iyyar 23, 141) made an even greater impression on that generation, for as long as it was occupied by the Hellenists the independence of Judea did not seem assured. The day on which the Acra was taken was appointed a festival. During Simeon's final years relations deteriorated between him and Antiochus VII Sidetes, the last great king of the Seleucid dynasty, who sought to curtail the influence of Simeon and bring him once more under the yoke of the Seleucid kingdom. Demanding in particular the return of Jaffa, Gezer, and the citadel of Jerusalem, Antiochus ordered his governor of the coastal plain to launch an attack on Judea from the base at Jabneh. A large Jewish force under the command of Simeon's sons set out against the king's army and put it to flight, pursuing it beyond Ashdod. Never again in the days of Simeon was there any open Seleucid intervention in Judea.

Hasmonean Rule. Simeon was anxious to obtain Jewish sanction for his rule and to secure for his house the status of a hereditary dynasty in Judea. In 140 B.C.E. a great assembly took place in Jerusalem which confirmed both Simeon and his sons after him "until there should arise a faithful prophet" as ethnarch, high priest, and commander in chief of the Jewish nation. This decision of the Great Assembly became the cornerstone of the Hasmonean regime and correctly reflected the union, in the hands of that dynasty's representatives, of the functions of the high priesthood, the civil rule, and the military command, a union of functions which was characteristic of the Jewish state's entire development under Hasmonean rule. Simeon endeavored to attract to himself circles that were at first opposed to the policy of the Hasmoneans, among these being men of local influence in various parts of the country, such as Ptolemy,

Simeon's son-in-law, whom he appointed governor of Jericho. Resolved apparently, with the support of Antiochus Sidetes, to supplant Simeon in Judea, Ptolemy murdered him and two of his sons. But the murder (134 B.C.E.) failed in its political purpose. Affection for the Hasmonean dynasty was deep-seated in the nation and Simeon's surviving son, John Hyrcanus, succeeded him as the ruler of Judea. The growth and expansion of the Hasmonean state of Judea were influenced by the processes which led to the increasing disintegration of the Seleucid kingdom. At the beginning of his rule, after he had overcome his internal enemies, John Hyrcanus was still faced with a threat from the central Seleucid government in the person of Antiochus Sidetes. The fighting was protracted (134–132 B.C.E.) and several of the king's advisors even tried to give it the character of a new religious war. After a drawn-out siege of Jerusalem the sides came to terms. Antiochus accorded official recognition to John Hyrcanus' rule of Judea, while the latter undertook to pay him an indemnity for the cities which his predecessors had taken outside the confines of Judea. He also undertook to assist Antiochus in his campaign against the Parthians, thus renewing for a time the relations between Judea and the Seleucid kingdom. But after Antiochus VII's death during his expedition against the Parthians (129 B.C.E.), the entire structure of the Seleucid kingdom collapsed, whereupon John Hyrcanus, having succeeded in regaining the complete political independence of Judea, initiated a policy of expansion in Erez Israel. His conquests were in effect a continuation of the war upon which his Hasmonean predecessors had embarked, his basic approach being that the country as a whole was the ancestral heritage of the Jewish nation. Under him the expansion, which took place in various directions—southward, northward, and eastward—had decisive consequences for the country's future.

Already in the 20s of the second century B.C.E. John Hyrcanus succeeded in annexing to Judea most of the territory of Erez Israel and especially that outside the limits **109** of Hellenistic cities. In point of its results for subsequent generations, particular importance attached to the expansion southward to Idumea (i.e., Edom), which, together with its two principal centers, Adora and Marisa, was annexed to Judea. Its inhabitants were converted to Judaism. The proselytization of the Idumeans was the first of its kind in that it was one of an entire race and not merely of a single or more individuals. The Idumeans soon became an inseparable part of the Jewish nation and their upper classes began to occupy important positions in the government and society of the Hasmonean kingdom. Henceforward the proselytization of the whole of Erez Israel assumed the character of a fixed aim of Jewish policy.

John Hyrcanus also undertook military operations in Transjordan and captured Madaba and Samoga; he attacked the Samaritans, took their capital Shechem, and destroyed their temple on Mount Gerizim. During his last years his conquests reached their zenith in the capture of the large Hellenistic cities of Samaria and Scythopolis (Beth-Shean), thereby opening to the Hasmoneans the way to Galilee, parts of which were, it seems, annexed to Judea already in his days.

His son and successor, Aristobulus I (104–103), completed the conquest of Galilee and defeated the Itureans who apparently ruled over part of Upper Galilee. As a result of the conquests of John Hyrcanus and Aristobulus the area of Judea was enlarged several fold. Almost all the population outside the confines of some Hellenistic cities now fell under Jewish rule and became part of the Jewish nation, and even some Hellenistic cities were captured.

This expansionist policy was continued chiefly by Alexander Yannai (103–76 B.C.E.) under whom all the foreign cities of Erez Israel, except Ashkelon, were taken. The Jews also made an onslaught on the cities of the Decapolis, and among other places took Gadara.

The Hasmonean conquests eradicated the main political impact of Hellenism from the territory of Erez Israel and transformed most of the country's non-Jewish inhabitants into an integral part of the Jewish nation. Judea now became the accepted designation of the country as a whole and continued as its official name until the days of the emperor Hadrian, thereby reflecting the ethnic and power changes engendered at the time of the Hasmonean rulers' conquests. Facts of great significance were established, and even after the downfall of the Hasmonean dynasty Erez Israel remained for centuries a country with a Jewish majority and all that this implied from various aspects.

At the basis of the constitutional development of Hasmonean Judea lay the decision of the Great Assembly of 140 B.C.E. which sanctioned the position of the Hasmoneans as the rulers of the Jewish state, and established the connection between the Hasmonean dynasty and the high priesthood. The status of the Hasmonean ruler as regards the outside world was at first expressed in the title of ethnarch, but a decisive change occurred in the days of Aristobulus I, who assumed the title of king in order to enhance the prestige of the Hasmonean ruler, since that of ethnarch no longer reflected his status as compared to that of other rulers in the region.

Judea's transformation into a monarchy enlarged the importance of the Hasmonean king as far as the traditional institutions that directed the nation during the preceding period were concerned. Yet despite the enhanced status of the rulers of the Hasmonean dynasty they did not officially regard themselves as absolute rulers, with the possible exception of Alexander Yannai at a certain period during his reign. At least internally they emphasized that, in the state, the entire nation was sovereign alongside the ruler, as clearly indicated in Hebrew inscriptions on coins.

At the outset of its career the Hasmonean dynasty was borne along on a tide of religious-national enthusiasm. For the Jewish masses it was the dynasty to which the deliverance of Israel had been entrusted. But already at an early stage of the accession of the Hasmonean dynasty it was evident that its supporters were not all of one complexion. Only with difficulty was a common language 111 found between the leaders of the priestly aristocracy that joined the Hasmonean dynasty and the Hassideans. At first the Hasmoneans were the natural leaders of the circles which were under the influence of the Pharisees, but during John Hyrcanus' rule a breach occurred between the Hasmoneans and the Pharisees which widened in the days of his sons. Several of the factors that marred the relations between the Hasmonean dynasty and the Pharisees may be conjectured. The atmosphere prevailing in the royal court and its external Hellenization, as also that of the kingdom, were incompatible with the outlook of the Pharisees. The gradual basing, too, of the Hasmonean dynasty on various social elements throughout the country which in part had nothing in common with the ideals of the holy war increased the tension. Some rejected the transformation of Judea into a monarchy. Among the opponents of the Hasmonean dynasty were also those who wanted to leave it in possession only of the secular government, on condition that the high priesthood was given to others. There were circles, too, that repudiated especially the assumption of the royal crown by the Hasmoneans, grounding their opposition on the outlook that this crown was reserved for the House of David only.

Nonetheless the nation greatly honored the Hasmonean dynasty and even its leading opponents showed a willingness for an accommodation. The gravest crisis in relations took place during the reign of Alexander Yannai, who came however to realize that a compromise had to be reached at least with a section of the hostile elements among the Jews. His last victories in his wars against the enemies of Judea in Transjordan likewise earned him great popularity among the masses of the nation.

The reign of his widow Salome Alexandra (76–67) was a period of close cooperation between the Pharisees and the throne. In her days the leaders of the Pharisees were given the direction of the state, and their traditions and ordinances, abolished under John Hyrcanus, became once more obligatory.

Alexandra's death (67 B.C.E.) left Judea in a state of civil war. Her elder son Hyrcanus, deposed by his brother Aristobulus from the kingship and the high priesthood, tried after a short time to realize his legitimate claims to them, and through one of his supporters, Antipater II, conspired with Aretas III king of the Nabateans. Their combined armies defeated Aristobulus and besieged him in Jerusalem. Meanwhile the Romans, having arrived in Syria, compelled the Nabateans to withdraw from Judea. The decision with regard to the succession to the Hasmonean throne was left to Pompey, the Roman commander, who was disposed to entrust the rule to Hyrcanus. After some hesitation Aristobulus surrendered to Pompey, and the Roman army advanced against Jerusalem, whereupon Hyrcanus' adherents opened the gates of the city to it. It was only on the Temple Mount that the Romans encountered any strong opposition. After a three-month siege the Temple Mount, too, was taken and thousands of its defenders were killed (63). An end had come to the independence of Hasmonean Judea, which had lasted for some 80 years and had achieved the political consolidation of Erez Israel under Jewish rule.

THE ROMAN PROVINCE. The Roman conquest led to decisive political changes in the country. Syria became a Roman province, while Judea, reduced in area, was granted limited autonomy and made dependent on the Roman governor of Syria. Judea was deprived of the whole coastal plain and of an access to the sea. Part of Idumea (Marisa) and of Samaria was severed from Judea. In this manner the territorial continuity of Jewish settlement in western Erez Israel was destroyed, the only road linking Galilee and Jerusalem being now by the way of the Jordan Valley. Pompey naturally freed from Jewish rule the large Hellenistic cities in Transjordan as well as Scythopolis, which were joined to the Decapolis and recovered their autonomous city life. The Greek cities on the coast also regained their freedom. The territory remaining under Hyrcanus II's rule thus comprised Judea and southern Samaria, most of

Idumea, the areas of Jewish settlement on the eastern bank of the Jordan, and Galilee. Hyrcanus was divested of his royal title, and the obligation to pay taxes to the foreign government reimposed. The Jews in the country did not willingly accept the new regime and the following years witnessed frequent insurrections usually led by men who represented Aristobulus' branch of the Hasmoneans.

A notable change for the better took place under Julius Caesar who was well disposed to the Jews and even regarded them as allies. After his victory over Pompey, Hyrcanus and Antipater went over to his side and helped him when he was in danger in Alexandria. The fact that Hyrcanus had joined Caesar's camp influenced the attitude of the Jews of Egypt who dominated key positions at the gateways to the country. When the danger threatening him had passed, Caesar took several decisions in favor of Hyrcanus II and the Jews in Erez Israel. Hyrcanus and his sons after him were confirmed as high priests and as ethnarchs of Judea, the walls of Jerusalem demolished in the days of Pompey were rebuilt, and the harbor of Jaffa was restored to the Jews. Under the new arrangements instituted by Caesar, Antipater rose to greater power, and his sons were given influential positions in the government, Phasael, the elder, being appointed governor of Jerusalem and Herod governor of Galilee.

The assassination of Caesar (44 B.C.E.) drew Judea, too, into the vortex of the Roman civil war. Cassius, one of the leaders of the pro-republican forces, went to the east and gained control of Syria and Erez Israel. Antipater and his sons now sided with Cassius who tried to extort as much money as possible from the population of Judea. While Antipater fell a victim in the internal struggle then taking place in Judea, his sons extended their influence.

Following the Parthian invasion in 40 B.C.E. of Rome's eastern provinces, momentous changes occurred. Mattathias Antigonus, Aristobulus' younger son, now considered the time opportune for entering into a compact with the Parthians and in this way regaining his ancestral throne.

As the Parthian forces advanced along the coast, the Jews in the neighborhood of Carmel and in the vicinity of Apollonia (Arsuf) flocked to join Antigonus. Hyrcanus and Phasael, who went out to negotiate with the Parthians, were taken prisoner by them, while Herod escaped from Jerusalem and made his way to Rome to obtain military and political assistance.

With the aid of the Parthians, Antigonus now became king of Judea, thus reestablishing the Hasmonean kingdom brought to an end 23 years earlier by Pompey. In the meantime Herod, the sole ally of the Romans in Erez Israel, was received with great honors in Rome by its rulers Antony and Octavian. To raise Herod's prestige above that of Antigonus, he was given the title of king. Returning to Erez Israel, he succeeded with the help of the Roman legions in capturing Idumea, Samaria, and Galilee. After the defeat of the Parthian armies in the east, large Roman forces became available for the war in Judea and the fate of Antigonus was in effect sealed. Following a siege of five months Jerusalem fell to the Roman army (37 B.C.E.) and Antigonus, the last king of the Hasmonean dynasty, was executed, to usher in Herod's rule in Judea.

Herod's Rule. Herod's reign was chiefly the creation of Rome's eastern policy. The Romans supported him as the ruler of Judea, seeing in him a powerful personality capable of preserving the existing order in the country and one whose loyalty to them was not in doubt. Since the Jews constituted the overwhelming majority of the population of Erez Israel, it also seemed proper from the Roman viewpoint that its king should be a Jew. However, in order to include within the borders of Judea a large non-Jewish population it was necessary that the character of the regime should not be theocratic, as had been the case with the Hasmoneans when the ruler combined the functions both of king and high priest. Herod thus fulfilled the demands of Roman policy in Erez Israel, and was a commander and politician who throughout his life cooperated fully with Rome's representatives in the east.

Herod's foreign policy faithfully mirrored that of Rome. He loyally carried out Antony's policy when the latter still enjoyed great power, and against the background of the policy of Antony and Cleopatra he became involved in a military struggle with the Nabatean kingdom (31 B.C.E.). After the fortune of war had gone first to Herod and then to the Arabs, his considerable military talents enabled him to gain a decisive victory over the Nabateans, thus proving to Rome's rulers his value as a leader capable of sustaining security and order in the region.

After Octavian's victory over Antony (30 B.C.E.), the former confirmed Herod as king of Judea and even extended the area under his rule. In the days of Augustus' principate in the 20s of the first century B.C.E., Herod's kingdom comprised almost the whole of Erez Israel, except for the enclave of Ashkelon and the coastal strip north of Carmel which were at no time during the Second Temple period incorporated within the Jewish state. In 23 B.C.E. Herod's kingdom was considerably enlarged when Trachonitis, Batanea (Bashan), and Auranitis (Hauran) were included under his rule. Further areas near the sources of the Jordan were annexed to his kingdom in 20 B.C.E. Rather than being based on official arrangements, Herod's political status in the Roman Empire was grounded on personal relations which he had prudently cultivated with the leaders of the Roman state and on the ties he had established with Augustus himself and with Agrippa, the greatest contemporary Roman commander and the princeps' right hand.

Herod's great influence with the Roman politicians enabled him to help Jewish communities in the Diaspora. When a serious dispute broke out about the rights of the Jews in the cities of Asia Minor, Agrippa, to whom the decision was entrusted, decided in favor of the Jews. Over his subjects in Erez Israel itself Herod exercised unlimited sway. Generally he succeeded in maintaining peace within the borders of his kingdom, nor did embitterment against him lead during his reign to open rebellion. With an iron hand and timely concessions, with a rigorous police supervision and the promotion of social elements dependent on him for their status, he succeeded in sustaining his regime until the day of his death.

Herod's conquest of Jerusalem spelled the end of the institutions of the old Hasmonean regime. He established a royal council which was not rooted in the Hasmonean past and which dealt with all important matters. The traditional Jewish Sanhedrin was divested of political power. Another notable Jewish institution whose prestige was curtailed was the high priesthood. Since Herod himself did not belong to the priestly class and was accordingly unable to serve as the high priest, he was constrained to appoint others to that office but took care that they should be his loyal supporters and not too deeply involved in the Hasmonean past. He also abolished the custom whereby the high priest was appointed for life.

The external splendor of Herod's reign found expression in his court, which was in every respect identical with those of other Hellenistic kings in the east. Many of his important ministers were Greeks and among his intimate friends were several luminaries of contemporary Greek literature. The tutors of his sons as well as his bodyguard were non-Jews. Herod's fame and extensive international ties attracted to his court visitors from various places in the Greek world who even played a certain part in the events that took place in the royal court. Herod married many wives who bore him sons and daughters. By his first wife he had a son, Antipater; by his second, Mariamne the Hasmonean, he had Alexander and Aristobulus. After he executed Mariamne he married various women, among whom were an Alexandrian Jewess, a Samaritan woman, and a native of Jerusalem. The presence of different wives' sons, all of whom entertained the ambition to succeed their father, vitiated the atmosphere of the court. Herod executed three of his sons, the two borne by his Hasmonean wife and his eldest son Antipater, on the charge of conspiring against him. These deeds, the outcome of an atmosphere of suspicion, clouded the success generally enjoyed by Herod 117 during most of his reign.

More than all Jewish rulers during the period of the Second Temple, Herod devoted himself to building new cities and erecting magnificent edifices, as was customary among the rulers of Rome. In this sphere his most important achievements were the establishment of Caesarea (on the site of Strato's Tower) and Sebaste (on the site of Samaria). At Caesarea he also built the largest harbor in Erez Israel which soon played a very significant part in the country's economic life. In Sebaste he settled many of his demobilized soldiers to whom he gave fertile allotments, and beautified the city. These two cities he organized on the pattern of the Hellenistic cities in the east and their establishment to some extent upset the balance of power that had existed in Erez Israel between the Jewish and the non-Jewish population. He also built the fortress of Herodium to the southeast of the capital, as well as Phasaelis in the Valley of Jericho, and Antipatris, improved and embellished Masada, and built the fortress of Machaerus. As a result of Herod's activities Jerusalem became one of the most resplendent capitals in the entire east. In it he erected a palace, rebuilt the Temple, and constructed the impressive towers of the Upper City, the fortifications of the stronghold of Antonia, as well as a theater and an amphitheater. He also built magnificent palaces in Jericho and in other places.

Under the Procurators. Herod's kingdom did not survive his death (4 B.C.E.). In his last will, subsequently confirmed by Augustus, he bequeathed Judea, Idumea, and Samaria to his son Archelaus; Galilee and Perea to another son Herod Antipas; and the northeastern parts of the kingdom to a third son Philip. For the nation, Herod's death was the signal to demand an alleviation of the burden of taxation and a change in the nature of the regime. When their demands were not met, a dangerous rebellion broke out which was only suppressed by the vigorous intervention of Varus, the governor of Syria. Augustus did not bestow
the title of king on Archelaus who had to be content with

that of ethnarch. He failed to win the support of his Jewish and Samaritan subjects, and they complained of him to the emperor, who ordered that he be deposed and that his inheritance, Judea, be organized as a Roman province (6 C.E.). Believing that there was no need to send Roman legions to Judea and that an *auxilium* would be enough to maintain order and security and to suppress disturbances, Augustus laid down that the governors of the province of Judea were to be of equestrian rank. At first the governors of Judea bore the title of *praefectus* and only after Agrippa I's death were they officially referred to as procurators.

Something is known of the origin of several procurators of Judea. One of them, Julius Alexander Tiberius, of Jewish parentage, was an apostate. Felix was a Greek and a freedman. The last procurator, Florus, came from a city in Asia Minor. Procurators of eastern-Hellenistic origin were naturally more friendly disposed toward the Hellenized urban population than to the Jews.

The governors of Syria intervened in the affairs of Judea. In several instances this intervention may be explained as resulting from the special authority granted by the emperor to the governor of Syria. At any rate, it is clear that the auxiliary forces stationed in Judea were not enough to suppress serious revolts and the procurator of Judea was in effect dependent on the help given to him by the governor of Syria, who was not merely governor of an ordinary province but the most distinguished of the Roman Empire's governors, the supreme commander of the Roman east, and responsible for the Parthian border. Accordingly, he regarded himself as responsible, to some extent, for the security of the province of Judea as well even though he was assigned no special authority over that territory.

As a rule the Roman administration granted a large measure of autonomy to the local Jewish institutions, which were charged with preserving peace and order, and which assisted the Romans in collecting the direct taxes. Foremost among the Jewish institutions was the Sanhedrin in Jerusalem, the Great Bet Din, which met in the Chamber of Hewn Stone. Whereas administratively its jurisdiction was restricted to the limits of Judea, its authority in the sphere of religion and as regards its enactments extended beyond these circumscribed territorial borders. Its functions were varied. It was the supreme institution of the Jewish nation in matters of religion and worship, issued regulations in the religious and juridical spheres, and supervised the religious life both in Ereẓ Israel and beyond its borders.

Under the earlier procurators relations between the Jewish nation and the Roman Empire had not yet become acute. Before the time of Pontius Pilate (26–36 C.E.) there is no mention of bloodshed in Judea. But from his days and onward there are increasing references to a messianic ferment, to disturbances, and to a gradual disappointment in the Roman administration, which had at first tried to find a suitable way of preserving order in Judea by respecting the religious feelings of the Jews, for example, by prohibiting the entry into Jerusalem of representations and images. But it was not often that the two sides reached agreement. The stationing in Jerusalem of part of the auxiliary army, usually inimical to the Jewish population, in itself led to clashes. There were also the heavy taxes and the inflexibility of several procurators which contributed to increasing the tension between the Roman administration and the Jews.

The first open breach between the Jews and the Roman Empire occurred during the reign of Gaius Caligula (37–41 C.E.). After the emperor's death, peace was indeed outwardly restored but there nevertheless remained a murky sediment that clouded the relations between the two sides. It had suddenly become clear to the Jews what evil lay in store from the rule of an omnipotent individual. The renewal of Antiochus Epiphanes' decrees had become a present reality. Taking advantage of the dangerous mood of Caligula who, sincerely believing in his own divinity, demanded divine honors from his subjects, the non-Jewish inhabitants of Ereẓ Israel erected in Jabneh an altar which the Jews demolished, thereby arousing the anger of the emperor who ordered that a massive golden image be set up in the Temple in Jerusalem, and delegated the task to Petronius, the governor of Syria. The implacable opposition of the entire Jewish nation and Agrippa I's intervention with the emperor prevented the execution of the order and only Caligula's death averted a yet graver situation.

The death of Caligula and the accession of Claudius (41 C.E.) ushered in great prospects for the advancement of Agrippa I, the grandson of Herod and of Mariamne the Hasmonean, who was appointed king of the whole of Erez Israel. For three years (41–44) the status of Judea as a province was annulled. Nor did Agrippa conform to the traditional policy of the Herodian kings who were always Rome's faithful servants. His personal ties with the emperor encouraged in him the hope that he would be permitted to do what others had not succeeded in doing. Of all the leaders of the Herodian dynasty, he alone in all his strivings gave primacy to the Jewish nation and its future, and became the most illustrious Jewish politician of his generation. The last years of his life were marked by a complete identification with the Jewish nation and with its needs as he saw them, and to this end he cooperated with the greater majority of the Jews of Erez Israel who regarded him as in every respect a Jewish king and the heir to the Hasmonean rather than of the Herodian dynasty. The non-Jews in Erez Israel however looked upon him as their enemy.

The death of Agrippa (44 C.E.) led to the reimposition of direct Roman rule in Judea. But the last 20 years of existence of the Second Temple were marked by a complete deterioration of the Roman administration, by a growing tension between the procurators and those under their rule, and by a breakdown of order and security throughout Judea. Typical in this respect was the procuratorship of Felix (52–60 C.E.). At first his rule was animated by a conciliatory attitude toward the Jews—whose leaders and especially the former high priest Jonathan b. Anan even strove for his appointment as procurator—but it eventually

Detail from model of Jerusalem at the beginning of the revolt against Rome, 66 C.E. Jerusalem, Holyland Hotel. Photo Werner Braun, Jerusalem.

122

ended in an open crisis between the Roman regime and the Jews. In his days there was an increase in the activities of the extremist freedom fighters, now a permanent feature of life in Judea. At the outset of his procuratorship Felix tried to arrest the spread of the movement, even as he acted energetically against those who inspired messianic hopes among the Jews. He suppressed, among others, a movement which arose under the inspiration of an Egyptian Jew's prophecies who promised to overthrow the walls of Jerusalem with the breath of his mouth. Outside the limits of Judea, too, the procuratorship of Felix was distinguished by disturbances and bloody clashes. The main focus of tension was at Caesarea, where the cause of the conflict was the struggle for civic rights between the Syrian-Greek majority and the large Jewish minority. While the latter enjoyed superiority in wealth and power, their opponents relied on the garrison whose soldiers were drawn from Sebaste and from Caesarea itself and naturally disposed to help their brethren. In the days of Florus (64–66 C.E.), the last procurator before the revolt, there was a decisive breach between the Roman administration and the Jewish nation. Neither the Roman authorities nor the Jewish autonomous institutions were able to preserve their influence and power. There was growing anarchy alike in the streets of Jerusalem and in the rural areas of Judea.

The Revolt (First Roman War). The great revolt which broke out in 66 C.E. was the result of a combination of several factors. In the realm of theory there was a conspicuous discrepancy between the Jewish belief in the Divine choice of the Jewish nation and in its glorious future on the one hand, and on the other the present reality of the Roman Empire's omnipotent rule. This discrepancy found vent in increasing messianic hopes and in expectations that the eternal kingdom of the Jewish nation would be established. The contrast was sharpened by the very essence and character of the Roman Empire with its tyrannical rule and its idolatry which extended even to political manifestations, such as emperor worship.

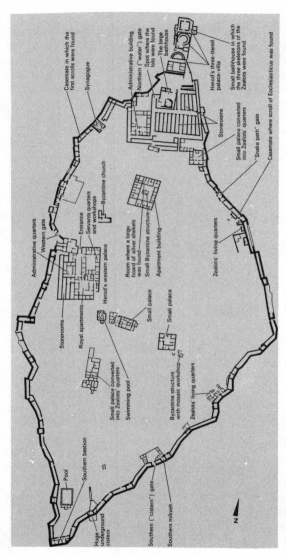

Plan of the fortress of Masada, which became a Zealot stronghold on the outbreak of the First Roman War in 66 C.E. After *Encyclopaedia of Archeological Excavations in the Holy Land*. Jerusalem, 1970.

Casemate in which the first scrolls were found
Synagogue
Administrative building
Northern ("water") gate
Spot where the lots were found
The large bathhouse
Herod's three-tiered palace-villa
Small bathhouse in which the three skeletons of the Zealots were found
Storerooms
Small palace converted into Zealots' quarters
"Snake path" gate
Casemate where scroll of Ecclesiasticus was found
Byzantine church
Administrative quarters
Western gate
Entrance
Servants quarters and workshops
Room where a large hoard of silver shekels was found
Small Byzantine structure
Apartment building
Zealots' living quarters
Storerooms
Royal apartments
Herod's western palace
Small palace converted into Zealots' quarters
Swimming pool
Small palace
Small palace
Byzantine structure with mosaic workshop
Zealots' living quarters
Southern bastion
Pool
Southern ("cistern") gate
Southern mikveh
Huge underground cistern

In addition to these feelings there were also several tangible features of the Roman regime which gravely offended the Jews. The presence of a Roman army in Jerusalem, the supervision by the authorities of Divine worship and of the Temple, the heavy burden of taxes and customs duties—these, but perhaps most of all the Roman administration's support of the non-Jewish population in Ereẓ Israel; made the rule of Rome hated by Jews.

The revolt also bore the aspect of a social revolution, its revolutionary social character being particularly prominent in those extremist groups in which messianic leaders, such as Menahem the Galilean and Simeon Bar Giora, were active. To them the revolt was not only a war against Rome. It was also a struggle against the upper classes of Judea who for many years had cooperated with the Roman regime.

The immediate events that led to the great revolt were associated with the tension in Caesarea and with the procurator Florus' conduct in Jerusalem which provoked a clash between the Jews and the Roman army. On the initiative of Eleazar b. Hanania sacrifices were no longer offered for the welfare of the Roman people and the emperor. The Roman garrison in Jerusalem was destroyed, and the Roman army in Syria under the command of Cestius Gallus, the governor of Syria, was defeated at the ascent of Beth-horon. A provisional government was set up which united under its rule the whole of Jewish Ereẓ Israel.

The emperor Nero could not remain indifferent to events in Judea and dispatched a huge Roman army under the command of Vespasian to suppress the revolt. Vespasian invaded Galilee and after overcoming stubborn resistance crushed Jewish opposition there (67) and in Transjordan. The significant events that took place in the heart of the Roman Empire after the death of Nero (June 9, 68) greatly delayed the continuation of military operations by Vespasian who at the beginning of July 69 proclaimed himself emperor of Rome. In the spring of 70 C.E. his son Titus laid siege to Jerusalem.

After a brave stand Jerusalem was taken by Titus'

armies, who burnt the Temple and so in effect terminated the war. Not long afterward Masada, the last fortress of the Jews, fell into the hands of the Romans (73).

6 DESTRUCTION OF THE SECOND TEMPLE TO THE ARAB CONQUEST (70–634 C.E.).

The Effects of the War of 66–70 c.e. The Jewish war against the Romans, which extended over a period of more than four years and encompassed the entire country, the continuing siege of the fortresses of Machaerus, Herodium, and Masada, the last falling only in 73, the capture of Jerusalem and the destruction of the Temple—all these gravely affected the Jewish people and the cities and villages of Erez Israel. Josephus (Wars, 6: 420) states that during the siege of Jerusalem alone more than a million Jews fell, while his contemporary Tacitus places the number at 600,000 (*Historiae*, 5: 13). To these figures are to be added those killed at various stages of the war in Judea, Galilee, and Transjordan. Many fell in the battles fought and the massacres perpetrated by the inhabitants of the Greek cities against the local Jews, such as in Caesarea, Beth-Shean, Acre, and Ashkelon. In addition to the slain, many were taken captive before the siege of Jerusalem; tens of thousands were sold into slavery, sent to toil in ships and mines, or presented to the non-Jewish cities adjacent to Erez Israel to fight against wild animals in the theaters. While the figures given by the early historians are undoubtedly exaggerated, it is certain that tens upon tens of thousands of Jews were killed or taken prisoner. Cities and villages were burnt and destroyed either in the course of the war or as an act of revenge and intimidation. Agriculture in particular suffered. Fruit trees on the mountains and in the valleys were cut down by the army for use in the siege or by military detachments in order to cow the population. That they might not be utilized by the enemy, many fruit trees were uprooted by the Jewish fighters, as were also the groves of balsam trees in the vicinity of Jericho which, of a quality unequaled in the world, were deliberately destroyed by the Jews, according to Pliny. Several cities and villages, which were demolished and of which Josephus tells that they were razed to the ground and burnt, were not actually destroyed but were damaged in one form or another. Some, like Jaffa, were already rebuilt during the war, others were completely destroyed or never restored.

With the destruction of the Temple, Jerusalem, although continuing to be inhabited by impoverished Jews, completely lost not only its spiritual significance but also its importance as a populated and economic center. Contemporary sages give distressing accounts of the plight of the surviving members of wealthy Jerusalem families. A considerable proportion of the inhabitants of Jerusalem and its immediate vicinity had derived their livelihood from the service and the supplies as also from other public duties associated with the Temple, as well as from the pilgrimages. With the destruction of the Temple and of Jerusalem they lost their sole means of support. The protracted war greatly increased the hostility of the soldiers and the authorities toward the Jews, undermining their position and bringing religious persecutions in its wake. The sources attest the destruction of synagogues and the building of theaters on their sites or their plunder, "so as to wound the feelings of the Jews." More grievous were the tortures inflicted on the Jews to compel them to transgress the commandments of their religion (Jos., Wars, 2:150ff.; Apion, 1:43). For a time after the destruction of the Temple that had unconditionally surrendered itself, its property, territory, and towns to the Roman state; they were deprived of their communal and religious rights by imperial edict; and were the arbitrary victims both in theory and in practice of unrestrained acts of lawlessness, as were also the Jewish communities in the immediate neighborhood of Erez

Israel. The authorities searched out the Jewish families

descended from the house of David in order to destroy them and thus eradicate the last remnant of the nation's hope of the restoration of the Davidic kingdom. There was also Vespasian's decree that, instead of the half shekel which each Jew contributed to the Temple in Jerusalem, a tax of two drachmas was to be imposed on every Jew in Erez Israel and the Diaspora, and given annually to the imperial treasury for Jupiter Capitolinus, the Roman god, whose temple was on the Capitol. More than being a serious financial burden, this tax, which was paid also by women and children, was humiliating and oppressive, in addition to indirectly enforcing idolatry on the Jews. Although levied until the days of Julian the Apostate in the middle of the fourth century, its connection with Jupiter was discontinued some years after the destruction of the Temple. The memory of the war against the Romans and of the subjugation of Judea, with all that these implied, was kept alive by the Flavian emperors who throughout that dynasty's reign struck coins commemorating the victory and emphasizing the fact that Judea had been conquered.

The Organizational and Spiritual Crisis. No less grave were the consequences in the spiritual and organizational spheres. The destruction of the country, the capture of Jerusalem, the burning of the Temple, and in their wake the abolition of the leading institutions—the high priesthood and the Sanhedrin—brought stupefaction and confusion in spiritual and communal life. Associated with the Temple and its divine service were communal and judicial institutions that had their seat in the Temple. There was the Sanhedrin which administered justice, proclaimed the new months, and intercalated the year. There was the high priesthood which had lost little of its commanding spiritual splendor despite its diminished prestige during the generations preceding the destruction of the Second Temple, its curtailed power, and the widespread criticism leveled at it. The destruction of the Temple brought an end to the sacrifices that atoned for Israel's sins and to the pil- **129**

grimages, and many categories of *mitzvot* connected with the Temple and its service fell into disuse, and so to some extent did numerous other *mitzvot* associated with festivals, such as the blowing of the *shofar* on the New Year and the waving of the *lulav* on Tabernacles, which were mainly observed in the Temple and only partially outside it. The Temple was also the political, juridical basis of the Jewish communal structure. Centering round it in the Persian and Hellenistic periods, Judea derived its constitutional power from the Temple, the nation's glory as far as the outside world was concerned and the focal point of the Jewish people both in Erez Israel and in the Diaspora. In the Second Temple period Jerusalem was not only the capital of the state but the theater of every spiritual creativity and political occasion. Coalescing as it were with the Temple, the city was intertwined in the practical life of the people and in the complex of the basic values of the nation's thought. The destruction of the city and of the Temple left a vacuum in the spiritual and practical life of the Jews. The crises that followed the revival and the fervent hopes aroused during the war against the Romans were calculated to undermine the nation's faith both in its teachings and in its future. One senses in the tannaitic literature and in the apocryphal works, composed in the generation after the destruction of the Temple and Jerusalem, the somber sorrow and pain that afflicted many contemporary circles. Some abstained from flesh and wine, for the altar had been destroyed on which flesh had been offered and wine poured out in libations. Many lived in caves, and in fasting and self-mortification awaited the messianic era which would soon dawn. There was no speedy transition to the spiritual, religious reality necessary to rebuild the sole basis of a hope of redemption—the life of the nation, now deprived of its Temple and its political framework.

The Administrative Changes and the Regime After the Destruction. With the destruction of Jerusalem and the Temple, Judea, except for those settlements (like Caesarea) which, within the confines of Jewish Erez Israel, enjoyed city status, passed under the direct control of the Roman administration. At Moẓa a colony was set up consisting of 800 Roman veterans, who received confiscated Jewish land. Jaffa and Flavia Neapolis, founded near Shechem, were granted city rights. No new cities were established within the limits of Jewish settlement, except Tiberias and Sepphoris which, having previously had city status, in the course of time regained their rights. The province of Judea, *provincia Judaea,* which was now founded, included all the coastal cities from Caesarea to Rafa, the whole of Idumea, Judea, Samaria, Perea in Transjordan, Galilee, and all the cities of the Decapolis, except Damascus and Canatha. After the death of Agrippa II (92), the last ruler of the Herodian dynasty, a considerable part of his kingdom, comprising territories in Perea, Tiberias, Magdala, and Gaulanitis, was added to Judea. In contrast to the period preceding the destruction, the province was now subject to the authority of a Roman senator who had formerly served as a *praetor* and whose title was *legatus Augusti pro praetore provincia Judaea.*

Contrary to the prevailing Roman imperial practice of stationing legions only in the provinces bordering on the empire, Vespasian stationed in Judea, an "internal" country, a permanent garrison, the tenth legion, *legio decima Fretensis,* that had taken part in the war against the Jews. During the entire period of the Roman imperial rule of Ereẓ Israel this legion was permanently stationed in the country, and inscriptions and seals of it have been uncovered at its various encampments. Its main camp, located on the city's ruins, was in Jerusalem; its commander was the governor, who resided in Caesarea. To facilitate contact between the military headquarters in the center of the country and the administrative seat of government at Caesarea, a branch of the coastal road was built from Antipatris to Jerusalem. Encamped near the legion were other military units, auxiliary troops, and so on, that had been brought from distant lands. The auxiliary forces which had been stationed in Ereẓ Israel before the destruction and which, consisting of soldiers from Caesarea and from Sebaste, were distinguished for their hatred of the Jews whom they had provoked to acts of war, were transferred by Vespasian to other provinces. Assisting the governor was a procurator who was in charge of financial affairs. It is doubtful whether the province of Judea became independent after the destruction and was not annexed to Syria, as it had been before the war, since civil, legal, and military issues of decisive importance still required the decision of the Syrian governor who resided in Antioch. Josephus tells that Vespasian ordered that all Jewish territory was to be hired out, for he founded no city in it (Wars, 7:216). Since in point of fact many Jewish farmers remained on their land as owners, Josephus' statement refers to that land which was confiscated and which indeed constituted a considerable proportion of Jewish territory. Contemporary literature echoes a poignant cry against the Roman tax-collectors *(conductores)* who held land throughout Erez Israel. Some was actually transferred to non-Jews, such as to the 800 veterans, and its former owners were dispossessed. Other land was given to favorites and loyal friends of the Jewish and non-Jewish authorities or to large tenants, the *conductores.* The former owners were not ejected from most of the confiscated land but cultivated their own as tenant farmers, for which they had to pay a high rental in kind, expecting nevertheless to be evicted at any time on the pretext of not paying the rent or some other excuse.

TAXES. On unconfiscated land a tax was levied which was increased after the destruction and from which only a few imperial court favorites, such as Josephus in the days of Domitian, were exempted. But whereas some in the territories of the Roman Empire were liable to a land but not to a poll tax, the Jews in Erez Israel had to pay both. A Roman writer of a generation or two after the destruction states that, because of their rebelliousness, the tax imposed on the Jews of Erez Israel was more severe than that demanded of the inhabitants of the neighboring countries. After the destruction the tax for the provision and maintenance of the army and of the enlarged Roman officialdom in the country, levied in kind *(annona)* from dough, animals, and all locally produced or imported agricultural and industrial products, was increased. There were bitter complaints against the excessive demands and the harshness employed in collecting them, as also against the various forms of forced labor, whereby the authorities and especially the army compelled the population, both urban and rural, to perform work, such as haulage, or repairing and making roads, with their own persons and with the help of their temporary or permanently requisitioned draught animals. A short time after the destruction small watchtower stations were erected along the borders and along the main roads in many places in Ereẓ Israel. In the years following the destruction, under the Flavian dynasty (until 96), a system of defense, known by its latter name of *limes Palaestinae* was established in southern Ereẓ Israel. Extending from Menois, north of Rafa, to the Dead Sea, the *limes* consisted of a series of fortresses connected by a road, along which, on allotments of land, military colonists enjoying a special status were settled. In the rear of the *limes* were two military bases: Carmel and Hebron. While its establishment brought security to the country's southern settlements, it further increased the already large non-Jewish population in the country.

The Inception of a Central Leadership. The renewal in post-destruction Ereẓ Israel of Jewish communal life— which also reconstructed Judaism in the Diaspora—without the framework of a state and without a Temple which was the foundation of Jewish religious and spiritual existence, is associated with the name of Rabban Johanan b. Zakkai and with his activities in the semi-Greek city of Jabneh. One of the greatest Pharisaic sages in Jerusalem before the destruction, he vehemently opposed the Sadducees and the Sadducean high priesthood. He was deputy to the president of the Sanhedrin, Rabban Simeon b. Gamaliel, who was the leader of the government set up after

Johanan b. Zakkai, weeping and rending his garments on hearing of the destruction of the Temple. From the *menorah* designed by Benno Elkan for the Knesset, Jerusalem. Photo Yizḥak Amit, Kibbutz Ẓorah.

Cestius Gallus had been forced to retreat and with whom he
signed the letters sent throughout Erez Israel and the

Diaspora in connection with tithes and the intercalation of the year (Mid. Tan. 26:13). To him is ascribed the abolition of the ceremony of the bitter water in the examination of a wife suspected of infidelity (Sot. 9:9). Although a priest, he is depicted as a scholar and teacher who in his statements and teachings protested and strove against the priests' haughtiness and aloofness. It is possible that he gave no support to the revolt against Rome. At any rate, warning the rebels against fanaticism and impetuous acts, he called on them to display moderation in their relations with gentiles and toward their sacred objects: "Be not precipitate in tearing down the altars of gentiles that you do not have to rebuild them with your own hands, that you do not tear down those made of brick and be ordered: Make them of stone . . ." (ARN² 31, 66). He was in besieged Jerusalem, but left the city during the siege, apparently in the spring of 68 when Vespasian was closing in on the city. His departure then left a deep impression on talmudic tradition, and there are different versions of his appearance before Vespasian when he prophesied that the latter would become the emperor (which Josephus ascribes to himself, and various sources to different persons in the east). According to later traditions in the Babylonian Talmud, he obtained from the emperor "Jabneh with its sages" and "the dynasty of Rabban Gamaliel" (Git. 56b). But this tradition, which contains much taken from somewhat later circumstances, reflects the time when "Jabneh with its sages" was already established under the leadership of Rabban Gamaliel, the son of Rabban Simeon b. Gamaliel, and the foundations had been laid for the succeeding dynasty of *nesi'im* who presided over the Sanhedrin and led the nation for more than 300 years. The earlier traditions embodied in the Erez Israel literature (Lam. R. 1:5, no. 31; ARN¹ 40, 22–23; ARN² 60, 19–20) indicate that Johanan b. Zakkai was first held in custody at Gophna and later transferred, apparently under duress, to Jabneh, which was used together with other cities such as Ashdod, on account of their large non-Jewish population, as a place for concentrating and imprisoning the Jews, and especially the prominent ones, who had surrendered to the Romans. According to one source, he only requested of the emperor, who granted his request, that certain persons be saved; according to others he succeeded in obtaining Jabneh "to teach his pupils" or "to observe the *mitzvot* and study the Torah" there.

The general circumstances prevailing during the war against the Romans, as also the usual procedures adopted by Vespasian and his son Titus, support these earlier versions of the origin of Jabneh. When requesting "Jabneh with its sages," Johanan b. Zakkai did not presumably ask of and receive from Rome permission to establish a national or even merely a spiritual center. Although the official permission he received was extremely restricted, he in effect began, with or without the authorities' knowledge, to rehabilitate Jewish life theoretically and to fill in practice the vacuum created by the destruction. He reestablished the Sanhedrin, and in Jabneh commenced to proclaim the new months and intercalate the years, on which the entire calendar of Jewish festivals depended. The proclamation of the new month, based on the testimony of witnesses, and the intercalation of the year, dependent on the decision of the *bet din,* which were previously done in the Temple in Jerusalem, were now transferred to Jabneh, and the information was transmitted to all the cities of Erez Israel and the Diaspora. By this action alone Jabneh became the leading center and place of assembly for all Israel. To it was transferred some of the authority and activities that pertained to the Temple courtyards in Jerusalem. Several of Johanan b. Zakkai's regulations deal with the proclamation of the new month at Jabneh. He decreed that the *shofar* was to be blown at Jabneh also on a New Year that fell on a Sabbath, which had previously only been done in the Temple and in Jerusalem. Another regulation lays down "that even if the head of the *bet din* is in some other place, the witnesses (who testify when the new moon appeared) should still go only to the place of the assembly" (RH 4:4).

His other regulations were likewise intended to fill the void created by the destruction and to rebuild Jewish life while retaining a remembrance of the Temple, so as to rehabilitate the former without the latter. He instituted that the *lulav* be waved all the seven days of Tabernacles, contrary to the situation that obtained during the existence of the Temple when it was waved seven days in the Temple and only one day in other parts of the country (*ibid*. 4:3). He ordained that the priests bless the people during prayers in synagogue without their shoes on, as had been done at the end of the service in the Temple. According to the *halakhah* a proselyte, on his conversion, had to bring a sacrifice to the Temple, but with its destruction he set aside a quarter shekel for a sacrifice to be offered when the Temple would be rebuilt, a regulation abolished by Johanan b. Zakkai (*ibid*. 31b). To the people, shaken by the destruction of the Temple, "where the sins of Israel were expiated," he taught: "My son, be not grieved. We have another means of expiation like it. What is it? It is deeds of loving-kindness" (ARN[1] 4, 21). He laid the foundations for the structure of organized life by instituting or renewing the ordination of sages and the title of "rabbi" for ordained sages, a fact of great significance not only for the religious life, law, and leadership in Ereẓ Israel, but also for the country's hegemony over the Diaspora, since the right of granting ordination was restricted to the leading institutions in Ereẓ Israel. The title of rabbi also indicated that its bearer was a member of the Sanhedrin and acted in its name. Furthermore, Johanan b. Zakkai began to work for the consolidation and unity of the nation amid the various trends and movements which appeared in all their destructive virulence during the last days of the Temple's existence. Nevertheless, Johanan b. Zakkai's activities are limited in comparison with those that marked the days of Rabban Gamaliel. This is not to be ascribed only to the difficult external conditions then prevailing and the Roman Empire's nonrecognition of the leadership at Jabneh. It is also due to the fact that many sages dissociated themselves from Johanan b. Zakkai and his actions at Jabneh. Conspicuous by their absence were not only the priestly sages who ministered in the Temple and ranked among the influential members of Pharisaic circles, but also many others, some of whom went to Jabneh after the days of Johanan b. Zakkai. Of his five pupils, only two, Eliezer b. Hyrcanus and Joshua b. Hananiah, accompanied him to Jabneh. Apparently a considerable number of the sages were unable to reconcile themselves with him, with his leaving besieged Jerusalem, his surrender to the Romans, and his throwing himself on the emperor's mercy. These circles, however, cooperated with Rabban Gamaliel, his successor and a member of the dynasty of the *nasi*.

In the Days of the Nasi Rabban Gamaliel. A change in the status of Judaism in Ereẓ Israel took place when the Flavian dynasty came to an end with the murder of Domitian (96). The policy of encouraging informers in Rome against those suspected of Judaism was abolished, as was that of persecuting proselytes. To this period is to be assigned the accession of Rabban Gamaliel to the position of *nasi* after having previously been compelled to go into hiding from the Romans. In contrast to Johanan b. Zakkai who according to the evidences had no contact with the authorities during his tenure of the office of *nasi,* Rabban Gamaliel traveled to Antioch where he obtained authorization from "the governor in Syria" (Eduy. 7:7). Roman imperial emissaries were sent to ascertain the nature of Hebrew civil law, then reintroduced and extensively in vogue. There were the journeys to Rome undertaken by Rabban Gamaliel together with the leading members of the Sanhedrin, Eliezer b. Hyrcanus, Eleazar b. Azariah, Joshua, and Akiva, their meeting with the authorities, and their visit to the Jews in the city. Under Rabban Gamaliel the center in Jabneh assumed most of the functions fulfilled by the Sanhedrin in Second Temple times. To it questions were addressed from all the cities of Ereẓ Israel and the Diaspora. During this period missions were reintroduced on behalf of the *nasi* and the Sanhedrin to the communities of Erez Israel and the Diaspora, some of the most eminent sages, such as Eliezer b. Hyrcanus, Joshua b. Hananiah, Akiva, and Ishmael, acting as emissaries and being sometimes accompanied by the *nasi* himself. These missions also had great economic importance, since the emissaries brought back with them the money collected in the Diaspora for the maintenance of the central authority in Erez Israel. The ties that the emissaries formed with the cities of Erez Israel and with the Diaspora had not only an organizational significance but also established a personal link between these places and the great teachers of the Torah acting in the name of the *nasi*. Wherever they went, they gave practical decisions on the questions submitted to them, brought with them the innovations decided upon in the *battei midrashot* in Erez Israel, supervised the communal arrangements and institutions, and established those essential for the life of a Jewish community, such as charitable, educational and other similar ones. The emissaries decisively influenced the appointment of leaders in the cities and villages of Erez Israel and the communities of the Diaspora, and even had the power to depose them if their leadership was found to be defective. During this period the character of the Sanhedrin assumed definite form as a *bet midrash*, a legislature and a dominant executive body.

Many discussions and actions that marked those years until the Bar Kokhba revolt (132) had not only then a decisive effect on the life of the Jews in Erez Israel and in the Diaspora but shaped and directed the existence of the nation throughout all subsequent generations. Amid much argument and conflict the *halakhah* was decided according to Bet Hillel, a fact of great influence on the entire history of the *halakhah*. A final decision was taken on numerous problems concerned with proselytization, priestly dues, tithes, and other subjects. At this period the concept crystallized that study is greater than action, since "study leads to action" (Kid. 40b). At one assembly which took place at Lydda in keeping with the custom of meeting on occasion elsewhere than at the permanent center at Jabneh, it was decided that a Jew, if forced to transgress the *mitzvot* of the Torah, may do so to save his life except in the three instances of idolatry, murder, and incest. But at a time of open religious persecution intended to compel Jews to sin against their religion, a Jew should suffer death and not transgress even a minor custom (TJ, Sanh. 3:6, 21a). At Jabneh the form of the festivals was laid down under the circumstances prevailing after the destruction, when there were now no pilgrimages, sacrifices, or Temple. The order was also fixed of the four fasts instituted after the destruction of the First Temple but either observed partially or totally disregarded in the Second Temple period. Under the direction of the sages of Jabneh, Aquila the proselyte of Pontus translated the Bible anew into Greek. The earlier Septuagint did not mirror the later halakhic and aggadic interpretation of the Pentateuch and the Prophets, thereby creating a barrier between the Jews who used it and the halakhic and aggadic expositions they heard from the sages. That the Septuagint had been adopted and canonized by the Church and several of its passages were used as a basis for the Church Fathers' interpretations may have influenced the sages to produce a new translation. The Jews did not entirely discard the Septuagint but Aquila's version was adopted in synagogues and in Jewish life. On Rabban Gamaliel's explicit instructions the order was fixed of the prayer of Eighteen Benedictions, known already in the time of the Second Temple. While it is not certain what precisely was done in the days of Gamaliel, at all events from this period the prayer was permanently instituted for private and public worship two or three times daily.

In the days of Jabneh, too, the breach and separation between Judaism and Christianity took place. Pharisaic Judaism had in the Second Temple period shown tolerance alike to Gentile and Judeo-Christians. But after the destruction came the separation. The Judeo-Christians dissociated themselves from the war against the Romans and from the tragedy that had come upon the nation. Nor did some share the hope of deliverance, which had, in their view, been fulfilled with the advent of their Messiah. Many of them saw in the destruction of the Temple and of Jerusalem a proof of the truth of Christianity, in that Israel had been punished for killing their Messiah, and Jesus' prophecy regarding the destruction of the Temple had been fulfilled. Some even held that with its destruction and the discontinuance of many commandments, all the *mitzvot* had been annulled and Judaism's hour had passed. Thus they used the destruction of the Temple for propagating Christianity. To this the sages of Jabneh answered with actions calculated to bring about a breach and a separation between the Jews and Judeo-Christianity and especially those trends in Judeo-Christianity that approximated to Gentile Christianity. A notable factor that had a decisive influence in the Jewish community's rejection of Judeo-Christianity was the introduction in the Eighteen Benedictions of an additional blessing directed against its adherents: "To apostates let there be no hope if they return not to Thy Torah, and may the Nazarenes and the sectarians perish as in a moment" (such or something similar was the ancient Erez Israel version). This prayer in effect excluded Judeo-Christianity from the Jewish people.

The Educational Activities of the Sages of Jabneh Outside the Confines of the House of Assembly. The sages of Jabneh succeeded not only in reconstructing the life of the nation but also in achieving the efflorescence of its spiritual and social existence. This was largely due to the activities of the leaders of the *bet midrash* and the Sanhedrin as also to the great personalities with whom that period was favored. Most of them were ordained rabbis and functioned officially as members of the Sanhedrin. But there were also those—and some of them represented the most outstandingly creative and constructive forces—who, unordained, continued as "disciples" and worked as itinerant teachers of the Torah in Erez Israel unhampered by any official obligations. Almost none of the personalities who established and consolidated the institutions of the communal national leadership at Jabneh emanated from the circles that, during Second Temple times, had constituted the social elite, whether of the priestly or the social-economic aristocracy. Some of the sages were indeed priests and even well-to-do or rich, but many, and they included some of the most eminent figures, were poor and of undistinguished birth, their standing being determined only by their learning and their rich personalities. In addition to the *bet midrash* at Jabneh, others flourished in the towns and villages, being found in all parts of the country from the south to the north, at Kefar Aziz in the south, where Ishmael was active; at Bene Berak, where Akiva lived; at Lydda, the seat of Eliezer b. Hyrcanus and of Tarfon; at Peki'in, which was under the leadership of Joshua b. Hananiah; and in Galilean cities, such as at Sepphoris, where Halafta was active, at Sikhnin, the seat of Hananiah b. Teradyon, and at Tiberias, where Yose b. Kisma taught. The heads of the local *battei midrashot* came regularly to Jabneh which some made their main place of residence, paying only short visits to their own *battei midrashot*.

Resettlement and Economic Recovery. Despite the considerable suffering endured as a consequence of the war Jewish Erez Israel made a rapid recovery. Many captives, freed with the help of the local Jewish population or by other means, returned to their homes. As a result of the teachings of the contemporary sages, the significance of Erez Israel, its settlement, and the redemption of its land now assumed the character of a basic principle in Jewish thought and action. Large tracts of land were redeemed from the non-Jews, plantations were restored, and new ones planted. Agricultural knowledge increased, and industry in Erez Israel, consisting of processed agricultural products, quickly recovered. Craftsmen's associations plied their trades; farmers reaped bounteous harvests; agricultural and industrial products were exported. Already toward the end of the first century C.E. the economic position had improved considerably. In general, Jewish cities destroyed during the war were rebuilt and rehabilitated. All the Greek cities, whose Jewish settlement had been destroyed during the war, were repopulated by Jews. By the end of the first century C.E. there were flourishing Jewish communities in places like Caesarea, Ashkelon, Acre, Beth-Shean, and elsewhere. Great assistance in the speedy rehabilitation of the Jewish nation in Ereẓ Israel was rendered by those cities which had not revolted against Rome or had at an early stage in the war stopped fighting, while the basis for the restoration of a normal economic life was provided by those cities and circles which had not participated in the war. By reason both of postwar military requirements and of the economic and commercial prosperity of the Roman Empire under the Antonines (96–180), the network of roads in Ereẓ Israel was extended and many bridges were built. In 106 the Nabatean kingdom was annexed to the Roman Empire, and in 111 a start was made with constructing a road linking Damascus and Akaba. A large part of the foreign trade with the Arabian Peninsula and with India passed along this route, to the benefit of the cities, including the Jewish settlements, adjoining this road and of the Jews in the Greek cities in Transjordan. The Jewish population increased too, in Akaba, that is, Ezion-Geber.

The War of Quietus. In 115–117 the Jews in the Diaspora rose in a widespread revolt which, embracing Libya, Cyrenaica, Egypt, Cyprus, and Mesopotamia, was marked by both battles between the Jews and the Greeks and uprisings against Roman rule in the east. The focal point of the revolt was in the Diaspora and the early historical sources speak explicitly only of the revolt and the destruction of Diaspora Jewry and especially of North African countries. But epigraphic evidences about military missions sent at that time to Ereẓ Israel and fragmentary literary information indicate that there were uprisings on a considerable scale in Ereẓ Israel too. In Jewish tradition these uprisings are known as "the war of Quietus" (Sot. 9:14), after the Moorish commander Lusius Quietus, who, having ruthlessly suppressed the revolt of the Jews in Mesopotamia, was sent to stamp out the revolt in Judea and was then ap-

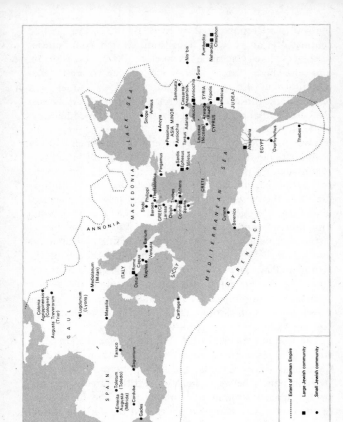

The Diaspora in the Roman Empire in the Mishnaic and Talmudic periods. Based on H. H. Ben-Sasson (ed.), *Toledot Am Yisrael*, vol. I, Tel Aviv, 1969.

pointed its governor until recalled to Rome, where he was executed at the beginning of Hadrian's rule (118).

Talmudic traditions tell of meetings on the Temple Mount in Jerusalem, of the revolt spreading to Galilee, the destruction of various cities in Erez Israel, and the execution of its leaders, Pappus and Lulianus, whose activities extended also to the Diaspora (Sifra 8:9). With the suppression of the revolt religious persecutions were reinstituted. In an act of deliberate provocation, an idol was set up on the Temple Mount (Ta'an. 4:6).

The Bar Kokhba Revolt. The accession of Hadrian (117) brought with it a trend to restore peace in the east and to rehabilitate and reconstruct the region on an extensive scale. Apparent in Hadrian's actions was a regard for the national character, predilections, and needs of the provinces. Erez Israel and the Jews, too, benefited from this trend. In his efforts to restore devastated areas, the emperor promised the Jews that he would rebuild and return Jerusalem to them, and permit the rebuilding of the Temple. Jews began to flock to Jerusalem, and organizational and financial preparations were made for rebuilding the Temple (Or. Sibyll. 5:252–4; Epistle of Barnabas, 16:1–5; Epiphanius, *Liber de Mensuris et Ponderibus,* 170; Gen. R. 64:10). A few years after his accession Hadrian, changing his mind, abandoned the plan of rebuilding Jerusalem as a Jewish city and instead decided to continue its construction as a pagan Roman city. Even the coins struck in Erez Israel in those days show a tendency to ignore the prevailing facts of Jewish existence. It is difficult to determine Hadrian's motives for this change of mind. He may have been prompted to adopt this new course by the profound echo which his promise produced among the Jews and by the political fears he entertained at restoring Jerusalem to the Jewish people. His attitude to Judaism may also have changed, for during his reign and already at the beginning of the twenties he displayed indubitable pan-Hellenistic tendencies, his policy being to introduce in the empire and particularly in its eastern regions the 145 later universalistic Hellenistic outlook and mode of life. This found expression alike in the erection of buildings and monuments, the passing of laws against oriental usages, and inclusion in the ban against castration which was punishable with death, of the prohibition of circumcision.

This last was not specifically directed against Judaism, since its practice was also forbidden to others in the east who circumcised their sons. But for no other people did circumcision occupy so significant a place in its thought. Nor did any other people so scrupulously insist on circumcising every single boy. Hadrian, who before becoming emperor had been the governor of Syria and had come into contact with the Jews and their sages, was undoubtedly aware of what these arrangements of his meant for the Jews. But in his resolve to reshape and reconstitute life in Erez Israel, he deliberately ignored the Jewish nation and its past in the country. No wonder that one historian, Dio Cassius, mentions this resolve of Hadrian as the cause of the revolt.

These actions, coming after the spiritual elation engendered by the permission to rebuild Jerusalem and the Temple, led to a profound agitation among the Jews and to military preparations against Rome, to the surreptitious construction of various fortifications, and to the accumulation of arms. Dio Cassius tells that the Jews purposely damaged the weapons they made for the Romans, so that these should be rejected and remain in the possession of the Jews without their stockpiling arousing suspicion. While Hadrian was in Erez Israel and its neighborhood (128–132) the Jews did not openly rebel, but the grave terrorist acts then committed in the country found the permanent Roman forces there insufficient to cope with the situation. An additional legion, the *Sexta Ferrata,* was brought to Erez Israel, and remained in the country after the revolt, being stationed in Kefar Otnai at the entrance to the Valley of Jezreel. The authorities were also compelled to reinforce the tenth legion by recruiting soldiers from nearby countries. When Hadrian left the east, the revolt broke out and assumed large proportions, since "the Jews throughout the entire world were in an uproar too, and joined them, inflicting openly or by stealth great losses on the Romans. They were moreover helped by non-Jews" (Dio Cassius loc. cit.). The Samaritans, or at least some of them, also joined.

In contrast to the rebellion against the Romans in 66–70, the revolt was distinguished by national unity and centralized leadership. There are references to local heroes and to various messiahs and pretenders to the royal title who flourished in the first stages of the revolt, but conspicuous during its course and until its end were the leadership and the central figure of Simeon bar Kokhba. It is he who is mentioned in the historical sources, round whose personality are centered talmudic traditions and legends, and in whose name—Simeon, Nasi of Israel—coins were struck. Documents and letters, dating from the time of the war and found in the caves of the Judean Desert, were taken there by fugitives from En-Gedi and its vicinity. In them it is "Simeon bar Kosiba, Nasi of Israel," who issues instructions and commands; in his name public lands are leased out. Christian sources state that he was called Bar Kokhba by reason of the messianic traits ascribed to him. Akiva, too, acknowledged his messiahship and declared: "This is the King Messiah" (TJ, Ta'an. 4:8, 68d). With Simeon the Nasi there also appears on some coins "Eleazar the priest," apparently Eleazar of Modi'in, a sage of Jabneh, whom talmudic tradition associates with Bar Kokhba. The headquarters of Bar Kokhba and of the commanders of the Jewish fighters was at Bethar situated at the extremity of a mountain ridge to the southwest of Jerusalem. In the intervening period between the war against the Romans and the Bar Kokhba revolt, the town, having been rebuilt after its destruction, flourished as a commercial and inhabited center for the region in place of Jerusalem. Shortly before the revolt, the Sanhedrin and the household of the *nasi* moved to Bethar, in which not only schools for the study of Torah were established, but also one for Greek learning. It is not known what connection the 147 household of the *nasi* had with the revolt or with Bar Kokhba, or to what extent the Sanhedrin was associated with the revolt, but it is clear that the sages supported it.

The revolt began with a great offensive. Bar Kokhba succeeded in gaining control of the whole of Judea, including Jerusalem, as well as of a considerable part of the rest of Erez Israel, and in introducing in the territory under his rule an independent Jewish order. The rebels defeated Tinnius Rufus, the Roman governor, and Publius Marcellius, the governor of Syria, who arrived with the legions stationed in Syria and to whose assistance the legions stationed in Egypt and Arabia had been dispatched. The 22nd Legion, which had come from Egypt, was annihilated. At this juncture the Jewish fighters invaded the coastal region and the Romans engaged in sea battles against the Jews. In those days Rome enjoyed complete security, peace prevailed on its borders, and hence it was able to mobilize large numbers of men and forces even from distant places. Hadrian summoned Julius Severus, the governor of Britain, who arrived with his forces and with legions from Danubian countries. There were about 12 legions in all, composed of their full complement or of detachments of them. Julius Severus, "refraining from engaging in open warfare," forced the Jewish fighters back step by step amid heavy losses to the Roman army, compelled them to retreat to fortresses which were taken one by one. "Fifty strongholds . . . and 985 of the most important settlements were destroyed"; hundreds of thousands were killed. In the first stage, Galilee, which was not seriously affected, was captured, and the main burden of war fell on Judea. Eventually the Jewish fighters were thrust back to their last stronghold, Bethar, which fell after a protracted siege. Tradition records that Bethar was captured on Av 9 (the summer of 135), on the anniversary of the destruction of the First and Second Temples (Ta'an. 4:6). With its fall and the death of Simeon bar Kosiba there came an end to the struggle which had lasted three and a half years, although there were sieges and skirmishes in the region of the Judean

Desert caves to which the fighters had escaped in the final stages of the revolt, even as had been the case with the fortress at Masada after the war against the Romans. In conformity with Roman custom, Jerusalem was now plowed up with a yoke of oxen, and thus the limits were fixed of the Roman colony, henceforth called *Colonia Aelia Capitolina* in Roman sources.

CONSEQUENCES OF THE REVOLT. In addition to the destruction of populated areas and the large-scale massacre, there were great numbers of Jewish captives who filled the slave markets in Erez Israel and in distant lands. Especially notorious was the market under the terebinth near Hebron where a Jewish slave was sold for the price of a horse's feed. Many settlements, especially in Judea, were not rebuilt. The central Judean Mountains were largely depopulated of their Jewish inhabitants. In Galilee, which suffered less from the aftermath of the revolt, the olive plantations were destroyed (TJ, Pe'ah 7: 1, 20a). Hadrian now resolved to launch a war of annihilation against the Torah and to expunge the name of Israel from the land. To this end decrees were issued against the observance of the *mitzvot,* gatherings in synagogues for the purposes of prayer or study were prohibited, *battei din* were forbidden to meet. In a description of those times a contemporary Babylonian sage commented: "'Of them that love Me and keep My commandments' (Ex. 19:6)—'These are the Jews who live in Erez Israel and jeopardize their lives for the sake of the *mitzvot.*' 'Why are you being led out to be decapitated?' 'Because I circumcised my son.' 'Why are you being led out to be burnt?' 'Because I read the Torah.' 'Why are you being led out to be crucified?' 'Because I ate unleavened bread.' 'Why are you being whipped with the scourge?' 'Because I performed the *mitzvah* of the *lulav*'" (Mekh., ba-Hodesh, 6). Jews were forbidden to stay in Jerusalem and only once a year, on Tishah be-Av (Av 9), were they permitted to enter the city to weep over the remains of their holy places. Desirous of blotting out, too, all reference to the Jews' association with Erez Israel, Hadrian changed the 149 name of Judea to Syria Palaestina, by which it henceforth came to be known in non-Jewish literature. The authorities confiscated land on an extensive scale on the strength of martial law or of offenses against the new decrees, such as the prohibition of circumcision. Large tracts of land lay waste, their owners having been taken captive or compelled to flee. The Jews in the country underwent a harsh period of persecution. Many, and they included the nation's most eminent men and sages such as Akiva, Ishmael, Hananiah b. Teradyon, Tarfon, and others, were killed in the persecutions, many went into hiding in Erez Israel, large numbers fled abroad and never returned or did so only after several years. There were numerous martyrs, this being the generation that gave the Jewish people the tradition of martyrdom known as *Kiddush ha-Shem*. From the end of the revolt until the close of Hadrian's reign (that is, from 135 to 138) the Jews of Erez Israel bore the full brunt of the anti-religious decrees.

The repressive measures were somewhat relaxed only on the accession of Antoninus Pius. He neither annulled them nor immediately restored to the Jews the status they had enjoyed before the revolt. Gradually however their situation improved. Apparently at the beginning of Antoninus Pius' reign, circumcision was permitted, a law enacted by him having allowed the Jews to circumcise their sons but not slaves or proselytes. For the Samaritans the prohibition remained in force, and for a long time they circumcised their sons at great risk. But alike in the days of the Antoninus as in those of Hadrian, a harsh military regime prevailed in Erez Israel.

RECOVERY AFTER THE REVOLT: USHA. The first signs of the recovery of communal life appeared in Galilee, to which the center of Jewish life henceforth passed and where the main population as also the seat of the Sanhedrin and of the *nasi* remained until the end of the period. The Sanhedrin had first gone to Usha, whence it moved for a short time to Shepharam and from there to Bet She'arim and Sepphoris. In the third century it finally settled at Tiberias, the capital of Galilee. But Judea still had its Jewish population, its *battei midrashot*, and sages—at Lydda there was a large *bet midrash*, which enjoyed independence in many spheres of Jewish life. But the central authority and the focal point of spiritual creativity were in Galilee, where the main work of collecting and of finally redacting the tannaitic and amoraic literature was done.

The leaders who restored the religious and communal life comprised several of Akiva's younger pupils who survived the massacre and who had not yet gained renown in the generation of Jabneh: Meir, Judah b. Ilai, Jose b. Ḥalafta, Simeon b. Yoḥai, and Nehemiah. The early meetings of the Sanhedrin were still held in temporary quarters and under semi-underground conditions in the Valley of Bet Rimmon, and only after many years, at "the end of the religious persecutions," did it meet at Usha (Song R. 2:5 no. 3). From the time that Tiberias was found (beginning of first century C.E.) many Jews and especially priests refrained from living there for fear that it had been built on a cemetery. Hadrian had wanted to give the city a pagan character but the temple which he had begun to build was not completed. After the revolt Tiberias was almost entirely Jewish. Simeon b. Yoḥai sought to declare it levitically clean and following protracted discussions it was recognized as such (TJ, Shev. 9:1, 38d). This facilitated the city's growth and enabled it to serve during the years as the spiritual center. Simeon b. Gamaliel, the son of Rabban Gamaliel of Jabneh, did not take part in the Sanhedrin in the early stages of its reestablishment, for he, too, had been compelled to go into hiding for several years. After some time he is mentioned as the head of the Sanhedrin at Usha.

The period not only of his tenure of the office of *nasi* (c. 140–170) but of the entire reign of the Antonines (until 193) was a difficult one both politically and economically. The authorities showed a growing contempt and suspicion of the Jews, and when Marcus Aurelius passed through Erez Israel in 175 he expressed himself in opprobrious terms about them. They, for their part, displayed considerable rebelliousness, hoping as they did for the downfall of Rome, a hope that grew with the latter's clashes and preparations for war with the Parthians. Simeon b. Yoḥai asserted: "If you see a Persian horse tied in the burial places of Ereẓ Israel, expect the Messiah" (Song R. 8:9). This rebelliousness was responsible for the fact that the Jews of Ereẓ Israel, like the other peoples of the east, supported Avidius Cassius who had proclaimed himself emperor and was assassinated shortly before Marcus Aurelius' arrival in the country. Brigandage, too, increased greatly at this time, and although this was due to economic difficulties, it also had overtones of political insurrection. In Ereẓ Israel as a whole the economic situation was quite good during this period, although the country suffered in 166 from a plague which spread in the east. Like other provinces, Ereẓ Israel profited from the expanded international trade. Roads were built and bridges constructed, public institutions were established, markets and grain exchanges were set up and wells dug, creating a sense of security and promoting commerce, so that many cities flourished at this time. There were Jews, too, who benefitted from this prosperity.

In Rome two inscriptions of Jews from Tiberias have been found that testify to commercial stations in the city, and some Jews, who were imperial court favorites, rose to positions of eminence. But the Jewish community as a whole lived in dire poverty. Thus reference is made to "the generation of R. Judah b. Illai . . . six of whose pupils covered themselves with one garment and studied the Torah" (Sanh. 20a). The nonrecognition of the Jews' religious rights brought in its train economic difficulties. Up to the Bar Kokhba revolt the authorities had exempted the Jews from land taxes during the sabbatical year, when they had no income from agricultural produce. After the revolt they had to pay these taxes, and were hard put to find a way of meeting the burden of taxation while observing, at least to some extent, the sabbatical year (Sanh. 3:3 et al.). This circumstance is the background to the *halakhah* which lays down that "if at the present time a man wishes to become a proselyte, he is to be addressed as follows: 'What reason have you for wanting to become a proselyte? Do you not know that at present Jews are persecuted and oppressed, despised, harassed, and burdened with afflictions ... and do not conduct themselves in public like other peoples?' " (Yev. 47a; Tractate *Gerim,* beginning). As a result of the harsh conditions there was an increasing emigration, either temporary or permanent, from Erez Israel. Seeking to stem it, the sages enacted *halakhot* to curtail this tendency.

Despite the difficult political conditions and the imperial nonrecognition, the sages of the generation of Usha and Rabban Simeon b. Gamaliel succeeded in consolidating the leadership of the central authority and in restoring to Erez Israel its hegemony over the Diaspora. During the persecutions, when the house of assembly ceased to function, one of the Erez Israel sages Hananiah, the nephew of Joshua, who had been sent to Babylonia, began to proclaim the new months and intercalate years there, and would not desist even when the central authority was reestablished in Erez Israel. Only by resolute persuasion, by appeasement, and with the support of the Babylonian sages was the *nasi* able to make the separatist circles in Babylonia cease their activities, whereupon the Jews there once again submitted to the authority of Erez Israel. In the days of Rabban Simeon b. Gamaliel, the office of *nasi* assumed the form of a triumvirate, consisting of the *nasi* himself, the *av bet din,* and a sage, who was the authorized halakhist. For some time, Nathan, the son of the exilarch, in Babylonia, was the *av bet din,* thereby enabling the *nasi* to associate with his office also a representative of that large Diaspora community. This set an example for future generations, the great majority of those occupying the position of *av bet din* in the tannaitic and amoraic period having been sages who immigrated to Erez Israel from Babylonia.

In the generation following the Bar Kokhba revolt the Samaritans began a large-scale expansion beyond the confines of "the land of the Cutheans." Their expansion to the north having been halted by Beth-Shean and Jezreel Valleys, they spread northwest along the coast and especially southwest along the southern coastal plain. The reasons for this may have been the Jews' diminished power as well as the plight in which the Samaritans found themselves on account of religious persecution. They therefore sought refuge among the Jewish population, perhaps because of the close contacts established between them during the Bar Kokhba revolt. The Samaritans' expansion into the Jewish areas led to considerable friction, and there were assertions by sages that, since leaving their villages, they had become lax in the observance of *mitzvot*. In contrast to the earlier *halakhah*, they were now more and more adjudged as non-Jews.

The Severan Dynasty. R. Judah ha-Nasi. A period of political and economic efflorescence came to the Jews of Erez Israel under the Severan emperors (193–235), coinciding largely with the tenure of the office of *nasi* by Judah I, the eldest son of Rabban Simeon b. Gamaliel and known as Rabbi. After the murder of Commodus (192) an armed struggle broke out between Pescennius Niger and Septimius Severus which divided the east, including Erez Israel and the legions stationed there. Pescennius Niger had, as governor of Syria, been ruthless in his attitude to the Jews. When they had asked him to lighten the burden of taxation, he had answered that were it possible he would tax the very air they breathed. He severely punished the cities which supported his rival. While the tenth legion sided with him, the house of the *nasi* and the Jews of Erez Israel supported Severus, whose victory was regarded as a deliverance. The good relations that existed between the Jews of Erez Israel and the Severans, which continued throughout that dynasty's reign, influenced several Severan emperors in their predilection and love for Judaism and for a syncretism in which it, too, was included. Alexander Severus was derisively called *archisynagogus* (head of the synagogue). The political position of the Jews in Erez Israel improved and they were able to occupy notable positions in the Greek

The body of Judah ha-Nasi being taken to heaven by the angels. Bronze by Milton Horn, 1962. 50×36 in. (127×91.5 cm.). River Forest, Ill., West Suburban Temple Har Zion. Photo Estelle Horn.

and Roman cities. Their more influential status found expression mainly in an increased autonomy, both public and judicial. The *nasi* was permitted to levy taxes for the maintenance of the central authority, civil and criminal cases were tried, and judgment could be enforced against the guilty party. When necessary, the *nasi* could also try capital cases. While this right was not officially recognized by Roman law, it was not exercised surreptitiously (Origen, *Epistola ad Africanum,* 28:14).

The relations between the Roman Empire and Judah ha-Nasi were particularly good. Extensive areas of state land in the Valley of Jezreel, Golan, and elsewhere were given to him as a gift or on lease. The *aggadah* frequently mentions the close ties between him and the Roman emperor Antoninus, but since several Severans bore this name, it is difficult to determine which of them is meant. From what is known of the stay of the emperors in the neighborhood of Erez Israel and their association with Judaism, this reference is probably to Caracalla (198–217 c.e.) or Alexander Severus (222–235 c.e.). The Jews were grateful to the Severan dynasty and both in Erez Israel (at Kaisan in Upper Galilee) and in the Diaspora synagogues dedicated to the emperors of that dynasty have been found. In their days there was a great expansion of settlement. Thus at this time there were included within the halakhic limits of Erez Israel areas in the north and south, which halakhically had not belonged to Erez Israel since the majority of their inhabitants had been non-Jews and to which the commandments applicable to Erez Israel, such as those relating to priestly dues and tithes, had not previously applied. At this time, too, there was established in Jerusalem a permanent Jewish settlement, known in talmudic tradition as the "the holy community in Jerusalem" *(kehilla kadisha de-bi-Yrushalayim).* While presumably the prohibition against Jews' settling in Jerusalem was not officially rescinded, the authorities chose to ignore it. At this time, too, the economic position of the Jews of Erez Israel improved. The extensive urbanization initiated by the Severan emperors had favorable economic repercussions. Septimius Severus bestowed city rights on Bet Guvrin, now called Eleutheropolis, and granted it large areas which included the whole of Idumea. Land was even detached from Aelia Capitolina and the *limes* and given to it. Lydda, too, obtained city status, was named Diospolis, and granted considerable areas of land. In 220–221 C.E. the district of Emmaus was made a city and named Nicopolis. This completed the urbanization of western Erez Israel. Except for the part of Upper Galilee known as Tetracomia (the four villages) and the imperial estates in the *limes* and in the Valley of Jericho, the whole of western Erez Israel became a city area enjoying special privileges.

Emigration from Erez Israel was now replaced by immigration from the Diaspora, among the immigrants being people with expert knowledge, initiative, and money, who developed new branches of the economy, such as flax-growing, and of agricultural industry, such as the manufacture of clothes and dyeing.

The improved economic and political position found expression in splendid synagogues which were built throughout the country and remains of which have been uncovered, chiefly in Galilee, such as at Kefar Naḥum (Capernaum), Korazim (Chorazin), Baram, and elsewhere.

The Jewish people in Erez Israel saw in the enlargement of their power and in the aggrandizement of the *nasi* the beginnings of the redemption. A messianic aura surrounded him. From the days of Judah ha-Nasi and onward the *nasi*'s court was distinguished by an outer splendor, great opulence, and regal pomp. He succeeded in attracting to his court and to a participation in public leadership the heads of the large cities and the financial aristocracy, whom he prevailed on to accept the responsibilities of public office and national displine. This led to a protest on the part of the popular Hasidean sages, the extremists among whom became estranged from Judah ha-Nasi. In internal affairs, too, Judah ha-Nasi's authority was extensive. The right to grant ordination and the control of the Sanhedrin were concentrated in his hands. Under him the central authority exercised increased supervision over the cities and communities in the Diaspora. Under him, too, there was 157 considerable legislation in the spheres of communal religion, of apportioning the burden of taxes, and the manner of levying them. While not charged with collecting the taxes, he, by virtue of the authority of his office and of being a rabbi, gave decisions on various financial problems, among them being some which impressed their stamp on Jewish communal arrangements for generations, such as exempting scholars, who devote themselves wholly to the study of the Torah, from taxes and civic obligations. He also exempted areas in southern and northern Erez Israel from priestly dues, tithes, and from the laws of the sabbatical year, from which last-named he sought to grant a total exemption, but due to the opposition of Phinehas b. Jair, a Hasidean sage, the question was not brought up for discussion and a final decision.

His activities included the final redaction of the Mishnah, which constitutes the summary and crystallization of most of the halakhic material of the Oral Law. Judah ha-Nasi was not the first to undertake the task of committing the Oral Law to writing and of summarizing it in an halakhic compilation. Already in Second Temple times, and especially in the generation of Jabneh, this was done by *tannaim* but their Mishnah collections were incorporated, either wholly or in part, in that of Judah ha-Nasi, whose compilation is the more comprehensive and extensive. Assembling the teachings and collections of preceding generations, he arranged them in *sedarim* and tractates according to subject matter, *Shabbat, Pesaḥim, Gittin, Kiddushin,* and so on, and subdivided these into chapters, generally set out in a logical development of the subject. The final redaction of the Mishnah constitutes a compilation of the Oral Law without deciding between the various views but including also the decisions arrived at and the laws enacted in Judah ha-Nasi's *bet midrash.* His humility in teaching the Torah and in halakhic judgments, his readiness to pay heed to and examine different opinions, his spiritual independence, his exalted status, and his

lengthy tenure of the office of *nasi*—all these contributed to the compilation of the Mishnah and its acceptance as the basic work for the study of the Oral Law and as the principal foundation of Jewish jurisprudence. Within a short time his Mishnah, having superseded and consigned to oblivion earlier or contemporaneous collections, became the basis and the prototype of the continued creation of the Oral Law. The close of the Mishnah represents a turning point and a landmark in the history of the Oral Law, which was further elucidated and defined throughout the generations. The literature created up to the close of the Mishnah, even if redacted shortly afterward, is the tannaitic, that which followed it the amoraic, literature. All *halakhot* mentioned in the Mishnah and in the other tannaitic productions are more authoritative than those in the amoraic works. Except for a number of Aramaic and Greek words and expressions, the language of the Mishnah is mishnaic Hebrew, reflecting the prevailing circumstances in Ereẓ Israel from Second Temple times onward. The death of Judah ha-Nasi (c. 225) initiated a process that led to a separation between the office of *nasi* and the Sanhedrin. The last testament ascribed to him states that Rabban Gamaliel, his eldest son, was to be the *nasi* and the sage Ḥanina b. Ḥama the president of the Sanhedrin (TJ, Ta'an. 4:2, 68a).

In the following generation the separation was almost complete. Then the Sanhedrin, presided over by Johanan (from c. 240), had its seat at Tiberias, while the office of *nasi* occupied by Judah ha-Nasi II, had its seat for a considerable time at Sepphoris. Under normal circumstances a sage was the president of the Sanhedrin or the Great Bet Din, which was independent, but not entirely so, of the *nasi,* since the latter was theoretically its president, and in certain areas, as also in particular instances, its dependence on the *nasi* was maintained. Thus the ordination of sages was contingent on the sanction of the *nasi,* who continued to exercise the sole right to enact regulations. There was also cooperation between them in political matters. Alongside the central *bet midrash* or the Sanhedrin at Tiberias there were in amoraic times other *battei midrashot* which, as the centers of 159 instruction and leadership for their immediate vicinity, taught the Torah and appointed *dayyanim* for the neighborhood. At Lydda there was the center, founded by Joshua b. Levi, for the southern settlements; at Caesarea one established by Hoshaiah; and a smaller one in Upper Galilee at Akbara, under the leadership of Yannai, where a considerable nucleus of his companions lived a communal life for several generations. Each of these *battei midrashot* was distinct in its teachings and method of instruction, but in special instances their heads were invited to assemblies, the sages of the south (Lydda) in particular often meeting with the members of the Sanhedrin at Tiberias.

The Period of Anarchy (235–289 C.E.**).** In this period of the frequent change of emperors, of chaos and collapse throughout the Roman Empire, Jewish Ereẓ Israel in particular suffered. There was indeed no religious persecution of the Jews, and even when the Christians and Samaritans were compelled to participate in emperor worship, the rights of the Jews were recognized and respected. The contemporary diatribes against the evil "Esau [3]" who oppressed "Jacob" were mainly directed against Esau, the robber and plunderer, a circumstance conspicuous, too, in the non-Hebrew sources of the nations neighboring on Israel. The rural population suffered greatly from economic hardship, from taxation, and from oppression at the hands of soldiers, and since the economy of Jewish Ereẓ Israel was largely agricultural, the Jews were affected more than the non-Jewish population. During the period of anarchy there was a decline in agriculture, not because of the diminished fertility of the soil but because of the corrupt administrative arrangements that led to a neglect of the land and lack of interest in fostering the cultivation of the soil. During this period, too, the country suffered from privation and an extremely severe famine. Emigration increased, and although there was also a considerable immigration to Ereẓ Israel, it was not large

[3] In other periods Esau and Edom were euphemisms for Rome.

enough to balance the number of those leaving the country. Despite the upheavals and wars which occurred in the east with the accession and onslaught of the Sassanid kings there were increasing contacts between Erez Israel and the Diaspora, especially that in Babylonia. In the days of the principal generations of the *amoraim* the contacts between these two Jewish communities were considerable, numerous, and frequent. As a result of the situation created by the fact that the Roman Empire was in the process of disintegration and by the Persian attacks, the kingdom of Palmyra (Tadmor) enlarged its power. This buffer state. situated between Persia and Rome, and subordinate to the latter, first forged ahead from 260 C.E. under Odaenathus within the ambit of the Roman Empire. Later, under Queen Zenobia (267–272), having proclaimed its independence and freed itself from Roman suzerainty, it initiated a policy of conquest and expansion directed against the countries of the east, including Erez Israel. The Palmyrene regime was not only a continuation of Roman rule but also contained elements conducive to creating an independent eastern state. Although wide circles in the east supported it, at the decisive moment, when Rome reconquered the east from Zenobia, the great majority of them refrained from coming to its assistance and instead helped the Romans. When Odaenathus was a client king under Roman patronage, Jewish tradition charged him with being "a brother" (because of the eastern elements in his regime) who had come to the aid of "Esau" (Rome) in the latter's hour of weakness. "Happy is he," declared R. Johanan, the leader of that generation of Jews, "who witnesses the downfall of Tadmor [Palmyra]" (TJ, Ta'an. 4:8, 69b). But with Zenobia, whose attitude toward them was one of protectiveness and esteem, the relations of the Jews were friendlier, the clash between her and Rome even raising messianic hopes in some circles.

Stability Returns to the Roman Empire. At the end of the third century (284) Diocletian became emperor and succeeded in transforming the regime and the system of the 161

Roman Empire into a despotic monarchy on the Byzantine pattern with its exaggerated hierarchy and extensive bureaucracy. By dividing each of the provinces into two or three, their number was increased. Erez Israel, one of the smallest among them, was likewise subdivided into several parts, so that from 358 to the beginning of the fifth century (429) it comprised Palaestina Prima, which consisted of Judea, Samaria, the Coastal Plain, Idumea, and Perea (Jewish Transjordan), and whose capital remained Caesarea; Palaestina Secunda, which embraced Galilee, the Decapolis, and Golan, and whose capital was Scythopolis (Beth-Shean); and Palaestina Tertia, which comprised the Negev and whose capital was Petra. As in other provinces, the civil ruler, the *praeses* was distinct from the military head, the *dux*. Instead of reforming the corrupt government system, the new regime perpetuated it, increasing its sway over the population. Participation in all the associations became compulsory and was enforced, ranging from performing municipal duties to the organization of craftsmen's unions from which all workmen were excluded, and to the obligation of children to continue in their parents' occupation. All the associations were at the disposal of the empire for levying taxes and providing services. During this period land tenancy assumed such proportions that the petty independent farmer, typical of Jewish Erez Israel, all but disappeared. The land passed into the possession of the proprietors of large estates and its former owners became tenant farmers. The imperial law of the *colonatus* was introduced, binding the farmer in perpetuity to the soil. This perpetual tenancy was hereditary and was marked by several expressions of the tenant farmer's servitude to the landlord. The imperial tenant farmers were similarly bound in perpetuity to their tenancy and their holdings. Because land in Erez Israel was retained in the possession of petty farmers for a longer time, the *lex colonatus* was introduced in the country at a comparatively late period, 383–388, about 50 years later than in the other provinces. At the beginning of the fourth century, the Jews were progressively becoming a minority in their ownership of land.

With the stabilization of the imperial regime, a new force emerged in the world: Christianity was gaining a commanding position, commencing with Constantine's recognition of the Christian religion (313). This was destined to have a decisive effect on the status of Erez Israel and of its Jews, henceforth called upon to undertake a joint political self-defense. Hitherto the Jews had struggled culturally against a pagan world, which by its very nature acknowledged the existence of national religions. Even the Roman regime recognized in theory, and for most of the time in practice too, the Jewish religious reality in Erez Israel. Christianity, which within a short period became the imperial religion, did not, as is the way of a monotheistic religion, recognize or tolerate other religions, and in this displayed a greater bigotry and inflexibility than Judaism. Although the Christian Church had a special interest in converting Jews, and particular those in Erez Israel, Judaism was not declared illegal either in that country or in the Roman Empire, which nevertheless fostered an enmity toward and a contempt for Judaism. In addition to the hostility originating in the separation between them the Roman Christians were the object of much of the contempt for Jews prevalent in circles of the pagan Roman aristocracy. The hostile attitude to Judaism was expressed in the emperors' anti-Jewish legislation with its insulting language, and in the attacks of fanatics on Jews and their institutions, such as the campaign of the bigoted monk Bar Sauma of Nisibis who, with his band, passed through Erez Israel in 419–422 C.E. destroying synagogues. Not only did Christianity have an interest in the holy places, such as the site of the Crucifixion, the sepulcher of Jesus, and others. It also based its gospel on the destruction of Jerusalem and God's rejection of the people of Israel, so that the whole of the patriarchal blessing, including Erez Israel, now belonged to it. Henceforward it was not the Jews alone who sought to have possession of Erez Israel. Many Christian congregations were established in the country. The inhabitants of villages and of the large cities, most of which remained faithful to Hellenism, had to fight for their continued pagan existence. Constantine and his mother Helena, who was devoted to Christianity and even immigrated to Erez Israel in her old age, set about building magnificent churches, one—the Church of the Nativity—at Bethlehem, and two—those of the Holy Sepulcher and of the Ascension—in Jerusalem, as also at Abraham's Oak. The Church Father Epiphanius has preserved a detailed account of the manner in which the emperor helped the apostate Joseph to build churches in the Jewish centers, at Tiberias, Sepphoris, and other localities holy to Christianity, such as Kefar Naḥum (Capernaum) and Nazareth, places inhabited exclusively by Jews. The Jews fought Joseph who consequently succeeded only in building a small church at Tiberias (Epiphanius, *Panarion adversus Haereses*, 1:2, xxx, 4). The Christian population increased by reason of the conversion of non-Jews in Erez Israel and of the arrival of Christians or pilgrims who settled in the country. The many monasteries which were first built in the fourth century and multiplied in the fifth and sixth also attracted devout Christians from abroad. There were instances of Jews who were converted to Christianity, as in the case of Joseph, but the number was not large either among them or among the Samaritans.

The Revolt Against Gallus. In June 351 a revolt of the Jews broke out at Sepphoris against Gallus, the Roman ruler in the east. The rebels had heard of various uprisings in the west and of Constantius' reverses in his campaign to suppress them. They also relied on obtaining assistance from the Persians whose attacks, some of them successful, had increased at that time. Having appointed a leader named Patricius, of whom little is known, the Jews defeated the Roman army in the city. From there the revolt spread through Galilee and reached Lydda in the south. It bore no anti-Christian character, nor were Christians or their institutions attacked, the revolt being directed solely against Gallus' corrupt rule. Ursicinus, an experienced commander, was dispatched against the rebels. The decisive battle took place near Acre. From there the enemy advanced against centers in Galilee inhabited by Jews, and several Jewish settlements and cities were destroyed. Some of them, such as Tiberias, Sepphoris, and Lydda, were rebuilt shortly after the revolt, but there were places like Bet She'arim which were now left with only a meager population. It is not known where the seat of the Sanhedrin and of the *nasi* was during the revolt, but not long after it they were once again engaged in their usual activities. During the years immediately following the revolt the authorities interfered with assemblies for the intercalation of the year and especially with emissaries sent to inform the Diaspora of it (Sanh. 12a). It was therefore apparently decided to draw up a permanent calendar (TJ, Er. 3:11, 21c) which, according to a later tradition, was done by Hillel II in 359 (*Sefer ha-Ibbur,* 97). Even after the calendar had been laid down and until it received its definitive form, questions were addressed to the sages of Erez Israel to elucidate various problems. In Erez Israel they continued even afterward to proclaim the new month and to celebrate the occasion as had formerly been done when its proclamation was made by the Great Bet Din.

Julian the Apostate. Excitement mounted in Erez Israel and the Diaspora during the brief reign of Julian (360–363). who endeavored to resuscitate Hellenism, to which he was devoted, by diminishing the image of Christianity in the empire. Wishing to reinstitute the sacrificial service of the Jews, which he regarded as more important than anything else in their Bible, he announced and promised in his letters to the "Community of the Jews" and to the *nasi* that he would rebuild "with great diligence the Temple of the supreme God" and "the holy Jerusalem which you have for many years longed to see rebuilt and which I shall restore." When he set out to fight the Persians, a special emissary, Alypius of Antioch, was appointed who filled important duties in connection with the rebuilding and to whom large sums of money were allocated. By this act the emperor may have sought, as he departed for war, to win over the Babylonian Jews, and assure their support, but all his letters are marked by friendship and sympathy toward the Jews. Moreover, he revoked the decrees relating to the special Jewish taxes, such as that of the two drachmas, and even asked the *nasi* to reduce the tax levied for the needs of his high office from the Jews. Julian's proclamations and actions created a ferment among the Jews, who flocked to Jerusalem and began to collect money from Italy and as far afield as Babylonia and Persia. Jews settled in the city, started to expel Christians from certain parts of it, and set up a synagogue in one of the colonnades on the Temple Mount. The Christians were furious, and their writers tell of a fire that broke out when the pagan shrines, abandoned with the rise of Christianity, were removed from the Temple site. It is possible that the Christians, desirous of interrupting the work of building, started the fire. When Julian was killed, apparently by a Christian Arab soldier, on the Persian front, the matter was ended.

After Julian's death, the Christians began to attack the Jewish settlements in the south where the Jews were greatly in the minority. Christian sources report the destruction "in the south of 21 cities of pagans, Jews, and Samaritans, who had had a share in Julian the Apostate's sin." Even after this the Jewish settlements in the south did not cease entirely but were reduced in number and impoverished. In the period between the death of Julian and the accession of Theodosius I (379) there was no anti-Jewish legislation, and several laws were even enacted which enhanced their status and that of the *nasi,* one law exempting officials of the communities subject to "the illustrious *nasi*" from sitting on municipal councils, another of 368 prohibiting the billeting of soldiers in synagogues. This period was a congenial one for the Jews either because Julian's personality and activities had fostered a tolerant attitude toward other religions and arrested the Church's domination or because the emperor Valens (364–378) acted with moderation due to his not wishing to add to his enemies, since the adherents of

Arianism, of which he was one, were already then in the minority. Under Theodosius I and his sons Honorius and Arcadius as also under Theodosius II until the abolition of the office of the *nasi* (that is, from 379 to 428) there was intensified anti-Jewish legislation which assigned an inferior status to Judaism and the Jews.

The Close of the Jerusalem Talmud and the Abolition of the Office of the Nasi. In the second half of the fourth century C.E. the Jerusalem Talmud was finalized and redacted in Ereẓ Israel, for the most part at Tiberias. In it was summarized all that was said, initiated, and thought in the world of Ereẓ Israel's sages in the century and a half that elapsed since the close of the Mishnah. No tradition is extant of the time taken to redact it or who its redactors were. The date of its redaction is fixed on the basis of the last sages and of the latest historical events—the revolt against Gallus and the emperor Julian's activities—mentioned in it (TJ, Meg. 3:1, 74a; TJ, Ned. 3:2, 37d). Dating from the end of the fourth century are evidences which combine to portray the firm status of the office of *nasi,* his right to collect money and to appoint and depose the leaders of communities in the Diaspora. At the beginning of the fifth century the position of the last *nasi,* Rabban Gamaliel VI, was undermined. Accused of contravening the imperial laws by building synagogues, circumcising Christian slaves, and acting as a judge in cases involving Christians, he was deposed from the rank of "Honorary *praefectus.*" The existence of the office of *nasi,* who claimed descent from the house of David, was not to the liking of the Church, which tried to diminish his image and spiritual stature. An order in the *Codex Theodosianus* of the year 429 mentions the death of the *nasi* and instructs the Sanhedrins in the two Palestines to transfer to the imperial treasury the money previously collected on behalf of the *nasi.* Taking advantage of the death of Rabban Gamaliel VI and of the "babes who died" (according to Jewish tradition), the authorities refrained from approving the appointment of another *nasi.* With the abolition of this office, the nation lost its leading institution which had persisted for three and a half centuries after the destruction of Jerusalem and the Temple. The Sanhedrin continued to exist, money was sent to it even without official permission, and Jewry was obedient to it and its leaders who were called "the heads of the school" *(rashei ha-perek)*, but it progressively lost its hegemony over the Diaspora. With the accession in 520 of Mar Zutra, the son of the exilarch Mar Zutra, the title of Head of the Sanhedrin was bestowed on him, and until the Arab conquest his descendants continued to occupy that position.

Byzantine Rule in Ereẓ Israel. During this period the economic position of the country improved. Many Christians, among them men of wealth and influence, immigrated to Ereẓ Israel. The visits, too, of Christians, as also the existence and export of the bones of patriarchs, prophets, and saints, whose graves were purported to have been discovered, brought much wealth to the land. In this period agricultural settlement, particularly in the Negev, was extended to areas never previously nor subsequently tilled, as evidenced by the remains not only of agricultural cultivation but also of cities in the Negev which flourished at this time. The period from the second half of the fifth century until the revival under Justinian (527–565) of the aggressive Christian policy was a tranquil one for the Jews in Ereẓ Israel. The Christians were absorbed in a theological controversy between the orthodox and the monophysites on the relation between the human and the divine nature of Jesus, a controversy which was associated with political, military, and communal clashes, so that they had no time to concern themselves with the Jews. The latter benefited from the economic prosperity that had come to the country, as attested by the building, extension, and renovation of synagogues whose remains have been found in the north (Bet Alfa, Hammath-Gader; and elsewhere) and in the south (Jericho, Naaran, Ashkelon, Gaza, and in other places). Although the erection and renovation of
synagogues were prohibited, the Jews were able to circum-

vent various repressive laws. The difficult position of the Samaritans and their hopes of receiving help from the Persians emboldened them to organize in 485 and in 529 two large revolts. At first successful, they set up their own brief government in a small area around Samaria, but the revolts were speedily suppressed with such ruthlessness that the Samaritans were considerably reduced in number. There followed a relentless religious persecution. Justinian's reign was the last glorious period of Roman-Byzantine rule in Erez Israel. He fortified the borders, provided the cities with a water supply, and built magnificent churches in various places in the country. But his reign was marked by the beginning of a harsh legislative attack on Judaism and by the Church's growing obduracy in its policy toward the Jews. When the old laws were selected from the *Codex Theodosianus* for inclusion in Justinian's new legal compilation, several which confirmed the rights of the Jews were omitted, while others depriving them of rights were added.

The Persian Invasion. In 603 the Persians renewed their attempt to assail the Roman Empire. In 611 they arrived at Antioch, in 613 they entered Damascus, in 614 they reached Erez Israel. The approach of the Persians inspired messianic hopes. Contact was made with the conquerors and the Jews gave them effective help in capturing Galilee. From there the Persians marched on Caesarea, proceeding along the coast, advanced against Lydda, and wound their way up to Jerusalem (May 614), in whose capture Jewish forces also took part. The Persians handed the city over to the Jews who, settling in it, began to remove from it the Christians and their churches. The leader in Jerusalem was one known only by the name of Nehemiah b. Hushi'el b. Ephraim b. Joseph, his messianic designation, and a beginning may even have been made to reintroduce sacrifices. His rule in Jerusalem lasted for three years. In 617 the Persians retracted, perhaps in order to gain the support of the Christians for their rule. The Jews did not acquiesce in this and the Persian regime was compelled to fight against them. Nehemiah and some of his closest adherents were killed by the Persians *(Sefer Zerubbabel)*. In the meantime Heraclius, the Byzantine emperor, having begun to grow powerful, set out in the spring of 622 on a campaign of conquest against Persia. In 627 the Persians, accepting their defeat, agreed to withdraw to their own country and the Byzantine army regained control of Erez Israel. In 629 Heraclius appeared at the gateways of the country. The Jewish leaders made a vain attempt to enter into a compact with him. They presented him with many gifts, he promised to overlook their past actions, and even made an agreement with them, binding himself by oath to observe it. One of the Jewish leaders, Benjamin of Tiberias, who was extremely wealthy, lodged the emperor in his home there, maintained him and the army accompanying him, and even joined him on his journey to Jerusalem. On March 21, 629, the emperor entered Jerusalem in a typically magnificent Byzantine procession and restored to their site the remnants of the cross given to him by the Persians. The emperor, who was not an anti-Semite, wished to keep his promises but under pressure from the Church revoked them. A decree was issued expelling the Jews from Jerusalem and its vicinity, and Jews were put on trial. Many were killed and many fled. In the period between Heraclius' return and the Arab conquest there were forced conversions and persecutions by the Byzantine Empire. The Arab conquest brought relief to the Jewish population, but in the Arab period the Jews of Erez Israel lost their central position in the leadership of Jewry.

7 ARAB PERIOD (634–1099)

The Arab Conquest. The armed raids against Syria and Ereẓ Israel which were carried out by Arab tribes from the Hejaz toward the end of Muhammad's lifetime differed little from the attacks mounted by the inhabitants of the Arabian desert against the agricultural and trading settlements of the border lands from the ancient period on. The Byzantines, heirs of Roman power in the Near East, founded an Arab "state" embracing the territory that had formerly belonged to the Nabateans and Palmyra. In reality, though, it was a drifting camp of nominally Christian (Monophysite) Bedouin of the Ghasān tribe that constituted a buffer between the settled lands and the desert. These semi-barbarians were hired to stand guard against the barbarians of the hinterland, but after defeating the Persians and expelling them from Ereẓ Israel (628) and other lands they had conquered, Heraclius did not think it necessary to spend any more on his Bedouin mercenaries. The Byzantines did not grasp the impact of the rise of Islam in Arabia and did not regard the events seriously. The advance of Arabian bands probing their frontier and raids and incursions into Transjordan and even into Ereẓ Israel, seemed no more than the usual Bedouin border attacks.

In 629 the Arabs suffered a defeat near Mu'ta (east of the southern extremity of the Dead Sea). According to Arab historians, after the death of Muhammad (632) three commanders were assigned the mission of occupying Syria and Ereẓ Israel. 'Amr ibn-al 'Aṣ was given the task of conquering "Filasṭīn," i.e., Judea and the southern Coastal Plain; Shuraḥbīl ibn-Ḥasana was to take Galilee and the valleys of the upper Jordan and Jezreel, an area later called

The Land of Israel under Arab rule, 8th century C.E. After *Atlas of Israel*, Survey of Israel, 1970.

172

Jund Urdunn (the military district of the Jordan); and Yazīd ibn Abī-Sufyān marched on Damascus. ʿAmr invaded Palestine by way of Elath, while the other two advanced along the caravan route from Tabūk to the Balqāʾ between the Jabbok and Arnon winter streams. The Byzantines suffered three serious defeats in 633–634, as the Arabs relentlessly pushed them back toward the sea from the east and south, and retreated to Beisan (Beth-Shean). For six months the Arabs raided towns and villages without capturing a single fortified city. When they marched on Beisan, the Byzantines withdrew to Fiḥl (or Faḥl-Pella) in Transjordan after destroying the Jordan River dams to impede the enemy's progress. Defeated near Fiḥl, the Byzantine troops fled to Damascus, with the Arabs in persuit. The Arabs then briefly occupied Damascus, which they abandoned—along with other cities taken in Syria—when they received news of a large Byzantine force gathering at Aleppo and Antioch. This army, however, composed of about 50,000 Armenian and Arab mercenaries, was crushed in a decisive engagement at the confluence of the Ruqqād and Yarmuk rivers (in Golan) on August 20, 636. By the end of the year, all of Syria as far north as Aleppo was in Arab hands.

In Erez Israel, Jerusalem, Caesarea, and Ashkelon were still garrisoned by Byzantine troops. Jerusalem surrendered in 637 or 638, after the Byzantine commander deserted, ending a two-year siege. Patriarch Sophronius conducted the negotiations with the Arabs, who promised not to harm the Christian churches there. Caesarea was apparently taken by Muʿāwiya in 640, ending a seven-year siege, after a Jew showed the Arabs a secret passage into the city. (According to an Arab historian, there were 700,000 "Roman" soldiers, 200,000 Jews, and 300,000 Samaritans inside the city.) The fall of Ashkelon followed soon after (641). The Arab conquest of Erez Israel was a major event in the history of the Western world. It opened a gateway to the West for the inhabitants of the desert and brought them into direct contact with a 2,000-year-old culture. Had they been satisfied with their conquest of the Persian Empire, it is doubtful whether their influence on civilization would have been any greater than that of the Sassanids or Zoroastrians.

The conquerors did not change the administrative system in Erez Israel. Northern Erez Israel (the Byzantine Palaestina Secunda) became the military province *(jund)* of Urdunn (Jordan), with Tiberias as its capital, and southern Erez Israel (the Byzantine Palaestine Prima) became *Jund Filasṭīn,* with Lydda as capital. The latter province comprised Judea and Samaria and, according to the Arab geographers of the tenth century, the Negev, as well as the southern districts of Transjordan, were annexed to it. The conquest was followed by the migration of Arabs into the area. When taking a town, the Arabs sometimes stipulated that half of its area be handed over to them. Arabic historians record that this was the case in Tiberias and Beisan. At first, most of the Arabs lived in great camps, e.g., al-Jābiya in Golan and Emmaus in the Judean plain, where they soon began to acquire estates and settle down. The number who became landlords and engaged in agriculture increased when Muʿāwiya became governor of Syria and Erez Israel. Arabs bought estates, settled down and became peasants throughout the country. Muʿāwiya also founded colonies of Arabs and other Muslims in the coastal towns as a military safeguard against Byzantine attacks on this vulnerable area.

The Ummayyads[4] also granted lands to Bedouin tribes. Whereas most of the Arabs living in Transjordan and regions to the north before the Muslim conquest belonged to south Arabian Kalb tribes, under Ummayyad rule the North Arabian Qays tribes became predominant. Many Qaysites moved into Galilee, Golan, Hauran, and al-Balqāʾ. On the other hand, the Arabs who settled in Tiberias and Bet Guvrin were Kalbites. The majority of the Arabs of southern Erez Israel belonged to the Lakhm and Judhām tribes (South Arabians). In the course of the ninth century, the number of Qaysites continued to increase in northern Erez Israel and Transjordan. After the dissolution

[4] Ummayyads: First Moslem-Arab caliphate, centered in Damascus.

of the military camps, their inhabitants dispersed and settled in the established towns, and both Islam and the Arabic language proliferated. Nevertheless, these towns did not change completely: a great portion of the town dwellers remained Christians, as borne out by Al-Maqdisī (985) in his account of Jerusalem. Ramleh was probably the one exception. Founded by the caliph Suleiman (715–17), who resided there, it became the flourishing capital of the south.

The decline of the Abbasid [5] caliphate began in the ninth century, when Turkish princes established semiautonomous principalities. Ahmad ibn-Ṭūlūn founded an independent kingdom in Egypt (868) and ten years later conquered Ereẓ Israel and Syria; his son defeated the caliph's brother in battle at the Yarkon River (*nahr* abī Fuṭrus—Antipatris) in 885. After Ahmad's death, the Qarmatians—one of the Shi‘ite sects from the Syrian desert—began to carry out fierce raids against Syria and Ereẓ Israel in 906. A bit later, Ikhshidi princes who became masters of Egypt (935) and Ereẓ Israel (942) set out to engage forces with the Turkish rulers of Aleppo. In the second half of the tenth century, the Fatimid Shi‘ite dynasty assumed power in Egypt. The Ikhshidis attempted to prevent the Fatimids from taking control of Ereẓ Israel, but were defeated in a battle near Ramleh in 969.

FATIMIDS AND SELJUKS. During the early period of Fatimid [6] rule in Ereẓ Israel, enemies of the dynasty carried out a number of incursions into the country. First to invade Ereẓ Israel were the Qarmatians, who captured the entire country except the coastal fortresses in 971. Although their attempt to penetrate into Egypt failed, they remained in control of Ereẓ Israel for three years. In 974 they were driven out by Fatimid troops, but after a short time they managed to reestablish their authority for a few months. The Byzantines, who exploited the confusion in Ereẓ Israel, attacked the Abbasid caliph and, under the emperor Tsimiskes, undertook what modern scholars have called the

---

[5] Abbasids: Second Moslem-Arab caliphate, centered in Baghdad.
[6] Fatimids: Militant Arabian dynasty that ruled for nearly 200 years.

Byzantine Crusade, penetrating as far as Beisan in 975. They were compelled to retreat from the areas conquered in Syria, but meanwhile, the Qarmatians renewed their attacks. After joining forces with the Turkish leader Alptekin, the ruler of Damascus, the Qarmatians defeated the Fatimid troops near Ramleh and laid siege to Ashkelon; however, they were vanquished in 977 by the Egyptian caliph al-Aziz in a battle near Ramleh.

Even after defeating the Qarmatians, the Fatimids could not establish a stable government in the country because of the rising power of Ṭayyi' Bedouin, who had been supported by the Egyptian caliphs in the hope that they would be useful against their governors in Damascus. In effect, the Bedouin chiefs of banū Jarrāḥ, who lived in Ramleh, were the real masters of the country, and the governors of the Fatimid regime were content to maintain their authority only in the coastal towns. In 998 the Bedouin chief Al-Mufarrij ibn Danfal ibn al-Jarrāḥ revolted against the caliph Al-Ḥākim and installed the sharif of Mecca as caliph at Ramleh. Later, the Bedouin were reconciled with the government, but Al-Mufarrij's power continued until his death in 1013, when the Egyptian Fatimids sent a large army to Ereẓ Israel to put an end to Bedouin rule. At first the caliph Al-Ẓahir maintained peaceful relations with Al-Mufarrij's son and successor, Hasan; however, when relations again deteriorated, Hasan concluded an alliance with a league of Bedouin tribes ruling Syria, intending to make himself master of the entire region from the Taurus to the Egyptian border. Initially, the Bedouin scored a number of victories, taking Ramleh in 1024 and ruling the country for five years. In 1029, however, they were defeated by a Fatimid army near Lake Kinneret. In 1042 the banū Jarrāḥ again attempted to conquer the country. Fatimid power was already unstable at this period and the first Seljuk forays into Ereẓ Israel had begun.

The Seljuks were a Turkish people that had established an empire in Western Asia in the middle of the 11th century. In 1071 the Seljuk general Atsiz captured Jerusalem and most of the rest of Erez Israel. Although his invasion of Egypt ended in failure, the rebellion that broke out in Jerusalem while he was occupied there was later suppressed. The Seljuk conquest brought an end to Arab rule in Erez Israel, although the struggle between the Fatimids and the Seljuks lasted until the end of the 11th century; the Fatimids held the Coastal Plain and in 1098, a year before the arrival of the crusaders, even recaptured Jerusalem.

The detailed description of the political events in the 10th–11th centuries indicates a gloomy picture of the living conditions in that period, which is also confirmed by contemporary letters found in the Cairo *Genizah*. Agriculture was predominant in the economic life of the country. The dams near Beisan were quickly repaired and the region soon became famous for its dates, rice, and indigo. Other sectors lost importance, compared to previous periods and neighboring countries. Erez Israel was self-sufficient in the growing of cereals and exported olive oil, dried figs, and raisins. In the Jordan Valley and the Coastal Plain sugar plantations developed considerably, and the Arabs introduced the lemon and orange to Erez Israel. In spite of the flourishing agriculture in the first centuries of Arab rule, heavy fiscal pressure exacerbated the peasants and provoked revolts, e.g., the uprising of Abu-Ḥarb, who in 842, caused turmoil in Erez Israel. The volume of industry decreased, however, when the coastal towns shrank in size as a result of the loss of overseas markets. The interruption of international trade in the Mediterranean area was a foremost phenomenon in the economic history of Syria and Erez Israel under the caliphs. Industry, therefore, produced mostly for local markets, although soap (made from olive oil) and glass vessels were sold in Egypt and Transjordan. On the whole, the decay of maritime trade in the Mediterranean world was outweighed by the intensification of commercial relations with countries that had belonged to other economic regions before the Arab conquest. Erez Israel's economy thus remained intact under the caliphs. Its 177 decline and the subsequent general impoverishment of the population began in the tenth century, due to changes in the political structure, as described above.

In the south (the Negev), however, the deterioration of the economy began even earlier. With the consolidation of the Muslim empire from Spain to India, it became safe for travelers to journey by land, a permanent postal system was established, and new overland trade routes between Europe and the East came into being. These developments eliminated the Negev trade routes, which had functioned as a factor in international commerce, during the Roman and Byzantine periods, and the Negev's key position disappeared for centuries to come. Its cities declined as their inhabitants lost the transit trade and their livelihoods from dyeing and weaving, and the population dwindled. As the markets for agricultural products disappeared, the farmers also moved away, and villages ceased to exist. Ramleh, the headquarters of the administration, was then an important commercial center, and other larger cities were Ashkelon, Caesarea, and Jerusalem. These cities, however, declined like the rest of the country during the period of Fatimid rule. The constant Bedouin raids made life quite difficult for the inhabitants, and, in addition to man-made disasters, earthquakes, which occurred in 1016 and 1033, contributed still further to the country's impoverishment.

The Muslim population of Ereẓ Israel was for the most part Sunni, and the Shiʿite propaganda of the Fatimid government met with little success. There were large groups of Shiʿites in Tiberias and a number of other places. Most of the inhabitants of Nablus and its environs were Samaritans. In Jerusalem, Bethlehem, Nazareth, and Tiberias, the majority of the population was Christian and enjoyed the protection of the Byzantines who cared for the Christian shrines. The spoken language of all the inhabitants, regardless of religion, was Arabic, although Arabic culture had not struck roots in the country. The intellectual level of the population was lower than that of the neighboring countries. In 985 the Jerusalem geographer al-Maqdisī wrote that it was difficult to find a Muslim intellectual in Erez Israel in his time. The cultural level of the Christians was higher than that of the Muslims, which explains the fact that Christians held most of the government positions. Talented and ambitious members of the population emigrated to the adjacent countries, where the chances of advancement in a number of fields were much greater.

THE JEWISH POPULATION. In the period preceding the Arab invasion, there were Jewish agricultural and trade settlements in the Negev, south of the Dead Sea, along the shores of the Gulf of Elath, and in Transjordan. Delegations sent to conclude protective treaties with Muhammad, once his fame had begun to spread, included Jews from Transjordan and the Gulf of Elath. Maqnā, a small port along the southern portion of the Gulf, was a Jewish community inhabited by the banū Janbā, warriors who earned their livelihood from agriculture, fishing, trade, and home crafts. From the clothing they pledged to deliver to Muhammad, it is apparent that they were wealthy. The delegation from Elath was accompanied by groups of Jews from the neighboring communities of Adhruḥ and Jarbā, between Petra and Maʿān in Transjordan. The region between Edreʿi and Jericho was inhabited by Jews as late as the 10th and 11th centuries, but they disappeared completely during the Crusades. Estori ha-Parhi, however, mentions a Jewish community in Edreʿi in his time (13th century).

The southern coastal towns continued to flourish after the Arab conquest. In the 11th century there were still Jewish communities in Gaza, Rafa, and El-Arish, but they disintegrated with the Crusades, when the population as a whole declined. Many villages and small towns were destroyed in the crusader wars against the Fatimids and the Ayyubids, but the disappearance of much of the population in the borderland was also due to the complete cessation of transit trade in the Negev during this period. Controversial reports exist about the resettlement of the Jews in Jerusalem after the Arab conquest. According to Arab sources, the treaty between the caliph Omar and Patriarch Sophronius about the surrender of Jerusalem to the Arabs contained the condition that the Jews should not be allowed to settle in the city. On the other hand, a document in the Cairo *Genizah* testifies that Omar gave 70 Jewish families from Tiberias permission to settle in Jerusalem. A later Arabic source reports that Jewish families attended the Mosque of Omar in the Temple area. The sources about Jerusalem as seat of the academy do not indicate the date of this event.

In general Jewish and Christian communities in Erez Israel prospered during the first 50 years of Arab rule. The founder of the Ummayyad dynasty, Caliph Mu'āwiya (661–680), devoted himself to organizing and expanding his realm. His regime displayed tolerance toward the people under Muslim protection and afforded numerous opportunities to both Jews and Christians. Mu'āwya settled Jews in Tripoli because he regarded them as loyal to the Arabs and wanted to strengthen reliable elements there. The situation changed for the worse when Omar II (717–720) became caliph and introduced numerous restrictions against non-Muslims (in the Omar Covenant). These laws severely affected the public conduct, religious observances, and legal status of the people under Muslim protection. During the Abbasid rule, Jews were sometimes forced to wear yellow turbans, Christians, blue ones, and Samaritans, red ones. These regulations, however, were not strictly observed and had to be stressed from time to time in public proclamations. In 1009–13 the Fatimid caliph Al-Ḥākim issued severe restrictions against the dhimmi (protected non-Muslim population) that affected the Christians more than the Jews. He also revived the regulations about prescribed garb and ordered the destruction of churches and synagogues. Finally, Jews and Christians were presented with the ultimatum of either adopting Islam or leaving the country. During this period, the Church of the Holy Sepulcher in Jerusalem was demolished. Soon afterward, however, while Al-Ḥākim was still alive, the orders were rescinded and permission was granted to rebuild the houses of worship and allow persons who pretended to adopt Islam to profess their own religions openly.

ECONOMIC CONDITIONS. Because of the heavy land taxes imposed on non-Muslim farmers, Jews ceased to cultivate the soil. They settled in the towns, where economic conditions were better and they were safer, and engaged in crafts such as dyeing and tanning, which became exclusively Jewish occupations for centuries to come. With the exception of Al-Ḥākim's decrees, the attitude of the authorities toward the Jews in the Fatimid period was generally favorable and better than the treatment accorded to the Christians, who sometimes provoked the Muslims with their arrogance. Whereas it was strictly forbidden to employ members of the protected faiths in government posts during the Abbasid period, under Fatimid rule, Jews and Christians were in the service of the caliphs, who had come to learn that the protected peoples were more loyal to them than the Sunni Muslims.

The Jews of Ramleh derived benefits from the trade caravans passing through the city. They traded with Egypt and Syria, as well as with North Africa. However, Bedouin depredations and severe earthquakes, which caused great damage to Ramleh, undermined the city's position. The economic status of Jerusalem was less satisfactory because of the city's distance from trade routes and its proximity to the desert. Whenever disorders and highway robberies increased, the number of Jewish and Christian pilgrims to the Holy City fell off. Also, the tax burden in Jerusalem was heavier than in other cities of Ereẓ Israel. Most of the Jewish population lived off contributions from foreign Jewish communities or visitors. Whatever Jewish merchants there were in Jerusalem were dependent on those in Ramleh. A number of copyists supported themselves from copying manuscripts to be sold abroad.

RELIGIOUS AND SPIRITUAL LIFE. In the last century of Byzantine rule, Tiberias was again the center of Jewish spiritual and religious leadership. Mar Zutra, a scion of the exilarchs, settled there in 520 and was appointed head of 181 the academy. Even the persecutions of the emperor Justinian (527–565) could not destroy the community that had fostered the development of Jewish scholarship. Tiberias was the center of the biblical text masoretes and the inventors of the Tiberian system of vocalizing Hebrew, the most important cultural achievement of the period. This system superseded two others, the Babylonian and the Palestinian, and came into current use in all Jewish communities. The Tiberian pronunciation became famous for its precision and clarity, and many scholars went to Tiberias to study the proper tradition of reading the Torah. The city also attained renown for its liturgical poets. One of the most famous of them was Yannai b. Yannai, several hundred of whose *piyyutim* have remained. Fragments from a halakhic work *Sefer ha-Ma'asim li-Venei Erez Yisrael* ("Book of the Deeds of the Erez Israel Jews"), in which important decisions on religious, social, and economic matters have been collected, provide a glimpse into the life of the period. Although the exact date of the collection is still controversial—the end of the Byzantine or beginnings of the Muslim period—there is no doubt about its importance as one of the few halakhic works of that period from Erez Israel to have survived. It is not known exactly when the academy passed from Tiberias to Jerusalem and Ramleh. From some hints in the letters of the Erez Israel *gaon* Aaron b. Meir, it can be assumed that the move occurred in the ninth century. It may also be ventured that the transfer of the academy to Jerusalem was caused at least partially by the settlement of the Karaites (see below) in the city. Among the outstanding heads of the academy during the period, in addition to Aaron b. Meir, were R. Solomon b. Judah (1025–1051) and Daniel b. Azariah (1051–1062), a scion of the Babylonian exilarchs who signed with the title "*gaon* of Tiberias," although his seat was in Jerusalem. The last *gaon* whose seat was in Jerusalem was Elijah b. Solomon. After the Seljuk conquest of Jerusalem (1071) he had to move the academy to Tyre, where it remained until the Crusades. It then moved to Hadrak near

Damascus and subsequently to Damascus itself. The academy existed in Syria for about a century and was still known as the Academy of the Holy Land.

The Karaites in Jerusalem. In the ninth century a number of Karaites left Iraq and Persia and settled in Jerusalem, which became an important center of Karaism. A letter written by Aaron b. Meir testifies that among them were *nesi'im* (princes), so styled because they belonged to the exilarchic family. The Karaites occupied a special quarter and called themselves "mourners of Zion"; the foremost among them were styled *"shoshannim"* (lilies). The rivalry between the Rabbanites and Karaites in Jerusalem was one of the reasons for the reestablishment of the seat of the Rabbanite academy in Jerusalem.

LEADERSHIP. After the extinction of the patriarchate (c. 429), the leadership of the Jewish population passed to the scholars and heads of the academy, rather than to descendants of the Davidic dynasty, although the Karaites attempted to revive the office of the *nasi* (patriarch) from the family of Anan, of the family of the exilarchs who were of Davidic stock. In the 11th century a Rabbanite descendant of the exilarchs, R. Daniel b. Azariah who styled himself "patriarch *(nasi)* and *gaon*," ascended to the leadership of the community. In an epistle to Egypt, he wrote: "Since we came to this holy place, we guide Israel, with God's help, in the whole of Palestine and Syria, and administer justice even to those in distant places. In all towns and settlements prayers are recited for us. The *Haverim* and judges in every place are authorized by us. Nobody else has any influence even over a small town . . ." (Mann, Egypt, 1 (1920), 179; 2 (1922), 216). Daniel concentrated the powers of the exilarch and the *gaon* in Iraq in his hands. From the many letters of Solomon b. Judah, Daniel's predecessor in the office as head of the Palestinian academy, it is assumed that he was the acknowledged representative of the Jewish population vis-à-vis the Muslim authorities. The *geonim* Elijah b. Solomon and his son Abiathar also assumed leadership beyond the boundaries of Ereẓ Israel.

The *ḥaverim* mentioned in Daniel b. Azariah's epistle were authorized to head the local communities and sometimes also served as *dayyanim*. The judges were paid by their communities, but it is learned from many letters that they did not always receive their fixed emoluments or collections made to pay their salaries. In one of his letters, Solomon b. Judah mentions how the Jerusalemites induced him to become their *ḥazzan* before he became the head of the academy, because he was satisfied with a small livelihood; but two years passed and his services went entirely unrewarded, due to the great distress prevailing in the Holy City (Mann, Texts, 1 (1931), 318). One of Solomon b. Judah's main tasks was to request support for his communities and their functionaries from the Ereẓ Israel congregations in Egypt. The *gaon* Josiah remarks in a letter (Mann, Egypt, 2 (1922), 69–70) that the academy used to be maintained by the Fatimid government, but this support ceased (during the Al-Ḥākim persecutions?), and the academy was in great distress. These financial problems increased with deteriorating political and economic conditions. At the end of the 11th century the Jewish population in Ereẓ Israel diminished and lost its firm organizational and spiritual features.

8 CRUSADER PERIOD (1099–1291)

In 1095 Pope Urban II issued an appeal to the French
at Clermont that they should rescue the Holy Land and
recover it for Christendom. The response was instantaneous:
Peter the Hermit, a Fleming from Amiens, harangued
crowds; fanatical bands of peasants streamed eastward,
passing through southern Germany, Hungary, and the
Balkans, destroying the Jewish communities on the
way; but this first mob "army" did not reach the Holy Land
and was destroyed by the Turks (July–October 1096). Two
years elapsed before the mailed Christian chivalry could be
organized, and it took another year before that military
expedition reached the coastal road leading from Lebanon
into Erez Israel (May 1099). The coastal cities agreed, out
of fear, to furnish the advancing expedition with provisions
and funds. The army made its way from Caesarea to
Ramleh (whose population fled) on the way to conquer
Jerusalem, the proclaimed aim of the Crusade movement.
The crusaders besieged Jerusalem from June 7 to July 15,
1099, and the city capitulated after Godfrey de Bouillon's
troops had broken through the northern wall and Raymond
of Toulouse's men had broken through at "Mt. Zion." The
conquerors carried out a mass massacre of the population,
which numbered between 20,000 and 30,000. The Jews, who
had heroically defended their quarter, were in part killed
and burned in their synagogue and in part taken captive
and sold into slavery in Italy. Only few managed to flee to
Ashkelon and Egypt.

Having conquered the capital, the crusaders proceeded
to occupy the rest of the country. Bethlehem had surrendered even before the conquest of Jerusalem; the city was in

Beirut

Sidon

Beaufort
Qal'at Namrūd
Belinas
Tyre   Toron (Banias)
                          (Tibnin)
                  Kh. Nabartein
              Kefar Baram   Almah
Montfort   Gush   Dalton
              Halav   Amkah
Kefar Yasif   Ein Zeitim   Fir'im
Acre   Meron   Biriyyah
              Kafr 'Inān   Safed
Haifa
              Kefar Mandi
                              Tiberias
Chastiau   Sepphoris
Pélerin   Kefar Kanna
(Athlit)
              Nazareth
                          Belvoir
              Zarain
Caesarea
                          Beth–Shean

                  Sabaste
                  (Samaria)
                                      Ajlūn
Arsur   Naples
(Arshaf)   (Shechem)
Jaffa   Mirabel
                                  Al-Salt
              Lydda
              Rames
              (Ramleh)
Toron des   Beit Nūbā
Chevaliers
(Latrun)
              Jerusalem

              Bethlehem
              Bethgibelin
              (Bet Guvrin)
                  St. Abraham
                  (Hebron)
Ascalon

Cadres
(Gaza)

MEDITERRANEAN SEA

DEAD SEA

186

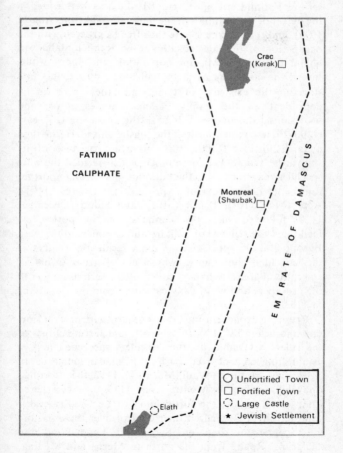

The Crusader kingdom at its greatest extent, 1187 C.E.

fact handed over to the crusaders by its Eastern Christian inhabitants, who constituted the majority of its population. Jericho and Nablus had also surrendered when Tancred took both Tiberias and Beisan without a battle, turning the former into the capital of a new principality. The last serious Fatimid attempt to combat the crusaders ended in the defeat of the Fatimids at the battle of Ashkelon (August 1099), and the crusaders were thus free to proceed with the occupation of the coastal cities. Like Ramleh, Jaffa was abandoned by its Muslim population and for a while, served the crusaders as their main port; during this first stage in the existence of their state, they were totally dependent on the supply of men, horses, arms, and provisions from overseas. It took the crusaders ten years (1100–10) to conquer most of the coastal cities. Haifa, then a small fortress (1100), was important because of its shipyards; the Jewish community, which resided there by special arrangement with the Fatimids, played an important role in its defense. Arsūf (April 1101), Caesarea (1101), Acre (May 1104), Beirut (1101), and Sidon (December 1110) followed suit. The conquest of the port cities facilitated the renewal of military and commercial ties with Europe and also provided the main residential centers of the crusader community, which never struck roots in agricultural areas. Ashkelon constituted a serious danger to the crusaders and was finally captured from the Egyptians in 1153.

Crusader expansion into the southern part of Transjordan had begun by 1100. In spite of the deterring efforts of the rulers of Damascus, the crusaders succeeded first in establishing control over the local nomad population. In 1107 they captured Wadi Mūsā; in 1112 they fortified Shawbak, calling it Montreal; in 1113 they conquered Elath; and, finally, the fortification of Le Crac (Kerak), captured in 1142, secured their control over the area, the land connection between Syria and Egypt, and the "Pilgrims' Road" from the north to Mecca and Medina.

Omitting further details it should be pointed out that from

the standpoint of territorial expanse, the Kingdom of Jerusalem (or the Kingdom of David and even Israel, as it was called during the period of Saladin's rise to power in Egypt (1174)) was at its height. Its border in the north went along the Muʿāmalatayn River (or Nahr Ibrahim) between Giblet (which belonged to the principality of Tripoli) and Beirut and continued in the west along the coast southward to Dayr-al-Balaḥ (Daron of the Crusaders). It extended eastward from Beirut to encompass the sources of the Jordan and reached the foot of Mount Hermon. From there the border turned southward and encompassed parts of Horan and Bashan, Gilead, and all the territory of Moab up to Elath. The desert region of the Negev (Grande Barrie, from the Arabic *bariyya* (desert)) completed the borderline between Elath and Daron.

Saladin, Ayyub's son, directed his policy toward the unification of Syria and Iraq with Egypt, a goal that was fulfilled with his conquest of Aleppo (1183). His halting attempts to attack the crusaders' borders during the lifetime of Nur al-Din (Gaza, 1170; Montreal and Elath, 1171; Crac, 1173) took on the appearance of a planned mission in 1177, when he attacked southern Gaza, captured Ramleh, besieged Lydda, and reached Arsūf. But at the battle of Gezer (Montgisard, as it was called by the crusaders), he was routed by Baldwin IV, and his attempts to impose a sea blockade on the crusaders (1179–82), accompanied by attacks on Montreal, Galilee, Beisan, and Beirut, ended in yet another crusader victory in the battle of Forbelet (1182). In 1183 Saladin captured Beisan and Zarʿīn, besieged Crac, and destroyed Nablus, Samaria, and Jezreel. His victories terminated in the battle of Hattin (July 1187) with the crushing defeat of the crusader camp, which had left Sepphoris to come to the aid of besieged Tiberias. As a result of this battle, all the crusader cities and fortresses, including Jerusalem (November 1187), surrendered to Saladin almost without a fight. Tyre, which was not conquered due to Conrad Montferrat, now became the center of the remaining crusaders, under the leadership of their king, Guy de Lusignan. The prolonged siege imposed on Acre by the crusaders (August 1189–July 1191) and their conquest of the city constituted the beginning of a renewed conquest under the leadership of Richard the Lion-Hearted; but, as a result of the conflict between the kings of France and England, this endeavor produced poor results. According to the peace treaty of September 1192, the crusader state was established in the area between Tyre and Jaffa (the Lydda-Ramleh area was divided between the two sides); in addition, the Christians obtained the right of pilgrimage to Jerusalem, which remained in Muslim hands.

Upon Saladin's death (1193), the Muslim empire was once again broken up. The crusaders, however, were no longer able to exploit this situation, despite the fact that their state continued to expand by virtue of the various Crusades (such as the German Crusade that succeeded in capturing Beirut in 1197). The treaty of 1204 returned Jaffa (which fell to the Egyptians in 1197), as well as part of the territories of Sidon and Nazareth, to the crusaders. The

Eastern moat and wall of Caesarea, built by the crusaders in 1251. Courtesy Government Press Office, Tel Aviv.

Fourth Crusade, which might have brought aid to the crusaders in Ereẓ Israel, turned to the capture of Constantinople and resulted in the diversion of the European forces to Cyprus (captured by Richard in 1189). The military Crusade of the kings of Hungary and Cyprus in 1217 spent itself in undirected missions in the Galilee, Beisan and Mt. Tabor, and its only positive results were the fortification of Caesarea and the founding of Athlit (Château Pélerins). The remnants of this Crusade joined the daring attempt to attack Egypt (the Fifth Crusade). Fear of the crusaders prompted the Muslims to destroy their fortresses at Tibnīn, Banias, Belvoir (Kawkab al-Hawā), Safed, Mt. Tabor, and Jerusalem simultaneously.

The crusaders now awaited the arrival of Frederick II, emperor of Germany and king of Sicily. His departure was delayed until 1228, when, meanwhile excommunicated by the Pope, he reached Acre. In the interim, the crusaders had captured parts of Sidon, built the walls of Caesarea, and fortified Qal'at al-Qurayn (Montfort). As a result of his connections with Al-Malik al-Kāmil, the sultan of Egypt, Frederick succeeded in acquiring the crusaders' territorial sovereignty without entering battle. Sidon (with the exclusion of Beaufort), Tibnīn, Sepphoris, Nazareth, Lydda, Ramleh, Bethlehem, the Ramleh-Jerusalem road, and Jerusalem itself—excluding the Temple area, which remained under Muslim jurisdiction—were transferred to the crusaders. The kingdom now included two enclaves connected to the coastal region: Nazareth and Jerusalem. Frederick proclaimed himself king of Jerusalem and then left the country. Frederick's excommunication, self-coronation, and departure from the country brought about civil war, with the opposition to Frederick under the leadership of the House of Ibelin. The war raged intermittently from 1231 to 1243 and depleted the strength of the kingdom of Jerusalem. The Italian communes and military orders carried out their own policy, and the country remained bereft of a true ruler.

The crusaders' attempt to reconstruct the ruins of

The caravansery, now Government House, in Gaza, built by the Mamluks in the 13th century. Courtesy Israel Department of Antiquities, Jerusalem.

Ashkelon terminated with their defeat in the battle of Gaza (November 1239). Meanwhile, the sultan Ismail of Damascus convinced them to enter into a treaty with him against Ayyub, ruler of Egypt and stipulated he would return to them Beaufort (Qal'at al-Shaqīf), Safed, and Tiberias in Galilee. During the period of mutual political intrigues, Egypt called upon the assistance of the Khwarizmian Turks, who were then in flight from the Mongols. They overran the country, captured Jerusalem from the crusaders (August 1244), and dealt them a crushing blow at the battle of Hirbiya (Forbie) near Gaza (October 1244), later destroying Galilee. Jerusalem, which was annexed to Egypt, and Judea and Samaria, which were annexed to Transjordan, were never again returned to the crusaders. Later still (1247), the Egyptians also captured Tiberias and Ashkelon.

The days of the crusader coastal kingdom were now numbered by the rise of the Mamluks in Egypt (1250), which brought to power a strong military class. With the appearance of a new factor in the Middle East—the Mongols, whose commander (Hulagu) conquered Baghdad in 1258—it appeared that a Mongolian-European Christian pact that would help the crusaders withstand the Muslims (rumors circulated that there were numerous Christians among the Mongols) was in the offing. The crusaders, however, did not exploit the presence of the Mongols and adopted a neutral stance in the severe clash between the latter and the Mamluks of Egypt. In 1260 the Mongols suffered a blow in the battle of Gaza and later a crushing defeat at 'Ayn-Jālūt (En-Harod), which routed their army. A result of the neutral stance of the crusaders was that they now faced Baybars, the great ruler of Egypt, who slowly but surely captured one fortress after another. Once again the remnants of the Kingdom of Jerusalem did not cooperate with each other and made separate treaties with the conqueror, in order to preserve their meagre possessions. Eventually Acre, the center of the kingdom, fell, after a period of siege (April–May 1291), to Al-Malik al-Ashraf the Mamluk. The period of the Crusades thus came to a close in Palestine.

THE JEWISH POPULATION. During the period of crusader conquests, the Jews cooperated with the Fatimid forces and the urban Muslim population. Rumors of the murder and pillage perpetrated by the crusaders upon the Jewish communities in the Rhine area reached the East and gave rise to messianic expectations, which were in turn nourished by the naive belief that the First Crusade served only to gather the nations of the world into the Holy Land in order to destroy them in war ("the war of Gog and Magog"). Christian sources from that period first mention Jews in connection with the defense of Jerusalem. The Jewish quarter, founded in the 11th century in the northeastern section of the city (between Damascus Gate and the Valley of Jehoshaphat), was the first to be attacked and invaded by the troops of Godfrey of Bouillon. Only a very few survived the terrible carnage and the burning of the synagogues (together with those who sought refuge within them). The Jews are mentioned again in connection with the defense of Haifa in 1100. The Jewish community there enjoyed special conditions conferred upon it by the Fatimids. It is said that Tancred, who retreated from the walls of Haifa, did not attempt to besiege it again until he was admonished that failure to conquer this city defended by Jews would make a mockery of the God of the Christians. The Haifa community was likewise slaughtered by the crusader armies and the Venetian sailors.

Contemporary letters and edicts and fragments thereof discovered in the Cairo *Genizah* (some of which have been published by S. D. Goitein; see bibliography) provide more than a glimpse into the life of the Jewish community in Erez Israel under the crusader rule; they add much to the (sometimes) later descriptions from the non-Jewish sources. A letter found in the *Genizah* describes the fall of Jerusalem, the ransoming of the captives, and the relief efforts on behalf of the refugees who fled with the Fatimid commander. Leaders of the Jewish community in Ashkelon dispatched the letter to the Alexandrian community, begging it to cover the debts incurred by the Jews of Ashkelon in connection with their relief work. A second letter was written by a pilgrim to Erez Israel, who, it may be presumed, came from the Maghreb (North Africa) or Spain. He proceeded as far as Cairo but could not move to Jerusalem because the Holy City had been captured by the "Franks . . . who murdered all who were in it—Ishmaelites and Israelites. The few who remained after the slaughter have been captured. Some of those have been ransomed and some are still in captivity." He goes on to express the hope that the sultan will defeat the enemies and he will be able to visit Jerusalem soon. Another letter, written in the winter of 1099/1100 by the *av bet din* of the academy, a scion of the Ben Meir family, deals with ransoming members of his family. The writer regards the conquest as an affliction. Indeed, a long letter sent from Erez Israel to Egypt in the first decade of the 12th century informs that conditions changed for the better for those who remained in the country, and the writer would like to renew business relations with his relative and friend. A letter written (in Tyre) to the *dayyan* of Fostat in 1100 includes a short description of the siege of Beirut as related by a fugitive who left the city by night. It seems that all of the 35 Jewish families who lived there were massacred.

Tyre and Banias in the north and Ashkelon and Rafa in the south, which still withstood the crusaders, absorbed many of the refugees from the massacred communities, while others fled to Egypt. It may be assumed that the communities located in the agricultural region, such as Galilee, suffered minimally from the crusader conquests. Despite their generally difficult situation, the Jewish settlements still made their influence felt and instances of conversion to Judaism were recorded, such as that of Obadiah the Norman, who remained for a time at Banias and Tyre (when those cities were in Muslim hands). Once the period of military conquest had ended, the Jewish communities began to reconstruct their lives. Their status was enhanced somewhat by the immigration movement from Europe, which was in turn encouraged by improved maritime transportation between the two areas. The legal status of the Jews under the crusader code, which did not differ from that of Syrian-Christians and Muslims, also helped renew Jewish life in Erez Israel, for inasmuch as the Muslims constituted the majority of the population and the crusaders' continued existence depended upon them, the crusader code was very tolerant with respect to infidels. This was in contrast to the hostile attitude of European Christianity toward the Jews that was taking shape in the 12th century. Only in Jerusalem did the crusaders revive the Byzantine edict that forbade Jews to live within the holy city, and, indeed, only a few families settled there by special permission of the king of Jerusalem.

Various travelers (including Benjamin of Tudela) who visited Palestine during the second half of the 12th century left descriptions of the conditions of the Jewish communities there. These descriptions are confirmed by the finds in the Cairo *Genizah*. The most important of these communities was Tyre, which apparently continued to exist even after the crusader conquest. It was an organized community whose leaders and scholars exchanged letters with Maimonides in Egypt on halakhic matters. Next in importance was the Acre community, whose scholars also maintained contact with Maimonides, and third came the Jewish community in Ashkelon, which may not have been destroyed after the surrender of the city to the crusaders in 1153. The remainder of the Jewish settlements of the period were very small. There were small communities in the coastal cities of Beirut, Sidon, and Caesarea. The cities of Galilee had only the isolated communities of Tiberias in the 12th century and Safed in the 13th century. A letter that mentions the "regnant Dame" of Tiberias (the allusion being to Eschive, who ruled in Tiberias before 1187) has been found in the Cairo *Genizah*. There were also rural Jewish settlements in Galilee: Gush Halav, Almah, Kefar Baram, Amkah, Kefar Hananyah, Kefar Tanhum, Meron, Dalta, Biriyyah. The small communities of Zar'in, Nablus, Beit Nuba, and Bet Guvrin were scattered in Judea and Samaria. Although the Jewish community in Erez Israel did not intentionally abandon its former settlements, it increasingly concentrated in the Christian area of the coast cities. This move may have been motivated by economic factors, as opportunities for artisans and tradesmen were more abundant in the ports.

Saladin's conquests and those of his successors, the Ayyubids and the Mamluks, diminished the territorial scope of the crusader kingdom and wakened messianic hopes among the Jews in Europe and the East. An important manifestation of the period was the immigration to Palestine from the Diaspora. Many of the refugees of the Crusades longed to return to the Holy Land. The scant information that has been preserved about the 12th-century immigration deals not so much with actual immigration as with visits to the Holy Land (in the 1260s and 1270s) by

Tiberias, with the traditional tomb of Meir Ba'al ha-Nes in the foreground. Courtesy Ministry of Tourism, Jerusalem. Photo A. Strajmayster, Jerusalem.

travelers such as Benjamin of Tudela, Pethahiah of Regensburg, and R. Jacob b. Netanel Hacohen. Parallel to the unceasing flow of visitors to Erez Israel during the 13th century, a trickle of immigrants began to settle. Furthermore, two rather short-lived spiritual centers were created in Jerusalem and Acre. This new movement was probably encouraged by the crusaders' inability to defeat Saladin and was likewise sustained by the waves of persecution that plagued European Jewry at that time. The Jewish population in Jerusalem, which was limited to a few families during the crusader occupation, expanded markedly after Saladin's conquest (1187). According to Judah Al-Ḥarizi, who visited Jerusalem (1218), Saladin immediately published a proclamation calling the Jews from all over the world to come and settle in the capital. In his time the Jerusalem community consisted of scholars from France; a fine congregation from Ashkelon (apparently refugees from the Jewish community destroyed there in 1191), led by a Yemenite "prince"; and a large congregation from North Africa, where there was an increase in persecution at the end of the 12th century.

Sources from the Cairo *Genizah* add interesting details to the observations made by Judah Al-Ḥarizi. The fragments published by Braslavi (*Ereẓ Yisrael*, 4 (1956), 156–9) include the names of other French scholars who lived in Jerusalem during the period. A proclamation by Saladin reducing the custom duties to be paid by non-Muslims by half, mentioned in a letter, was no doubt an invitation for Jewish merchants to settle in the conquered area. A letter from 1214 clarifies some of Al-Ḥarizi's remarks about the Jerusalem community. It expressly mentions the synagogue of the "Son of the Yemeni" and ends with greetings for the "Ashkeloni and Maghrebi elders." The first immigration wave from Europe included the "300 French and English rabbis" who immigrated in 1210–11 and settled in Acre. Among them were learned scholars from the ranks of the tosafists, such as R. Jonathan ben David ha-Kohen from Lunel and R. Samson of Sens.

The renewed Jerusalem community was short-lived. During the occupation of Jerusalem by the Christians (1229–39, 1243–44), the Jews were not initially allowed access to the city. In about 1236 a special agreement permitting them to visit the Holy City was arranged; it included a special permit for Jewish dyers to settle in Jerusalem, and their presence in the city is mentioned by Benjamin of Tudela and Pethahiah from Regensburg. It may be assumed that the destruction of the city in 1244 by the Khwarizmian Turks ended Jewish settlement. The immigration to Jerusalem of the Spanish scholar Naḥmanides in 1267 stimulated efforts to revive the community, and many students flocked to him from distant places in the East. He completed his commentary to the Pentateuch in Jerusalem. He left Jerusalem for Acre and his death in 1270 apparently brought the Jerusalem community's revival to a halt. At a later period a legend arose about the "Naḥmanides synagogue" in Jerusalem that attempted to ascribe the revival and uninterrupted existence of the Jerusalem community to Naḥmanides.

The development of the Acre community stood out in

contrast to Jerusalem's deteriorated condition. Part of the 1210–11 immigration settled in Acre, and later waves were also absorbed there for the most part. Among its important settlers was R. Jeḥiel of Paris, who immigrated after 1257 and apparently succeeded in founding a yeshivah in Acre called *"midrash ha-gadol"* of Paris. Emissaries from Acre collected funds in various European communities. The Acre community also maintained ties with European rabbinical authorities. The *nagid* David ben Abraham, grandson of Maimonides, lived in Acre for a considerable time during his exile from Egypt (1284–89) and there met R. Solomon Petit, the most active opponent of Maimonides' doctrines. David used all his influence to procure the issue of a ban (1287) against Solomon by the *nasi* of Damascus as well as a letter against him from Samuel ben Daniel ha-Kohen, the *gaon* of the Baghdad Academy (1288). This controversy confirms the existence of a religious center at Acre. The community was almost completely wiped out during the conquest of the city by Al-Malik al-Ashraf in 1291.

As to the economic activities of the Jewish community at the time, the majority of the Jews were artisans, particularly dyers of woven fabrics (dyeing was then a royal monopoly). Another skill practiced particularly by Jews was the blowing of the famous Tyre glass. They also figured among ship owners, as well as druggists and physicians. In contrast, Jews played a minor role in the great Mediterranean international trade (an Italian monopoly), although there were Jewish merchants and peddlers among the local tradesmen.

9 MAMLUK PERIOD (1291–1516)

MAMLUK RULE: When the complete Ereẓ Israel again returned to the total rule of the Muslims, its importance in international politics was lost for hundreds of years. Al-Malik al-Nāṣir Muhammad was ruler in Egypt and his governor, Tangiz, longtime omnipotent ruler in Syria and Ereẓ Israel, maintained order and security in the country and constructed waterways and public buildings. Mamluk rule was undermined after the death of Al-Malik al-Nāṣir, and at the beginning of the 15th century disagreement among the chief ministers led to civil wars that wreaked havoc in the Syrian territories. In the middle of the same century, during the rule of the sultans Al-Malik al-Ashraf Barsbāy (1422–38) and Al-Ẓāhir Sayf-al-Dīn Jaqmaq (1438–53), Ereẓ Israel again enjoyed a short period of respite, followed by the increased disintegration of Mamluk rule.

The two-and-a-half centuries of Mamluk domination in Ereẓ Israel brought about little change in the administration of the country. Syria and Ereẓ Israel were divided into large provinces *(niyāba)*, which in turn were divided into districts. Each province was headed by a "deputy king" *(nā'ib)* and each district *(wilāya)* by a governor *(wali)*. The province of Safed included the districts of Safed, Nazareth, Tiberias, Tibnīn, Athlit, Acre, Tyre, al-Shāghūr, al-Iqlīm al-Shaqīf, and Jenin. It was, in effect, an enclave in the larger province of Damascus, which included a great part of Ereẓ Israel, i.e., the northern districts of eastern Transjordan (Edrei, 'Ajlūn, al-Balqā', Banias), the Beth-Shean district, and the districts of central and southern Ereẓ Israel (Shechem, Qāgūn, Jerusalem, Hebron, Ramleh, Lydda, and Gaza). Various changes were introduced in the administration of the southern districts in the second half of the 14th century. The status of the governor of Jerusalem was raised, and Hebron was added to his district; a special governor, directly responsible to the government in Cairo, was appointed for Ramleh, and Lydda and Qāqūn were added to his district. Because Gaza periodically became an independent province, the status of this district underwent frequent changes. Eastern Transjordan was under the jurisdiction of a special province, Kir Moab (al-Kerak).

Sources from the 14th and 15th centuries attest that the economic structure of Ereẓ Israel remained essentially unchanged during the last centuries of the Middle Ages. The author-prince Abu al-Fidā', who visited the country in 1312, describes the fruit of Ereẓ Israel as export produce. The geographer Al-Dimashkī and a traveler, Ibn Baṭuṭah, both of the 14th century, report that olive oil and soap made from it were the most important products of Ereẓ Israel. Al-Qalqashandī (15th century) relates that there were sugar plantations in the Jordan Valley, and the Burgundian traveler Bertrandon de la Broquière, who visited in 1432, recounts that cotton was cultivated in the Beth-Shean Valley. When the last vestiges of crusader rule were eliminated, Ereẓ Israel again had no share in the international spice trade, which in the past had been a source of great profits for its inhabitants.

The Mamluks destroyed Acre, Jaffa, and the other coastal cities for fear that they would be used as aids in renewed Crusades. Jaffa remained in ruins until the end of the Middle Ages, while a small settlement was established in Acre in the 15th century. Tiberias and Ashkelon were also partly in ruins at the end of the Middle Ages. Fabri, who visited Ereẓ Israel in 1480 and 1483, found many places in Jerusalem in ruins. According to Obadiah of Bertinoro, who reached Jerusalem in 1488, the city contained about 4,000 householders, among whom the 70 Jewish heads of families were the poorest of all, lacking any livelihood (A. Yaari, *Massa'ot Ereẓ Yisrael* (1946), 127). According to information from the period of early Mamluk rule, Ramleh **201**

The old city of Ramleh, founded by the caliph Suleiman, 715–17. Government Press Office, Tel Aviv.

was a large city with a flourishing trade; but visitors to Ramleh from the end of the 15th and to the beginning of the 16th century related that it, too, was progressively declining into ruin. All the sources attest that Gaza was a flourishing trading town, about twice the size of Jerusalem. Gaza, Ramleh, and Nablus (Shechem) were apparently the largest towns in Erez Israel at the end of the Middle Ages.

Erez Israel did not play an important role in Arabic cultural life during the period, but various sources attest that there was no lack of learning and education in its towns. The Mamluk sultans and their ministers continued to establish *madrasas* (schools) for instruction in religion and allocate funds for the maintenance of their teachers and students. The number of *madrasas* established in Erez Israel by the end of the Middle Ages reached 50, of which 43 were in Jerusalem. From a religious point of view, the Mamluk period stamped Erez Israel with the characteristic that has distinguished it up to modern times. It became an orthodox Muslim country, while the number of its Shi'ites progressively decreased. Its distance from the ruling centers, on the one hand, and the espousal of religious fanaticism in the *madrasas*, on the other, gave rise to the prominent role played by religion in the daily life. There were periodic complaints by Muslim extremists, which often resulted in lengthy controversies, that the Christians had enlarged their churches in disregard of the Muslim law. Similarly, Jerusalem (from 1473 on) was the scene of a prolonged controversy between the Muslims and Jews over the latter's right to a particular synagogue, which was eventually destroyed by the Muslims (see below). At the same time, the more gifted among the inhabitants would leave Erez Israel for Egypt and Syria. Arabic sources mention a number of Muslim religious scholars who were born or were active in Erez Israel and several local Arabic writers in different areas. Only a few of them, however, were of any significance. Among these, special mention should be made of Mujīr al-Dīn al-'Ulaymī (1456–1521) who was a judge in Jerusalem and Ramleh and wrote a work on the history of Jerusalem and Hebron.

A number of magnificent buildings were constructed by the Mamluk sultans and their representatives out of a desire to perpetuate their names, even in a forsaken province such as Erez Israel. Fine examples of Muslim architectural art of the period are the tower on the site of the White Mosque in Ramleh, of which only remnants have remained: Bāb al-Qattānin in the Haram area of Jerusalem ("the cotton-workers' gate"); Qā'it bāy Sabīl ("the fountain of Qā'itbāy") on the Temple Mount; and the Tankiziyya *madrasa* near the Western Wall (first half of the 14th century). Also worthy of mention are the Mamluk bridge, the "Jisr Jindās" (second half of the 13th century), which still serves traffic near the town of Lydda.

At the end of the Mamluk period, the security of Erez Israel was undermined, and a worsening of the economic situation ensued. The wars against the Ottomans compelled

The Mamluk tower of Ramleh, built c. 1318. Courtesy
Government Press Office, Tel Aviv.

the Mamluk rulers to seek additional sources of income (for
example, confiscating oil from the farmers in the Nablus
district and then forcing the residents of Jerusalem,
Hebron, and Ramleh to buy it at exorbitant prices) and to
conscript the Bedouin tribes for military service. Such
actions caused rebellions among the populace who sometimes even left their permanent places of residence to hide in
204   the mountains and deserts. In the last decade of the 15th

The Land of Israel under the Mamluks, 14th century C.E.
After *Atlas of Israel,* Survey of Israel, 1970.

The Mamluk bridge near Lydda, built in 1278. Courtesy
Government Press Office, Tel Aviv.

century the Bedouins in the Beth-Shean district and
Transjordan rebelled. Apart from political and economic
upheavals, there were also natural disasters. Arabic sources
record the outbreak of plagues in 1438, 1469, 1476, and
1492; a locust plague in 1484, which laid the land waste;
and earthquakes in 1458 and 1497. The hardships endured
by the people and their dissatisfaction with the authorities
gave rise to the general hope that the annexation of Erez
Israel to the Ottoman state would result in a change for the
better.

Jewish Community. After the wave of bloodshed
perpetrated by the crusaders at the beginning of their
conquests, there was a period of respite and gradual
recovery among the small and impoverished Jewish communities that managed to survive the difficult times.
Gradually, pilgrims began to visit the land and refugees
returned to settle there. However, as the Mamluks
destroyed the ports that had served the crusaders as
important centers of trade with Europe and the inland

towns lost their importance in overland international commerce, the Jews had difficulty in supporting themselves in the large settlements and were scattered in small towns and villages throughout Ereẓ Israel and even Transjordan. R. Estori ha-Parḥi, a refugee from France (1306) who settled in Beisan during the first half of the 14th century and was the first to study the land, several times makes mention of small Jewish communities in Ereẓ Israel in his book *Kaftor va-Feraḥ*. He even made trips into Transjordan and became acquainted with the communities in Edrei, ʿAjlūn, Salka, Ḥabram (Amrawa). In western Ereẓ Israel he found Jews in Jerusalem (where he lived for some time), Lydda, Ramleh (which he calls Gath), Gush Ḥalav, and Safed. In addition to Rabbanite Jews, he also mentions the Ṣaddu-cees, i.e., Karaites, as well as the Samaritans. He makes special mention of -pilgrimages to Jerusalem from the neighboring countries: Sin (i.e., Syrian Tripoli), Hama, Aleppo, Damascus, Cairo, and Alexandria. There is information from the second half of the 14th century about Jews who lived in Miẓpeh Shemuel (i.e., Nabī Samwīl) near Jerusalem. It is evident, however, that these settlements lacked the economic basis required for peaceful develop-ment.

Despite the difficult political and economic conditions in Ereẓ Israel, the Jewish community began to strengthen and consolidate from the beginning of the 15th century, especially in Jerusalem. This caused a reaction on the part of the Franciscan friars, who held the cenaculum above the Tomb of David on Mt. Zion. Properties belonging to the Jewish community were also situated on Mt. Zion. The Franciscans accused the Jews of having dispossessed them of their share of the tomb, and in 1428 the pope issued an order forbidding the fleets of Italian towns to transport Jews to Ereẓ Israel. The dispute over ownership of the alleged Tomb of David in Jerusalem continued for an extended period and resulted in great difficulties in Jewish immigration by sea and the renewal of the prohibition against transporting Jews in Christian ships (c. 1468). R.

Isaac Sarfati (second half of the 15th century), in a famous letter (whose exact date is unknown), calls on the Jews to settle in Erez Israel, suggesting that they make their way overland for "indeed the way of Turgemah is the way to the land of life, all of it overland until Jerusalem, there is only a passage of six miles through the sea" (A. Jellinek (ed.), *Zur Geschichte der Kreuzzuege* (1854), 20–21). The German traveler Ruter (1479) gives the details of this route: "Following is the description of the overland route from Nuremberg and its neighboring districts to Jerusalem, as described to me by a Jew in Jerusalem who took this road a long time ago. The route can be traveled in great safety. Most of the Jews who come from the lands of Germany to Jerusalem make their way overland . . . from Nuremberg to Posen . . . Lublin . . Lemberg . . . through Wallachin to Chocim (?) . . . Akerman (on the shore of the Black Sea) . . . Samsun (Turkey) . . . Tukat . . . Aleppo . . . Damascus . . . Jerusalem" (J. Braslavsky, *Le-Ḥeker Arẓenu* (1954), 142; R. Roehricht and H. Meisner (eds.), *Deutsche Pilgerreisen nach dem Heiligen Lande* (1880), 112–3). This description explains the presence of settlers from Central and Southern Europe in Jerusalem.

The suffering of the Jews of Spain and the Balearic Islands at the end of the 14th and the beginning of the 15th century, even before the expulsions in 1492 and 1497, increased the immigration from hostile countries, and members of their communities could be found in the major cities of Erez Israel even before it was conquered by the Ottoman Turks. It appears that some of these settlers were Marranos. Obadiah of Bertinoro explicitly states that he found Marranos in Jerusalem and Hebron who had "returned to the fold" (the Spanish refugees in Safed will be discussed below). Many of the details about the population at this time are known from the letters and travelogues of Italian Jews who were then living in Erez Israel: R. Elijah of Ferrara (1435); R. Meshullam of Volterra and R. Joseph de Montagna (both 1481); R. Obadiah of Bertinoro and his anonymous disciple (1490–95); R. Israel of Perugia

(1517–23); R. Moses Basola (1521–23). In addition to the settlements already noted, mention should also be made of Kefar Kannā (near Nazareth), where about 38 families lived. R. Obadiah records that 70 families were living in Gaza. According to R. Joseph de Montagna (A. Yaari, *Iggerot Ereẓ Yisrael* (1943), 91) in 1481 there were 300 Jewish families in Safed, more than four times the size of Jerusalem's Jewish population. A "letter about the Sabbatical Year from the sages of Safed to the rabbis of the holy yeshivah of Jerusalem" from 1504 has been preserved and shows that even before the great influx of refugees from Spain into Safed, there were revered scholars in the town, headed by R. Perez Colombo and R. Joseph Saracosti of Saragossa.

According to the detailed description by Obadiah of Bertinoro, the economic situation of the Jews of Jerusalem was severe. The heavy tax burden led the wealthy and the scholars of the community to leave the city. Out of 300 Ashkenazi and Sephardi families, only 70 of the poorest remained, of whom only the artisans—strap makers, weavers, or smiths—and traders in spices and medicines made a scant living. The burden of taxes and levies, to the extent that Torah scrolls and religious objects had to be sold, was connected with fines and bribes that the community had to pay in order to save the synagogue (named after Naḥmanides, near the Ḥurvah Synagogue) from the Muslims, who destroyed it in 1474.

In view of the poor moral and economic situation, the *nagid* Nathan Sholal also left Jerusalem and returned to Egypt, where he met Obadiah of Bertinoro. Nevertheless, Obadiah praises the relations between Muslims and Jews in Jerusalem and emphasizes that in all his travels he did not come across Muslim hostility toward the Jews. According to him, if there had been a wise Jew possessing political acumen in Ereẓ Israel, he could have been "a minister and judge both for the Jews and for the Ishmaelites" (Yaari, *ibid.*, 128). Obadiah also reveals some of the ignorance and crudeness rampant in Jerusalem in his time. Learning had decreased in these generations, and the scholars who are still remembered are very few. At the beginning of Mamluk rule, Tanḥum b. Joseph ha-Yerushalmi (d. 1291 in Cairo), an exegete and grammarian who wrote his works in Hebrew, lived in Jerusalem. He also composed a lexicon to Maimonides' *Mishneh Torah,* of which only the introduction is extant. The importance of R. Estori ha-Parḥi's work *Kaftor va-Feraḥ* lies not only in the geographic-historical information it contains, but also in the opinions and decisions on the *mitzvot* of Ereẓ Israel, discussed therein. R. Elijah of Ferrara (settled in 1435) disseminated the teachings of Maimonides, the Mishnah, and the Talmud with *tosafot* in Jerusalem and was also appointed a *dayyan* and received questions from Cairo, Alexandria, and Damascus. Obadiah of Bertinoro, according to his own account, served as a gravedigger, for there was no one to perform the rites of burial. He was, in effect, the rabbi of Jerusalem—where he also wrote his commentary to the Mishnah. Two Sephardi pupils studied with him regularly, and there were two Ashkenazi rabbis in the city. According to the testimony of his anonymous pupil, the situation in Jerusalem greatly improved because of Obadiah's activities.

The system of *takkanot* in Jerusalem continued after Obadiah's death (c. 1500) and lasted until the Ottoman conquest. The extant version of the *takkanot* was preserved by R. Moses Basola (d. 1572) who copied them from the calendar of the synagogue in Jerusalem. One of the most important *takkanot* was that according to which scholars were exempt from taxes, even if they were wealthy, except for the head tax. In matters of controversy their cases would be brought to the court of the *nagid* in Egypt. This *takkanah* was apparently first formulated by the *nagid* R. Isaac Sholal (nephew of R. Nathan Sholal) in 1509.

Isaac Sholal went to Jerusalem a short while after the Ottoman conquest of Cairo. R. Abraham ha-Levi had settled there even earlier and had been known before his immigration as an outstanding scholar and kabbalist. The expansion of the Ottoman Empire in the time of Selim I indicated to him the forthcoming downfall of the "Edomite" kingdom, and he prophesied the coming of the messiah in 1530 or 1531.

10 OTTOMAN PERIOD (1517–1917)

The Golden Period of Ottoman Rule (1517–1574). The sultan Selim I (1512–20), who manifested similar qualities to those of his grandfather, Muhammad (II) the Conqueror, did not continue his predecessor's attack on Europe. He was "a man of the Eastern front," as one historian describes him, and during his rule the Ottoman territories were doubled through conquests in Asia and Africa. His first campaign was waged against the Persian shah Ismail I, founder of the Safawid dynasty. After defeating him in 1514, Selim pretended he was preparing for a second military campaign against Persia and complained that the Mamluk sultan was conspiring against him together with the "infidel" Safawids, who belonged to the Shi'ite sect. Selim apparently received authoritative reports about the decline of the government in Egypt and intended to entice the Mamluks into leaving their country, extending far from their supply bases in Africa, and attacking him in Asia. This stratagem succeeded: in May 1516 the aged Mamluk sultan Qanṣūh al-Ghawri went to Syria to fight against Selim and in the battle that broke out on Aug. 24, 1516, in the Valley of Dābiq (near Ein Tāb) in northern Syria, the Egyptians were decisively defeated. As a result, Selim gained all the large cities of northern Syria: Aleppo, Ḥama, Homs, and Damascus. From Damascus, Selim sent out commanders to take control of the neighboring districts. Druze chiefs and Bedouin sheikhs from all over Syria arrived there to swear allegiance to the new ruler and the great vizier Sinān Pasha, who left Damascus to conquer Gaza. Even before the end of 1516, the entire country was apparently under Selim's control. At the beginning of 1517,

The Land of Israel under Ottoman rule, 17th century C.E.

213

Inscription over the Jaffa Gate in Jerusalem, dedicated to the Ottoman Sultan Suleiman and dated 1538. Courtesy L. Sowden, Jerusalem.

when Selim embarked on his campaign against Egypt (of which he gained control after a military victory), he visited Jerusalem.

At the beginning of the rule of Selim's son, Suleiman (I) the Magnificent (1520–66), the wali of Syria and Ereẓ Israel, Jan-Birdi al-Ghazālī, rebelled against him, believing the time had come to overthrow the yoke of Ottoman rule and establish a sovereign kingdom in Syria and Ereẓ Israel. Some scholars maintain that he exploited the ferment among the population that resulted from the poor economic situation. The wali was murdered by the Ottomans, however, and his head was sent to Constantinople. Calm was restored in the rebellious districts, the roads that had been impassable during the war were again safe, and the movement of trading caravans to Egypt was renewed. A letter by R. Israel of Perugia (written shortly after the conquest) indicates that the Jerusalem community suffered from the general disorder that resulted from the rebellion (A. Yaari, *Iggerot Ereẓ Yisṟael* (1943), 177). Subsequent to the rebellion, all native-born walis were removed from their posts, and thereafter all responsible positions in the government were held only by Ottomans. The military and civilian administration was established according to the Ottoman system evolved by Suleiman the Magnificent. The conquered territories were divided among the Ottomans as military feudal states, and the feudal lords were required to join the battle as cavalry, bringing with them auxiliaries in proportion to the size of their states. The cavalries of the entire region were united under a standard (Turk. *sanjak*, Ar. *liwā'*) and in battle were under the command of the *sanjak bey* (Turk. "lord of the standard") or the *mir-liwā'* (same in Ar.). This commander was at first appointed from among the cavalry. The external symbol of his position was a banner, with a golden ball on top and a horsetail below it.

With the growth of the Ottoman Empire and its expansion beyond the regions of Anatolia, it was necessary to adapt the administrative organization to the new conditions. The number of the sanjaks increased, and it was useful to appoint deputies to the sultan with a rank higher than that of the *sanjak bey*. They were placed in charge of an area including a number of sanjaks and served as intermediaries between the highest authority and the districts. The first 50 years after the conquest of Ereẓ Israel were the decisive years in the evolution of the new organizational framework of the empire. The organizational framework of the *iyāla* (i.e., the authority) or the *wilāya* or vilayet (the "rule" of the district) was probably also established then.

Ereẓ Israel was divided into four sanjaks: Jerusalem, Gaza, Nablus, and Safed. Each sanjak was an organizational, military, economic, and judicial entity. For practical purposes the sanjak was divided into a number of rural regions *(nāḥiya)*. In the sanjak of Jerusalem there were two regions: Jerusalem and Hebron. The sanjak of Gaza was at first divided into three regions: Gaza, Ramleh, and Lydda, but according to the second *deftar* (assessment), Lydda was joined to the Ramleh region. In the sanjak of Nablus (Shechem) there were four regions: Jebel Shāmī (the northern mountain, i.e., Mt. Ebal), Jebel Qiblī (the southern mountain, Mt. Gerizim); Qāqūn, and Banī Sa'ab. The *deftar* of 1533–39 also mentions the region of Marj Bani 'Amir (Valley of Jezreel), but according to the *deftar* of 1548/49 this was annexed to the Tiberias region. In the sanjak of Safed there were at first six regions: Safed, Tibnīn, Tyre, Shaqīf, Acre, and Tiberias; later Tyre was annexed to Tibnīn.

The constitution of the province of Damascus, which included Erez Israel, was established in the *qanun-name* of Suleiman (1548). In contrast to the disorganization and lack of security that characterized the end of the Mamluk period, Erez Israel now enjoyed a secure rule and regulated organization. The improvement in the general condition was also manifested in agriculture, which was improved where it previously existed but was not expanded into desolate areas. Censuses conducted during the first 50 years after the conquest show that the population of Erez Iṣrael doubled, reaching approximately 300,000, and only a fifth to a quarter of the population lived in the six towns: Jerusalem, Hebron, Gaza, Ramleh, Nablus, and Safed. The remainder were primarily farmers living in villages, and some were Bedouin and seminomad, who worked the land only seasonally and temporarily. The Bedouin also engaged in collecting a variety of plants for medicine, resin, and the production of potash, using it for the manufacture of soap. The major agricultural products of the field were wheat, barley, maize, and different strains of beans (which served as food for man and beast (vetch)), vegetables, cotton, and sesame. The orchards produced dates, figs, pomegranates, berries, olives, apples, pears, and nuts. Fruit was also used for fruit honey. The Jews and Christians produced grape wine, as well as grape honey, which were permitted for the Muslims. The sources also make frequent references to beehives. Cattle breeding was undertaken mainly by the Bedouin, as well as by the fellahin and the residents of urban settlements. There were many jamus (buffalo) in the area of the Ḥuleh swamps, and fishing was popular in the settlements near the Ḥuleh and Lake Kinneret, as well as a few points on the shores of the Mediterranean (Acre, Jaffa).

The growth of the population, the expansion of cultivated lands in villages and the outskirts of cities, and the cultivation of orchards and olive trees led to the expansion of agriculture. There was an increase in the number of oil presses for the production of olive and sesame oils and for extracting fruit juices for the preparation of fruit honey. Together with oil production was the manufacture of soap, which was well known for its quality throughout the Middle East. The windmills operated regularly. Apparently at the initiative of the Jewish immigrants, new branches of industry were established in Safed, e.g., the manufacture and dyeing of cloth and felt. Information about these fields is also supplied by the tax lists in the canuns and the *deftars* of private censuses of the centers of these industries and the countries to which the products were exported. Especially noteworthy were the taxes that were levied on olive oil produced in Jerusalem and Ramleh and on the soap from Jerusalem exported to Egypt. The soap factory in Hebron was the property of the *waqf.* The center of the weaving and cloth dyeing industry was in Safed and its environs, although dyeing was also carried out in Kafr Kānnā, Nablus, and Gaza. In addition there were tanneries in Nablus and Ein Zeitim. The special tax which was levied on mulberry trees indicated that they were apparently cultivated for the feeding of silkworms. In fact, silk spinners are mentioned in a number of places. With the expansion of the cultivation of cotton in Erez Israel, spinning began in Majdal, Lydda, Nablus, and Acre. Apart from the crafts undertaken by the Jews during the period of Mamluk rule, the Christians in Jerusalem, Bethlehem, and neighboring villages engaged in the home manufacture of religious objects (from wood and mother-of-pearl), which were sold to pilgrims on their visits to Erez Israel or exported for sale abroad.

NEW DEVELOPMENTS IN THE JEWISH COMMUNITIES. The writings of R. Moses Basola (who visited Erez Israel in 1521/22) testify that Jerusalem grew in his time as a result of the Spanish immigration. According to his estimate the Jews of Jerusalem numbered about 300 families, not including widows, who numbered no more than 150 and were not subject to taxes, thus enjoying a comfortable income. About 200 people were supported by charity from public funds and from funds collected in the Diaspora. From 1502 to 1524 the community was headed by the *nagid* R. Isaac Sholal. The detailed Ottoman *deftar* of 1525–26 dealing with the *jamᶜāti yahudyiān* (the Jewish community) contains a detailed listing of 199 names of householders, excluding bachelors, and it can be assumed that not all of Jerusalem's Jewish residents were included in this census. The community was then composed of four groups: (1) the Ashkenazim, numbering 15 families descended from the Ashkenazim who had lived there since the time of Maimonides, joined by immigrants from Europe (the Italians were counted together with the Ashkenazim at that time); (2) the Sephardim, refugees of the expulsion who were the majority in the city; (3) immigrants from North Africa, known as Maghrebis; and (4) Mustaᶜrabs (the Moriscos), longtime residents, descendants of the local inhabitants who had never left Erez Israel. Among the *dayyanim* and scholars, including members of all the communities, there were often differences of opinion regarding the arrangement of prayers, the synagogue, etc. According to R. Israel Ashkenazi, after the conquest spiritual hegemony passed from the Mustaᶜrabs and Maghrebis to the Sephardim.

In the center of the country there was still a Jewish settlement in Nablus, and in the south there were settlements in Hebron and Gaza. The community of Safed comprised more than 300 householders, whose economic situation, according to R. Moses Basola, was good. There were three synagogues: a Sephardi, a Musta'rab, and a Maghrebi. With the aid of the Jews of Egypt, the Jews of Safed managed to survive the difficult transition period of Mamluk retreat and Ottoman conquest. Jews also lived in the villages of Galilee: Ein Zeitim (four householders); Birya (Biriyyah, 19 families); 'Almāh (18 families); Peki'in (33 householders); Kafr Kannā (40–50 families); Kefar Ḥananiah (14 families); and Kefar Yasif, Shepharam, and Kābūl. It is estimated that there were about 1,000 Jewish families (i.e., 5,000 persons) in Ereẓ Israel at the beginning of the Ottoman conquest. The transition period gave rise to messianic hopes among the Jews of both Ereẓ Israel and the Diaspora. In 1523 the pseudo-messiahs David Reuveni and Solomon Molcho arrived in Jerusalem foretelling the redemption. When he was in Portugal (1526), David Reuveni asked the king John III: "Help us and let us go out to battle against the provoking Suleiman and take the Holy Land from his hands" (Joseph ha-Kohen, *Emek ha-Bakha,* ed. by M. Letteris (1895), 113). Such hopes, as well as the improvement in the economic situation, gave rise to increased immigration, especially among the refugees from Spain. A few of them went to Jerusalem, whose population, according to official Turkish *deftars,* increased from approximately 200 families in 1526 to 338 families in 1554. R. Levi b. Ḥabib also settled there and cared for the community's spiritual and material needs. Among other great teachers who lived for a long or short period in Jerusalem were R. David ibn Abi Zimra (c. 1485; died in Safed, c. 1575) and R. Bezalel Ashkenazi, a native of Jerusalem (beginning of 16th century) who headed the yeshivah in the city.

The majority of the new immigrants settled in Safed, which developed into an important commercial and industrial town. According to R. David de Rossi, who settled in Safed in 1535: "Whoever saw Safed ten years ago and sees it again now is amazed, for the Jews are constantly coming in and the clothing industry is expanding daily **219**

There is no *galut* here like in our country [Italy] and the Turks respect the important Jews. Here and in Alexandria [cf. Egypt], those appointed over the taxes and incomes of the king are Jews" (A. Yaari, *Iggerot Erez Yisrael* (1943), 184, 186–7). In the middle of the 16th century, the Jews of Safed apparently numbered 10,000, i.e., the majority of the Jewish population of Erez Israel was concentrated in Safed and its environs—Ein Zeitim, Birya, and other villages in Galilee. During the 16th century Safed became known as a large and important center of Torah and teaching. In 1524 R. Jacob Berab settled there and sought to renew the system of ordination, which had not been used for hundreds of years. His plans aroused the violent opposition of the sages of Jerusalem, especially R. Levi b. Ḥabib, guardian of the spiritual and material needs of that community. They argued, inter alia, that the renewal of ordination required the authorization of all the scholars of Erez Israel. Nevertheless, R. Jacob Berab ordained four of the great scholars of his day, who were his students and colleagues: R. Joseph Caro, author of the code Shulḥan Arukh; R. Moses Trani (the Mabbit); R. Abraham Shalom; and R. Israel di Curiel (1538). Furthermore, these four ordained a number of their own disciples. This attempt to renew ordination and reinstate the full authority of the *battei din* of Erez Israel ultimately failed, but the spiritual influence of the scholars of Safed continued, as evidenced by Caro's *Shulḥan Arukh*, which has been accepted by the Jewish world.

Safed became the center of mysticism during this period. In fact all the great halakhic scholars who lived there at the time studied Kabbalah and the Zohar. *Maggid Mesharim*, dialogues between the author and the mystical inspiration *(maggid)* who guided him, was written by R. Joseph Caro. Before the arrival of R. Isaac Luria (ha-Ari) in Safed (1569?), mystical scholars and formulators of new methods, such as R. Moses Cordovero and R. Solomon Alkabeẓ, author of the Sabbath hymn *Lekhah Dodi*, became known there. The system of practical Kabbalah established by

Luria soon acquired many adherents throughout the Diaspora. His teachings were disseminated by his outstanding disciple, R. Ḥayyim Vital, and other disciples.

The yearnings for redemption and messianic hopes which increased during this period, especially among the Spanish refugees, found ultimate expression in the bold attempt by Doña Gracia Mendes Nasi and her nephew Don Joseph Nasi, the wealthy Marrano statesman and Jewish leader, to rebuild Tiberias from its ruins. Don Joseph and Doña Gracia leased from the sultan the area of Tiberias, which was then desolate. Joseph sent his representative Joseph b. Ardict, or Joseph Pomar (presumably identical with Joseph Cohen, his secretary at about this time), to deal with the settlement of Jews in Tiberias. The area, intended to become a city, was surrounded with a wall (1564). As there are few sources, it is difficult to determine whether Don Joseph intended to establish a Jewish state in Ereẓ Israel or create a limited haven for the Spanish refugees and derive economic benefit from the establishment of a new economic center in which wool and silk cloth would be manufactured. Whatever the original intent, the rebuilt Tiberias began to attract settlers from near (even from Safed) and far (Yemen). At the end of his life, Don Joseph displayed less enthusiasm in dealing with Tiberias. After his death, Solomon Abenaes received new rights over Tiberias from the sultan Murad III and erected a number of buildings in Tiberias. Finally, however, the plan to reconstitute the city disintegrated and was abandoned because of various political and economic factors.

In connection with these messianic trends and hopes during the time of Sultan Suleiman, when Ottoman rule was at its peak, Christian priests in Syria, still adhering to crusader ideas, suggested to Emperor Charles V that he conduct a campaign to regain the holy places. This plan was never realized. Once again, during the rule of Selim II, the Greek patriarch Sophronius (1570) asked the German kaiser to deal mercifully with Jerusalem by renewing Christian rule there.

Beginning of the Decline. During the rule of Murad III (1574–95), his son Muhammad III (1595–1603), and succeeding sultans—Ahmed I (1603–17), Mustafa I (1617–18; 1622–23), and Murad IV (1623–40)—the Janissary army lost the strict discipline instituted by Selim I and became a constant source of danger to the sultan by its frequent rebellions and exaggerated demands over salaries and various grants. The situation in the political center was quickly reflected first on the borders of the desert through signs of overthrowing the yoke of the empire. Sheikhs and small princes began to entertain a hope of rebuilding from the ruins wrought by the Ottoman rulers. Prominent among the emirs of the Druze who ruled in Lebanon was the Ma'an family, whose head, Fakhr al-Din II (1590–1635), conquered the Safed region and 'Ajlūn in eastern Transjordan while Muhammad III's army was engaged in battles with the Persians. Fakhr al-Din successfully uprooted the robbers who had spread throughout the land, and he turned Galilee into a tranquil and secure area. The same period saw the growth of the idea to establish an independent crusader state in Syria, Erez Israel, and Cyprus. Fakhr al-Din utilized this idea to expand the scope of his influence in Erez Israel with the help of the Christians. He occupied territories in the area of Jenin, came close to Mount Carmel, and signed agreements with the Bedouin in the mountains of Hauran. This activity aroused a violent reaction from the Turkish throne. In 1613 the grand vizier Mansur instructed the wali of Damascus, Ahmad al-Ḥāfiẓ, to engage Fakhr al-Din in battle. The Druze emir passed on the administration of his political affairs to his brothers and left for Italy, where he spent a number of years in the courts of the prince of Tuscany and other rulers; he visited the knights of Malta and returned to Lebanon in 1618. Immediately upon his return, he renewed his efforts to regain all the territories lost while he was in exile. Eventually he conquered the sanjaks of Safed, 'Ajlun, **Nablus,** and **Gaza.** At that time the sultan had no statesman or commander who could instill fear into the

Druze emir, who even dared to renew the plan for establishing a Christian state in Erez Israel through negotiations with the representatives of the king of Spain.

The expansion of the Ma'an family's rule over almost the entire area of Erez Israel led to clashes with other local rulers, especially the members of the Ṭarābāy. According to tradition, they received the Jenin region from the conquering Selim and expanded their sphere of influence gradually to Haifa, along the seacoast, and up to Gaza, sometimes even enforcing their rule over certain areas in Galilee. The al-Furaykh family, a Bedouin family from the Lebanon valley, established their rule by force in Safed, Nablus, and 'Ajlun. Under their influence, the wali of Damascus, Ahmad Kūtshuk ("the Small") was ordered by the central authorities to wage battle against Fakhr al-Din whom the kapudan pasha (commander of the fleet), Ja'far, was ordered to besiege from the sea, thus preventing Christian boats from rendering assistance. Fakhr al-Din attempted to conciliate the wali of Damascus by giving him Sidon (Saida) and Beirut, and in the meantime he sent Bishop Maroni to Italy to seek aid. Disappointed by his allies, he decided to surrender to the Ottoman rulers. In 1634 he was imprisoned in Constantinople and a year later was killed together with his two sons, who had been taken captive with him. His death, however, did not terminate the Druze's attempts to gain control of Erez Israel. The settlements in Galilee, especially Safed and Tiberias, suffered from the renewed attempts by several Druze emirs to reconquer the region.

The total defeat of the Ma'an family did not improve the situation in the country. The gradual decline of the Ottoman Empire was reflected in repeated rebellions by the Janissaries, the increasing burden of taxes, and the loss of large areas in Europe. Clearly the general situation had a negative influence on the population of Erez Israel in general and on the Jews in particular.

JEWISH POPULATION. During the last quarter of the 16th century the security situation of Erez Israel deteriorated. Safed and Galilee suffered particularly from robbery raids 223 by Bedouin and Druze tribes eager for the wealth of this industrial commercial town. Several sources give evidence that such acts were repeated several times. A Turkish decree of 1576 ordered the expulsion of 500 or 1,000 wealthy Jewish families of Safed, forcing them to move to Cyprus. This decree was annulled later, but the very existence of the order undermined faith in the authorities. Safed began to be depleted of its wealthy residents, a phenomenon which sometimes took on the form of actual flight. The scholars also began to abandon the town. R. Joseph Trani (son of R. Moses Trani) went to Constantinople in 1599 and R. Ḥayyim Vital moved to Damascus. R. Isaiah ha-Levi Horowitz (kabbalist, author of the famous moralistic work *Shenei Luhot ha-Berit*) decided not to settle in Safed and went to Jerusalem in 1621.

Although Safed was not totally abandoned, as was the case with Tiberias (where not one Jew remained by the end of the 17th century), the decline was evident.

A short time after R. Isaiah Horowitz' arrival in Jerusalem, the community was harmed by the greed of a Bedouin sheikh, Muhammad ibn Farukh, who achieved the position of *sanjak bey* of Jerusalem (1625) and began to tyrannize the population, and especially the Jews, through the imposition of heavy taxes. After a year of persecution, the pasha in Damascus finally dismissed ibn Farukh, but the heavy debts remained in force and many emissaries went out to the Diaspora to collect funds to save the community. The situation was not as favorable as envisioned by R. Isaiah Horowitz, but Jerusalem was rebuilt to some extent, as were other communities in the south—notably Hebron, in which a few of the disciples of R. Moses Cordovero and R. Isaac Luria settled.

During periods of trouble in Jerusalem, Hebron and Gaza served as temporary refuges from persecution and oppression. The number of Jerusalem's residents increased especially after the decrees of 1648, when some Jewish war refugees from the Ukraine arrived in Ereẓ Israel. The rulers of the city exploited the situation by imposing a heavier burden of taxes on the Jews, especially affecting the poor. Many awaited aid that was usually sent regularly by the Diaspora communities. When this assistance did not arrive in time and was insufficient, emissaries would be sent abroad to arouse the sympathy of the Jews. One of these emissaries was Shabbetai Ẓevi, who left Jerusalem shortly after his arrival there in order to collect funds in Egypt (1664). On his way to Egypt he stopped in Gaza. The Gaza community was a very important one at that time because the city was regarded as the capital of the Negev and Sinai (Beersheba was established only at the end of Ottoman rule) and was a large commercial center and a stopping place on the route between Africa and Asia. It was an asylum for Jewish refugees because it enjoyed an independent administration and was also even a refuge in times of plague. In the 16th–17th centuries there were outstanding scholars there. Shabbetai Ẓevi also made the acquaintance there of Nathan of Gaza who became his "prophet." The city became an important centre for the dissemination of Shabbateanism.

Jerusalem, which was then the center of most of the scholars of Ereẓ Israel and even attracted some of the great scholars from the countries of the East, again took over the spiritual leadership, which it had relinquished during the previous century to Safed. Despite the difficult material situation and the harsh attitude of the local rulers, in the 17th century the Jewish population succeeded in consolidating its position in Jerusalem and in the entire southern section of the country.

New Developments in the 18th Century. At the turn of the century, during the reign of Mustafa II (1695–1703), there was a change in the political status of the Ottoman power in Europe. The Treaty of Karlowitz (Jan. 26, 1699) forced the sultan to make many territorial concessions in his border regions. Russia demanded, inter alia, control of the holy places in Jerusalem and all Orthodox Christians in the Ottoman Empire, be they Greeks, Serbs, Bulgarians, or others. This control was expected to provide personal immunity and exemption from taxes and Muslim jurisdiction. With the decline in the military power of the Janissaries, the central authority was compelled to allow its walis to conscript soldiers in another way, in order to put them to use locally. Thus cavalry and infantry troops, composed of Albanian, Bosnian, and Maghrebi mercenaries were founded. Their salaries were derived from the incomes of government estates and special taxes levied on the population, usually without basis in religious tradition and regarded as illegal by religious scholars. These private armies were one of the sources of the anarchy in Turkey during the 18th century. The walis used them for the purposes of tax collection and expanding their rule at the expense of weaker neighboring provinces.

At the beginning of the 18th century, Ẓāhir al-Omar received the *"iltizām"* (the right to levy taxes) for most of the districts of Galilee (in the regions of Nazareth, Tiberias, and Safed) from the tribe of Zaydān. He very soon overcame some of his opponents and extended his rule over the district of Tiberias, where he fortified himself as the tax farmer of the pasha of Sidon. In 1742 the pasha of Damascus was ordered by the sultan to fight against Ẓāhir. This episode was described in Hebrew by the son-in-law of R. Ḥayyim Abulafia, who rebuilt the Jewish settlement in Tiberias (1740). The attack on Tiberias failed, and in 1743 the pasha tried again. A short while later he died. Thereafter Ẓāhir was able to overcome his remaining opponents and annexed their estates (such as Shepharam) to his territories. He then turned to the sea and conquered Acre. His control of Acre and Haifa (and economically also of Dar-Ṭanṭūra) brought him in direct contact with the traders and agents of Europe who had established bases in the coastal towns to conduct trade with inland regions.

Ẓāhir formed an alliance with the ruler of Egypt, Ali Bey, and the Russian fleet, which arrived in the Mediterranean to the surprise of the Turks. In 1771 almost the entire country was under his control, and his Egyptian allies captured Damascus. Ẓāhir captured Gaza, Lydda,

Ramleh, and Jaffa, but the Egyptian commander joined the sultan's army, regaining what Ẓāhir had captured and perpetrating a massacre in Jaffa (1775). The Ottomans attracted to their side Ẓāhir's mercenary forces, who betrayed their master and murdered him (1775). On the same day Acre was captured by the sultan's army and Ahmad Pasha al-Jazzār ("the Butcher") was appointed *sanjak bey* of the Sidon area.

Ahmad Pasha was wali of the Sidon area, whose capital he transferred to Acre, for 29 years (1775–1804). He also became the ruler of the Tripoli area and in 1790–99 and 1804 was the wali of Damascus. He organized a private army of Albanians, Bosnians, Maghrebis, and Bedouin and fortified the walls of Acre, and the value of these fortifications was proven during Napoleon's siege.

Napoleon's invasion of Egypt in 1798 came as a complete surprise for Constantinople, which had considered him an ally when he was conquering Malta and putting an end to the activities of the pirates. At the beginning of 1799, Napoleon's army was advancing toward Ereẓ Israel. He attempted to bribe Ahmad al-Jazzār into joining his side, but the pasha refused to receive Napoleon's delegation. The French then conquered Gaza, Ramleh, Lydda, and Jaffa without difficulty, despite the presence of a large garrison in Jaffa. The population welcomed the conquerors, for Napoleon had incurred their affection through various promises and a humane attitude. Napoleon's army did not turn to Jerusalem because he was interested only in strategic conquests that would open the way to the centers of the Ottoman Empire. The French military forces conquered Haifa and then besieged Acre. The English fleet came to the aid of al-Jazzār and remnants of the Ottoman army engaged the French in battle but were ambushed near En-Harod by the French general J. G. Kleber. This victory opened the way to Safed, but the opportunity was not exploited. In contrast, Acre defended itself, and Napoleon could not destroy its fortifications because he lacked heavy cannon. In the meantime, plagues broke out

Northwest tower, known as the "English Bastion," at the seawall of Acre, built by the pasha Aḥmad al-Jazzār in the late 18th century. Courtesy Israel Department of Antiquities, Jerusalem.

in the French camp, and the famous commander was forced to retreat with his army to Egypt.

The situation of the farmers who worked the lands of the government was, at the beginning of Ottoman rule, not unfavorable. The "miri," or the land of the emirate which was taxed, was not a burden on the fellahin, while the land was populated and they benefited, directly or indirectly, from profits made through international trade. With the impoverishment of the Ottoman Empire, however, the tax burden increased and the people began to abandon the villages for the towns. The various payments demanded from the villages became an intolerable burden in the absence of working hands. Furthermore, the Bedouin harassed the villagers in the plains and the valleys and robbed them of the fruits of their labors, which was an added reason to abandon the fertile lands.

According to the French traveler C. F. de Volney (in 1783–85), the decisive majority of the population were fellahin. Nevertheless, this traveler, and others who visited the country, noted the strange contrast between the fertility of the land and the poor state of the few farms. This was the situation in the southern plain (between Gaza and Ashkelon and Hebron) and in the area between Bethlehem and Jerusalem. The broad Acre plain and the region around the Kinneret, which were known for their abundance of water, were overgrown with reeds. The naturalist T. Shaw (1722), who investigated the flora and fauna of North Africa and the Middle East, records that the soil of many valleys was fertile and good; if the land had been cultivated as in the past, it would have yielded a larger crop than the best lands on the shores of Syria and Phoenicia. Cotton grown in the valleys of Ramleh, Jezreel, and Zebulun was of a better quality than that cultivated near Sidon or Tripoli. It was difficult to find beans, wheat, or other grains superior to the produce sold regularly in Jerusalem. The desolation about which travelers sometimes complained was not a result of the natural character of the country, but rather of the sparsity of the population and the indolence of the inhabitants.

Ẓāhir al-Omar attempted to improve the condition of agriculture in Galilee. He encouraged the fellahin to work their lands by granting loans and he especially tried to protect them from bandits. He favored the settlement of Jews and they reestablished themselves in Peki'in, Shepharam, and Yasif. In contrast, a traveler accuses Ahmad al-Jazzār, Ẓāhir's successor in Galilee, of not being concerned with the development of agriculture in the Acre plain, which remained a swampland.

RECONSTRUCTION OF THE JEWISH COMMUNITY. The messianic ferment that increased in the Diaspora at the end of the 17th century was connected with increased immigration to Erez Israel. At the beginning of the 18th century it was headed by Judah Ḥasid and Ḥayyim Malakh, both Shabbateans—the former covertly and the latter overtly— who arrived in Jerusalem at the end of 1700 at the head of a convoy organized in Europe. Before their arrival, the Jewish community of Jerusalem numbered 1,200, of whom **229**

200 were Ashkenazim weighed down by a burden of debts. Of the people who left with this convoy, which took two routes (one through Venice and the other through Constantinople), about 500 died on the way and only about 1,000 reached Jerusalem. Its leader, Judah Ḥasid, died almost immediately after the convoy's arrival, and conflicts arose with the veteran settlers, who were opposed to the Shabbatean movement. The new arrivals were a heavy burden on the Ashkenazi community of Jerusalem. The Arabs had lent money to the members of the convoy and now demanded reimbursement from the veteran Ashkenazim, who in turn appealed for aid from the Polish communities in their battle against the Shabbateans and sent emissaries to Frankfort and Metz, where financial help for the poor of Ereẓ Israel was concentrated. Help did not arrive, due to political reasons unconnected with Ashkenazi Jewry. The Arab creditors broke into the Ashkenazi synagogue on a Sabbath (Nov. 8, 1720), set it on fire, and took over the area, which they held until 1816. For several years after the burning of the synagogue, Ashkenazi Jews, who were recognizable by their dress, could not settle in Jerusalem for fear of being held for the old debts. Those who dared to do so a generation later had to disguise themselves as Jews from oriental communities. The European immigrants settled mainly in Hebron, Safed, and even Tiberias.

At that time the Jews lived mainly on charity received from abroad and, in a few cases, on income from businesses in their lands of origin. Any slight change in the situation of the contributors, or any delay in sending aid, could bring disaster upon the poor. The extreme poverty led R. Moses b. Raphael Mordecai Malkhi, a scholar and famous physician in Jerusalem (end of 17th century), to speak out against the immigration of very poor people, arguing that Ereẓ Israel needed immigrants who could be self-sustaining. In order to supervise the distribution and use of funds and also facilitate the payment of the numerous debts burdening the Jerusalem community, the "officials for Jerusalem" in Constantinople, sent a special *parnas* to act as a kind of administrator for the community and take care of Jewish pilgrims. For those Jews who wanted to devote themselves to the study of the Torah, yeshivot were established in Jerusalem, where outstanding scholars studied. Ḥayyim Joseph David Azulai, R. Sar Shalom Sharabi, and R. Abraham Gershon of Kutow (brother-in-law of Israel b. Eliezer Baal Shem-Tov) were in the yeshivah Beth-El, where kabbalistic studies were also pursued.

The Jews of Hebron suffered because of constant civil wars between the Arabs of Hebron, who belonged to the Qays faction (of north Arabian origin), and those of Bethlehem, who belonged to the Yemen faction (from south Arabian tribes). The Constantinople officials extended their activities to include Hebron, whose situation had been aggravated by debts owed by the community. Ḥayyim Joseph David Azulai went to Western Europe in 1753 and in 1773 on behalf of the Hebron community. Another emissary was Ḥayyim Isaac Carigal, who reached North America. In the 1880s the number of the Jews in the city of the patriarchs reached about 300.

The community of Gaza was smaller than that of Hebron and suffered from repeated incursions made by the various armies. It was decimated after the conquest of the town by Napoleon (1799), and in 1811 no one remained there. Many Ashkenazim from Poland and Lithuania settled in Safed and Tiberias, which were centers of Ḥasidism from the second half of the 18th century, establishing a new link with the greatest Diaspora community of the time. Thus Galilee and Tiberias, which had been almost depleted during the 17th century, were settled by immigrants from Eastern Europe. Tiberias was rebuilt by R. Abraham Abulafia (1740) with the help of the sheikh Ẓāhir al-Omar. After the Ḥasidim came a wave of their opponents, disciples of R. Elijah, the *gaon* of Vilna. According to tradition, the *gaon* himself wanted to immigrate but halted his journey in the middle. In 1770–72, his most important disciples, R. Ḥayyim of Vilna and R. Israel b. Samuel of

Shklov, arrived and a few years after his death many of his disciples, called *perushim,* immigrated. The immigration of the *perushim* was brilliantly described by R. Israel of Shklov.

1800–1882. The beginning of this period saw the end of the district system of administration, during which time Erez Israel displayed all the characteristics of a neglected province of a disintegrating empire and after 1840 there was a turn for the better. The population increased appreciably. The administration of the country was changed and there was an increase in Western influence, resulting from the revolution in means of communication, which brought the Ottoman Empire closer to Europe. The increased rivalry among the European powers turned Erez Israel into a focal point of the "Eastern problem."

According to estimates, which tend to be exaggerated, the number of the inhabitants in Erez Israel in 1800 did not exceed 300,000. The number of Jews apparently did not exceed 5,000, most of whom were Sephardim. Most of the Jewish population was concentrated in Jerusalem, Safed, Tiberias, and Hebron. The Christians, who apparently numbered about 25,000, were scattered over a wider area. Their main concentrations—in Jerusalem, Nazareth, and Bethlehem—belonged primarily to the Greek Orthodox, Greek Catholic, and Roman Catholic Churches. The remaining inhabitants were Muslims, almost all of them of the Sunnite sect. The size of the Jewish population was doubled in about 1840, with the Christian and Muslim elements unchanged. Between 1800 and the end of 1831, Erez Israel was divided into two Ottoman vilayets (pashaliks). The borders of these changed from time to time, but in general the eastern central mountain region from north of Nablus to south of Hebron (including Jerusalem) belonged to the vilayet of Damascus (al-Shām) and Galilee and the Coastal Plain, to Khan Yunis, belonged to the vilayet of Acre. The coastal region from Khan Yunis to Caesarea was divided into three *nāḥiyāt* (sub-districts): Gaza, Ramleh, and Jaffa. Most of the Negev was at that time outside

Ottoman jurisdiction.

The structure of the Ottoman state should not be analyzed from a Western point of view. Even during its zenith, no attempt was made to Ottomanize non-Turkish conquered regions. The children of ruling groups often married local women and assimilated into the local population. Thus local traditions and officials were maintained in Ereẓ Israel and a subject of the emperor had to maintain his prime allegiance not to the imperial government, but to the religious group or the social class into which he was born. The Christians and Jews, as members of special millets, even had limited direct contact with the Turkish government. Even the head tax, which exempted one from military service, was collected by means of the millet. Only those non-Turkish subjects belonging to the Sunni sect of Islam could identify to some extent with the higher (though only nominal) function of the sultan: the defense of the Muslim faith against apostasy.

The vague connection between Ahmad al-Jazzār and the supreme authority continued during the rule of Ahmad's successors—Suleiman, Ismail, and Abdallah (1804–32), who were less active and cruel than he. Of a similar nature were the relations between the supreme authority and the pashas who ruled in Damascus and Gaza. Public welfare had no significance in the view of the rulers, who regarded as their prime function the collection of taxes derived from three major sources: the "miri" land tax (from Muslims); the "kharāj," head tax; and customs. When these sources proved insufficient, various crop taxes were levied arbitrarily on Muslims and non-Muslims alike.

At the beginning of the 1880s, Ramleh and Acre derived their income from the sale of raw cotton and plain cotton cloth to the French traders in the Levant. Clothes, dyes, sugar, and coffee (from the West Indies) were bought from the French traders. These traders, however, disappeared from the country after the French Revolution and returned only after the Napoleonic wars. The (British)

Levant Company, which filled the gap created by the disappearance of the French traders, was not interested in the cotton of Ereẓ Israel. When the French traders returned to the East after 1815, they did not succeed in reestablishing their former trade connections. In 1821, when the long-fibered strain of cotton was introduced into Egypt, the manufacture of cotton in Ereẓ Israel became relatively useless, except during the U.S. Civil War, when it enjoyed a brief revival. Acre and Ramleh never regained their primary position in the economy of the country. In 1825, when the concession to the Levant Company and privileges granted the Trade Bureau of Marseilles were abolished, the way was opened for free trade.

The period of Egyptian rule in Syria and Ereẓ Israel, which lasted nine years (1832 40), marked the peak of provincial government. This was the first time that an independent pasha had rebelled against the Sublime Porte, conquered territories from other pashas, and compelled the sultan to admit the "legality" of his conquests. Nevertheless, after consolidating his position in Syria and Ereẓ Israel, Muhammad Ali, the pasha of Egypt, agreed to pay to Sultan Mahmud II the "accepted quota" of the tax (1834). Ibrahim Pasha (stepson of Muhammad Ali), who successfully conducted the military campaign, became the general ruler of the conquered area and established his residence in Damascus. The whole of Ereẓ Israel, whose northern border reached Sidon, now became one district. The few forests remaining in the valleys and on the mountain slopes in central Ereẓ Israel were cut down to supply wood for Muhammed Ali's fleet. Ibrahim Pasha forced the Muslim farmers to join the Egyptian army. Rebellions, which occurred in most of the towns, were put down by force and law and order established. Swiftly executed punishments halted the incursions of the Bedouin and travelers from Jaffa to Jerusalem no longer had to pay taxes to the Circassian sheikhs of Abu Ghosh. Attempts were made, with varying degrees of success, to eradicate bribery in the courts, institute a fair

234

A public hanging in Jerusalem toward the end of the Ottoman regime. Courtesy Jerusalem Municipality Historical Archives.

division of taxes, and avoid discrimination against the Jews in favor of the Muslims.

For more than a decade before Egyptian rule in Erez Israel, Protestant missionaries from Britain and the United States tried to obtain permission to establish regular institutions in Jerusalem and other parts of the country. These attempts met with the strong opposition of the provincial rulers and their representatives. Ibrahim Pasha allowed the missionaries not only to preach but even to establish schools. The Egyptian period also saw the beginning of extensive activity in biblical geography and archaeology, especially by the U.S. scholar Edward Robinson. Moreover, in 1838 the Egyptian government permitted Britain to open a regular consulate in Jerusalem; previously, consular representations were limited—apart from ephemeral French attempts in Jerusalem in 1699-1700 and 1713-15—to the coastal towns (Acre, Haifa, Jaffa) and Ramleh, and even in these places the powers would appoint local agents as their representatives. Twenty years later, all the important Western nations, including the United States, were represented in Jerusalem by regular consular delegations.

The intervention of the European powers in 1840-41 in the Egyptian-Turkish conflict forced Ibrahim Pasha and his forces to leave Erez Israel and Syria, which returned to the direct control of Turkey. Egyptian rule did not last long enough to have any lasting influence. The Qays and the Yemen factions again caused disturbances in the rural areas and the people of Abu Ghosh reinstated the collection of taxes from travelers (lasting until 1846). Former pashas, however, were not returned to their posts and a new administration was established on the basis of strict centralization.

 The increasing administrative changes were finally expressed in the Vilayet Law of 1864, which unified the whole provincial administration into one framework. Most of Erez Israel was covered by the sanjaks of Nablus (which, until 1888, included the area of Balqā', east of the Jordan) and Acre, which were part of the vilayet of Beirut, and the independent sanjak or mutaṣariflik of Jerusalem (previously part of the vilayet of Damascus), which was now placed directly under the authority of Constantinople. Each district was divided into sub-districts (Ar. qaḍā', plural aqḍiya) and each qaḍā' into sub-districts (Ar. nāḥiyāt). The provincial administration was composed of a strict hierarchy of Turkish officials: mudīr (head of a nāḥiya), qāymaqām (head of a vilayet). Each official was subordinate to the head of his administrative region, while the Wali was subordinate to the ministry of the interior in Constantinople (established in 1860). Turkish officials of every grade who headed an administrative unit were aided by a council (majlis) representing all sectors of the population, both Muslim and non-Muslim. This administrative system, of course, did not terminate all corruption and abuse or institute representative rule, but it greatly curtailed the arbitrary actions of the provisional rulers and even granted the various religious communities a small measure of influence in public affairs.

Missionary organizations, representing almost every sect in Western Christianity, increased quickly after the departure of the Egyptians. They were concentrated mainly in Jerusalem, which had, toward the end of the 19th century, the greatest proportion of missionaries per capita of any city in the world. Some of the missionary groups developed an increasing number of educational, medical, and charitable institutions. The number of those converting to the new faith, even among Eastern Christians, was negligible, but the establishment of schools and clinics by Protestant missionaries stimulated the Latin and Greek Orthodox communities, as well as the Turkish government and even the Jewish community, to establish similar institutions.

Political considerations led to increased rivalry among the missionary groups from various countries. The great European powers, which made attempts to gain areas of influence in every part of the Ottoman Empire as potential holding points in a future division of the empire, exploited the missionary activities of their subjects in Ereẓ Israel for the advancement of their political aims. Austria-Hungary, France, Prussia, and Russia rendered financial assistance to missionary activities. After the signing of the Treaty of Kutchuk-Kainarji (1774), Russia claimed the right to protect the Arabs who belonged to the Greek Orthodox Church and even granted its protection to the Greek Orthodox patriarchate in Jerusalem. The czarist government, which was aided by the Russian Orthodox Company for Palestine and the delegation of the Russian church in the country, contributed funds for the establishment of schools, churches, and hostels. France, which claimed similar rights in relation to the Roman Catholic community, institutions, and holy places, reinstituted the Roman

Catholic patriarchate in Jerusalem in 1847. The status of France as the protector of Roman Catholicism in Turkey was officially confirmed in Article 62 of the Treaty of the Congress of Berlin (1878). This status, however, aroused increasing rivalry on the part of other Catholic countries. In 1841 the Protestant missions of England and Prussia established a joint bishopric in Jerusalem, which the Germans stopped supporting in 1881.

The activities of the Protestant powers within the Ottoman Empire were conducted under less favorable conditions than those of Russia and France since the former had no millets in Erez Israel to "adopt" for religious reasons. Thus, during the Turkish-Egyptian War of 1839-41, Britain became the "defender" of the Jewish and Druze communities in Erez Israel, as a sort of countermove to France's identification with the Maronite community. One of the causes for the outbreak of the Crimean War (1853-56) was the conflicting claims of France and Russia to the guardianship of the holy places. After 1868 the German Templer movement established settlements in Jaffa, Sarona, Haifa, and Jerusalem, reaching over 500 in the course of time. The Templer settlements, which continued to expand, later supplied William II with the means of political penetration. Of the U.S. groups of Millennarians who lived in Artas (near Bethlehem) in 1852, in Jaffa in 1866/67, and in Jerusalem in 1881, only the last remained. This was called the "American Colony," although after 1896 it comprised more Swedes than American subjects. Archaeological investigation of the biblical period expanded. A U.S. naval unit headed by Lt. W. F. Lynch explored the Jordan and the Dead Sea. The Palestine Exploration Fund, established in 1865, completed a survey map of the area west of the Jordan, before embarking on the exploration of ancient sites. The American Palestine Exploration Society, which was short-lived (1870–81), concentrated on eastern Transjordan.

With the appearance of steam boats in the Middle East in the 1830s, regular communications between Erez Israel and Europe were established for the first time. In 1837 Austria and France gained licenses to operate postal services in the Asian provinces of Turkey. The Turkish-Tatar postal messengers, who traveled between Constantinople and the capitals of the provinces at approximately six-week intervals, were finally replaced in the mid-19th century by a Turkish service which, although more frequent, was no less confused. In 1865 telegraphic communications were set up in Jerusalem and other important towns of Erez Israel with the capital of the empire and Europe. Three years later the provincial administration completed the first road in Erez Israel (between Jerusalem and Jaffa) that was suitable for wheeled carriages. Improvements in transportation and communications led to an increase in the number of pilgrims and tourists, who brought new sources of income. By 1880 the population of Erez Israel had increased appreciably, reaching 450,000, of which 24,000 were Jews and 45,000 were Christians. Jerusalem, which had expanded beyond the walls of the Old City following the Crimean War, became the largest town in the country. Its population was estimated at least at 25,000, more than half of whom were Jews.

THE JEWISH POPULATION. In the history of the Jews of Erez Israel there is a distinct contrast between the periods 1800–40 and 1841–80. In the first 30 years of the 19th century the corruption of Ottoman rule reached heights of perversion. The eight years of the Egyptian conquest (1832–40) were a kind of transition period. After 1840 the Jews were drawn into international conflicts connected with the Eastern problem, but began to enjoy the protection of Western powers. Their numbers increased considerably, as did their economic and cultural influence, although Napoleon's campaign in Egypt and Erez Israel and his call to Eastern Jewry to come to his aid and thus pave the way for the political renaissance of Erez Israel—if such a proclamation was indeed made—made little impression on the Jews of the country. The restraining influence of Hayyim Salim Farhi, scion of an ancient Jewish family from Damascus, was felt in the country for 20 years. As the financial official and general adviser of Aḥmad al-Jazzār and his successors in the pashalic of Damascus, Farḥi somewhat eased the lives of not only the Jews, but the Muslims and Christians as well. After 20 years of rule he was murdered in 1820 by Abdallah Pasha, whom Farḥi had aided in his rise to the status of governor.

At that time most of the Jews of the country lived in the four holy cities: Jerusalem, Safed, Tiberias, and Hebron. Although they were sustained by funds from the *halukkah*, they labored under a heavy yoke of taxes imposed by the Turkish officials. Thus J. Conder wrote in 1831: "The extortions and oppressions were so numerous that it was said of the Jews that they had to pay for the very air they breathed." Nevertheless the population continued to increase, especially as a result of immigration from Europe. This flow increased with the introduction of steamboat transportation on the Odessa-Jaffa and other routes. The age-old attraction of Erez Israel, which was then felt especially among Eastern European Hasidim, brought a constant stream of ḥasidic settlers to Jerusalem and other holy cities. The first Ashkenazi community was established in Hebron in 1820 by Ḥabad Ḥasidim influenced by Ber, the son of R. Shneur Zalman of Lyady. Jaffa, which had been rebuilt by the Turks in 1810–20, attracted a considerable number of Jews from 1830 on. The development of the community, interrupted by the bad earthquake of 1837, was renewed after 1839 and especially after the establishment of the rabbinate in 1841. Most of the Jaffa Jews came from North Africa; in 1857 there were only three Ashkenazi families there. In 1874 their number increased to 20, and the total Jewish population of Jaffa numbered 500. Safed, which competed with Jerusalem for spiritual hegemony, suffered greatly in the earthquake of 1837, when some 2,000 Jews lost their lives and never regained its former position of leadership. The first Hebrew printing press in Erez Israel, which was established there in 1831, moved to Jerusalem

after nine years.

Letter of recommendation for Israel Halevi, emissary from Hebron to the Italian community of Carpi, 1811. Jerusalem, C.A.H.J.P.

Egyptian rule did not greatly ease the burden of taxes, but Muhammad Ali's efforts to institute Western methods opened the way for vital internal and external changes. Although the promises in the sultan's decree of 1839 to grant equal rights to members of the three faiths—Jewish, Christian, and Muslim—were never fulfilled, there was a considerable improvement in the situation of the Jews. The high-flown proclamations of the Turks, such as that of 1841 ("Muslims, Christians, Israelites, you are all the subjects of one ruler, you are all the sons of one father"), also had some influence on the status of the oppressed minorities. Of similar significance was the fact that the Western powers, in their struggle for the hegemony of the Middle East, displayed a certain interest in the Jews of Erez Israel. According to the system of Capitulations (agreement granting special rights to foreign powers in Turkey), the Western consuls in the country "protected" the interests of their citizens. Great Britain, and often Russia as well, became (for the reasons mentioned above) the patrons of the Jews of Erez Israel. Britain intervened on behalf of Jews who were Turkish subjects, but primarily on behalf of Jews from European countries when their own consuls refused to provide assistance. This was so not only during dramatic events, such as the Damascus Affair [7] of 1840 and the Christian massacre in Syria in 1860, but even under normal conditions. The British government even ventured, in connection with the Damascus Affair, to suggest that the sultan allow the Jews of the "ra'āyā" class (non-Muslim subjects of the sultan) to address their complaints against local Turkish authorities to him through the mediation of the British consuls.

Although this suggestion was rejected by the Turks, the British consular authorities found opportunities to intervene on behalf of the Jews. In 1849 R. Isaiah Bardaki, the leader of the Russian Jews of Jerusalem, requested that the British consul in Jerusalem grant protection to Jews who had become stateless as a result of discriminatory legislation in Russia. Thirty years later Russia relented in its hostile attitude toward the Jews of Erez Israel and even granted

[7] Damascus Affair: Case in which several Jews were accused of a ritual murder. International rivalries prevented the truth being established but eventually the accused were cleared.

them some protection, while persecuting the Jews in Russia itself. Laurence Oliphant reflected: "Had Russia encouraged Jewish immigration to Erez Israel and protected the immigrants, she could have had an excellent pretext for political interference in the country" (*Haifa* (1887), 49).

The idea of establishing a Jewish state or, at least, an autonomous Jewish settlement under supreme Ottoman control became a subject for serious discussion. In 1839, during the second of his visits in Erez Israel, Sir Moses Montefiore opened negotiations with Muhammad Ali to gain a charter for Jewish settlement in Erez Israel in return for a large loan to Egypt. These negotiations failed, however, because of the downfall of Muhammad Ali, in 1841. The idea of establishing a Jewish buffer state between Egypt and Turkey, however, gained supporters during the conflict between the two powers. The first who advocated this solution was Rev. Wilson Filson Marsh (see *Der Orient* (1840), no. 48, 372–3). A detailed plan for Jewish settlement was advanced at that time by Abraham Benisch, a Bohemian Jew who became editor of the London *Jewish Chronicle*. The memorandum he composed on the question was made available to the Foreign Office by the British consul in Jerusalem, William Young, and gained the support of Montefiore and other British Jewish leaders. Similar plans, though less detailed, were offered at that time on the European continent. The idea was supported by English notables such as Col. Charles Henry Churchill (1840–56), Col. George Gawler (1845), Laurence Oliphant (1879), and others.

Relations between Jews and non-Jews in Erez Israel were not at all amicable. Religious disputes were always common and the Jews were in a state of conflict with the missionaries, who were prohibited by law to convert Muslims, although the London missionary society for the dissemination of Christianity among Jews usually fought for the rights of Jews in Erez Israel. This group was supported by British consuls such as James Finn, whose autobiographical account, *Stirring Times* (1878), is an important source of information. Although contemporaries often remarked that missionary progress in Ereẓ Israel was slow, Ludwig August Frankel, who visited Jerusalem in 1856, found 134 converts there. According to the estimation of Goodrich-Freer, no less than 523 Jews converted in 1839–96, and the expenses for baptizing one Jew amounted to £1,000. In their battle against the missionaries, the Jews often came into conflict with the British and other consuls.

There were also serious internal conflicts within the Jewish community itself. Recipients of *ḥalukkah* funds often complained about discrimination, real or imagined, in their treatment by the *ḥalukkah* officials. The Jews of Germany and Holland were the first to establish a separate *kolel* for themselves, known as "Kolel Hod" (Holland-Deutschland), which served as a model for *kolelim* established by other factions of the community. By the beginning of the 20th century, there were 30 such *kolelim*. This division aroused internal controversies and also damaged the work of the *meshullaḥim*, the emissaries who were sent to collect money for the welfare funds.

Although the authority of the Ashkenazi rabbis was solid within their own community, they did not enjoy the legal recognition accorded the Sephardi *ḥakham bashi*, as most of the Ashkenazim were foreign subjects. The first Sephardi chief rabbis, including Solomon Moses Suzin (in the time of Muhammad Ali), Jonah Moses Navon (1836–40), and Judah Navon (1840–41), lacked governmental recognition, but from the time of Ḥayyim Abraham Gagin (1842–48), the *ḥakham bashi* received an official status by governmental appointment, or rather by the sultan's confirmation of his election by the Sephardi community of Jerusalem.

The number of Ashkenazim gradually exceeded the Sephardim in most of the communities of Ereẓ Israel, and while the old settlements grew from decade to decade, new ones were established. Nablus, the old center of Samaritanism, began to attract Jews when it became a trading center. In 1864 there were in Nablus about 100

Jews, 150 Samaritans, 600 Christians, and 9,400 Muslims. According to Ludwig August Frankl, there were about 100 Jews in the renewed community of Haifa in 1856. The influence of the Jews grew, especially in Jerusalem, which came to have a Jewish majority. When the Old City could no longer contain them, the Jews set up the first suburb outside the walls in 1861, and during the 25 succeeding years they established seven additional quarters, including Naḥalat Shiva (1869) and Me'ah She'arim (1872), which became the nucleus of the New City.

The economic situation of the Jews of Ereẓ Israel remained generally unchanged, despite several attempts to settle some Jews on the land and teach them useful trades. In 1839 and again in 1849 Montefiore responded to requests by the Jews of Ereẓ Israel to implement far-reaching plans to settle Jews on the land. Montefiore, together with the Rothschilds of Paris, who worked mainly through their adviser, Albert Cohen, and other European philanthropists, helped to establish a Jewish hospital in Jerusalem (1854) and supported the Laemel school, founded by Frankl in 1856 to teach Jews professions and to remove Jewish children from the mission schools. Since the teaching methods of this school were new from several points of view, and since European languages were also taught there, it met with the fierce opposition of extreme Ashkenazi Orthodox Jews and their supporters in the Diaspora, so that Frankl had to turn over the administration of the school to Sephardim, who were more tolerant.

The process of the Jewish community's transformation into a productive factor did not cease, but rather increased in pace. Even the missionaries thought of establishing an agricultural settlement for apostate Jews. In 1861 the first land purchase for agricultural purposes in modern times was made at Moẓa. Finally, in 1870, the French Jewish Organization, Alliance Israélite Universelle established the Mikveh Israel agricultural school. Agricultural settlements were established at Moẓa (1873) and Petaḥ Tikvah (1878), which, although they were abandoned after a short time, opened the way for future development and were reestablished later. In 1881 the U.S. consul wrote that about 1,000 Jews in Ereẓ Israel earned their livings through agricultural labor, and therefore many of them were no longer "paupers and beggars." On the other hand, the appearance of the first Hebrew journals—*Ha-Levanon* in 1863 and *Havaẓẓelet* in 1870—attested the expansion of the cultural horizons. In this way the population became ready to open its gates to new immigrants, ways of life, and ideas, which were brought to Ereẓ Israel by the Ḥibbat Zion movement.

The Land of Israel in International Affairs, up to 1880. After the Crusades, the European powers attached no great significance to the Land of Israel, and its conquest by the Ottoman Turks reduced its importance still further. The name "Palestine" had only a historical, archaeological, or antiquarian connotation; it did not denote any clearly defined political entity, or even a separate administrative subdivision of the Ottoman Empire. The country was part of Turkey; sometimes it was regarded as a part of Syria. As far as international affairs were concerned, it was no more than a remote territory, a bone of contention among unruly pashas and a prey to Bedouin banditry. Although certain European commercial interests, such as the Levant Company, did pay some attention to it at one period, their operations were designated to extend to the Ottoman Empire as a whole, and Palestine did not play a special role in their plans; nor has this competition been shown to have had any appreciable effect on the policies of the powers.

NAPOLEON'S CAMPAIGN. This situation underwent a drastic change when Napoleon made his surprising move to land an expeditionary force in the East and succeeded in conquering Egypt (1798; see above), followed by an invasion of Palestine which, after initial success, was frustrated by the failure of his efforts to take Acre. The reasons that presumably prompted Napoleon to undertake this campaign are of great significance, for they were the same that were henceforth to induce all major European powers to vie with one another for influence in the area.

The predominant consideration was the territory's geographical position at the crossroads of the three commercial and strategic routes of the modern world, which link the Atlantic Ocean and Mediterranean Sea with the Indian and Pacific Oceans, the Mediterranean with the Persian Gulf, and the Eurasian continent with Africa. When Ottoman rule in Asia entered into a decline at the end of the 18th century, every power felt obliged to deny exclusive control of the crossroads to any of its rivals. For Napoleon, the country was of equal importance for both defense and attack: its conquest would enable him to defend Egypt against Anglo-Turkish attempts to wrest it from his hands and provide him with a springboard for campaigns directed at Anatolia and Constantinople, Iraq, the Persian Gulf, and India.

Another factor that was to enter into the considerations of every power planning to replace the Ottoman Empire in the control of the area was the presence of ethnic and religious minorities that would presumably be prepared to accept the protection of a European power. At the time of Napoleon's campaign in Palestine, the idea of establishing a Jewish state in the area was mooted in Paris and during the siege of Acre Napoleon was said to have issued a proclamation to the Jews, apostrophizing them as "rightful heirs of Palestine" and calling upon them "to take over that which had been conquered" (some scholars, however, regard the proclamation as apocryphal). Napoleon was known to have had plans for fomenting unrest among the Druze and Maronites in the north and exploiting the existence of Christian and Muslim holy places for his purposes.

MUHAMMAD ALI'S CAMPAIGNS. For these and other reasons the future of Palestine became an issue of general European importance during the wars conducted by Muhammad Ali, an ally of France, who sought to base his rule in Egypt on the innovations introduced by the Napoleonic conquest. In order to ward off a possible direct 247 attack by the Ottoman forces, and as a first step toward the creation of an Arab empire that would include Syria, Iraq, and the Muslim holy places in Hejaz, he dispatched Ibrahim, his stepson, to Palestine and Syria. In 1832–33 Ibrahim overran both territories, and for the next seven years the area remained in the center of European political interest, especially as a result of Turkey's repeated attempts to reconquer it.

It was at this point that Britain (under Lord Palmerston) and, to a lesser degree, Austria decided that it was in their interest to shore up the sultan's tottering power. From their point of view, it was a timely decision, for otherwise there was a danger of Russian hegemony over the Ottoman Empire or French control of the Mediterranean. Furthermore, by this time Syria and Palestine had become a factor in their own right in the policy pursued by the powers. The growing significance of modern means of transportation—steamships and railroads—lent significance to an area that served as a crossroads and control of which would facilitate the construction of interoceanic canals and intercontinental railroads. This aspect was already recognized by Palmerston. The possession of Palestine would secure control of the Suez route, which was in use even in those pre-canal days (the early steamers preferred to cruise along the Mediterranean coast rather than risk the stormy passage around the Cape of Good Hope, transferring their cargoes overland across the Suez Isthmus to be shipped to their destination through the Red Sea and the Indian Ocean—the traditional route since early historical times). The eastern Mediterranean coast was also regarded as the proper place for the terminal of a land route—a railroad leading to Iraq and the Persian Gulf; in fact, the vision of such a route was to have an ever-increasing effect upon the imperialist policies of Britain and France.

From the French point of view, these considerations required the extension of Muhammad Ali's domain in Syria as far north as possible; the British, on the other hand, were interested in pushing him back as much as

248

possible toward the Nile Valley and denying him access to the main lines of communication to the Persian Gulf. In 1840, when Muhammad Ali, with French support, rejected a demand that his rule be restricted to Palestine, the other powers, led by Britain, intervened by force of arms and compelled him to give up Palestine as well as restrict himself to Egypt.

PROTECTIVE· RIGHTS. In the following two decades, Palestine retained a place in international affairs due to its importance for those powers that wanted the right to protect one or the other of the religious minorities in the decaying Ottoman Empire. Russia had long had such rights, confirmed in the Kutchuk-Kainarji Treaty of 1774 (Article 7), over Orthodox Christians in Turkey and the Orthodox Christian holy places in Palestine; France's rights to protect the Catholics (Latins) and their holy places, which had their roots in the age of the Crusades, were confirmed by Capitulations. Britain and, to some extent, Prussia sought to counter these advantages by extending their protection to the insignificant Protestant minority (which accounts for the creation of the Jerusalem bishopric in 1841). Palmerston and his successors also sought to extend unofficial British protection to the Jewish minority. Throughout the 1840s and 1850s, fierce competition ensued among the powers to improve their position as protective powers. The struggle was carried out mainly through their consular representatives in Jerusalem, which was an ideal arena in which to press their claims; their real purpose, of course, was to give the powers exercising these rights a hold on the Ottoman Empire that they could exploit whenever its collapse would lead to the ultimate disposition of its territories. It will be recalled that the contradictory claims of Russia and France with regard to the holy places were the direct cause of the outbreak of the Crimean War.

THE STRUGGLE OVER COMMUNICATIONS. Developments in Egypt between 1860 and 1890 again put the emphasis on the control of communications. The Suez Canal was opened in 1869 and France's hegemony in Cairo assured her control of the new waterway. This was a situation that the British felt they could not tolerate; finally, they took Egypt by military conquest, ousting the French and maintaining their position for many decades to come. The two powers now switched roles: it was Britain that now aspired to extend its influence to the north, by way of Palestine and southern Syria, while France, which had struck roots in the Lebanon and in central and northern Syria, sought to confine British influence to Egypt.

CHRONOLOGICAL TABLE

c. 17th century: The Patriarchs
c. 1250 Conquest of Canaan under Joshua
c. 1200 Philistines settle in Erez Israel
c. 1125 Deborah
c. 1100 Gideon
c. 1050 Fall of Shiloh; Samuel
c. 1020–1004 Saul
 1004–965 David
 965–928 Solomon

Judah	Israel
928–911 Rehoboam	928–907 Jeroboam I
911–908 Abijah	907–906 Nadab
908–867 Asa	906–883 Baasha
	883–882 Elah
	882 Zimri
	882–71 Omri
867–46 Jehoshaphat	871–852 Ahab Elijah
	852–51 Ahaziah
846–43 Jehoram	851–42 Jehoram
843–42 Ahaziah	842–14 Jehu
842–36 Athaliah	
836–798 Jehoash	
798–69 Amaziah	814–800 Jehoahaz
Amos	800–784 Jehoash
Hosea	
769–33 Uzziah	784–48 Jeroboam II

758–43 Jotham
(regent)
c. 740–c. 700 Prophecies of Isaiah
758–43 Ahaz
(regent)

733–27 Ahaz
727–698 Hezekiah

748–47 Zechariah
748–47 Shallum

747–37 Menahem
737–35 Pekahiah
735–33 Pekah
733–24 Hoshea
722 Samaria captured by Shalmaneser V
720 Sargon makes Samaria an Assyrian province Mass deportation of Israelites

701 Expedition of Sennacherib against Hezekiah
698–42 Manasseh
641–40 Amon
639–09 Josiah
609 Battle of Megiddo
627–c. 585 Prophecies of Jeremiah
609 Jehoahaz
608–598 Jehoiakim
597 Jehoiachin
597 Expedition of Nebuchadnezzar against Judah; Jehoiachin deported to Babylonia
595–86 Zedekiah
586 Destruction of Jerusalem; mass deportation to Babylonia
585? Murder of Gedaliah
538 First return under Sheshbazzar
c. 522 Zerubbabel governor
520–15 Temple rebuilt
458? Second return under Ezra
445 Walls of Jerusalem reconstructed under Nehemiah; Ezra reads the Torah.
428? Second return under Ezra
c. 408 Bagohi governor
398? Second return under Ezra
348 Artaxerxes III deports a number of Jews to Hyrcania

332 Alexander the Great conquers Erez Israel

301 Ptolemy I conquers Erez Israel

219–17 Antiochus III conquers most of Erez Israel

217 Ptolemy IV defeats Antiochus III in the battle of Rafah and recovers Erez Israel

198 Battle of Panias (Banias): Erez Israel passes to the Seleucids

175 Onias III deposed by Antiochus IV

175–71 Jason high priest

c. 172 Jerusalem becomes a *polis* (Antiochia)

171–167 Menelaus high priest

c. 170 Book of Ben Sira written

169 Antiochus IV plunders the Temple treasuries

168 Antiochus IV storms Jerusalem; gentiles settled on the Acra

167 Antiochus IV outlaws the practice of Judaism; profanation of the Temple; the rebellion of the Hasmoneans begins

166–60 Judah Maccabee, leader of the rebellion, victorious over several Syrian armies

164 Judah Maccabee captures Jerusalem and rededicates the Temple

162–59 Alcimus high priest

161 Judah Maccabee defeats Nicanor and reconquers Jerusalem; treaty between Judah and Rome

160 Judah Maccabee falls in battle against Bacchides; Jonathan assumes the leadership; guerilla warfare

157 Treaty between Bacchides and Jonathan; withdrawal of Seleucid garrisons, Jonathan enters Jerusalem

152 Jonathan high priest

142 Jonathan treacherously murdered by Tryphon

Simeon assumes leadership; Demetrius II recognizes the independence of Judea; renewal of treaty with Rome

141 Simeon captures the Acra

140 Great Assembly in Jerusalem confirms Simeon as ethnarch, high priest, and commander in chief

134 Simeon assassinated

134–104 John Hyrcanus

134 Treaty with Rome renewed

134–32 War with Antiochus VII; Jerusalem besieged; treaty between John Hyrcanus and Antiochus VII

Latter second century: First Book of Maccabees written

107 John Hyrcanus' sons capture Samaria

104–03 Judah Aristobulus

103–76 Alexander Yannai

76–67 Salome Alexandra

67–63 Civil war between Hyrcanus II and Aristobulus

63 Pompey decides in favor of Hyrcanus II. Temple Mount besieged and captured by Pompey

63–40 Hyrcanus II ethnarch and high priest. Judea loses its independence

56–55 Revolts of Alexander b. Aristobulus and Aristobulus

48 Caesar confirms Jewish privileges

40 Parthian invasion

40–37 Antigonus II (Mattathias)

37 Jerusalem captured by Herod

37–4 B.C.E. Herod

Shemaiah and Avtalion

19 Temple rebuilt

4 B.C.E.–6 C.E. Archelaus ethnarch

4 B.C.E –34 C.E. Herod Philip

4 B.C.E.–39 C.E. Herod Antipas

6C.E.–41 Judea, Samaria, and Idumea formed into a Roman province (Judaea) under a *praefectus*

Beginning of 1st cent., d. of Hillel

26–36 Pontius Pilate *praefectus*

30 Jesus crucified; d. of Shammai

37–41 Crisis caused by Caligula's insistence on being worshiped as deity

41–44 Agrippa I

66 Beginning of revolt against Rome

67 Vespasian conquers Galilee; the Zealots take over in Jerusalem

c. 70 Destruction of Qumran community

70 Siege of Jerusalem; destruction of the Temple

70 Sanhedrin established at Jabneh by Johanan b. Zakkai

73 Fall of Masada

c. 115 d. of Gamaliel II

c. 116–117 "war of Quietus"

132–35 Bar Kokhba war

254 135 Fall of Bethar; Aelia Capitolina established; Akiva executed

1244 Jerusalem captured by the Khwarizms

c. 1265 d. of Jehiel b. Joseph of Paris at Acre

1267 / 70 Naḥmanides in Erez Israel

1488—c. 1515 Obadiah di Bertinoro in Jerusalem

1516 Erez Israel conquered by the Turks

1538 Jacob Berab renews *semikhah* in Safed

1555 Joseph Caro's *Beit Yosef* published

c. 1561 Joseph Nasi leases Tiberias from the sultan

1564 Joseph Caro's Shulhan Arukh published

1569–72 Isaac Luria in Safed

1572 d. of Isaac Luria

1575 d. of Joseph Caro

1620 d. Ḥayyim Vital

1630 d. of Isaiah Horowitz

1700 Judah Ḥasid and his group arrive in Jerusalem

1742 Ḥayyim Attar and his group arrive in Jerusalem

c. 1751 d. of Moses Ḥagiz

1777 Menahem Mendel of Vitebsk and his group of Ḥasidim
     settle in Galilee

1799 Napoleon's campaign

1808–10 Disciples of Elijah Gaon settle in Erez Israel

1831 Erez Israel taken by Muhammad Ali

1837 Disastrous earthquake in Safed and Tiberias

1839 Citizenship to Turkish Jews

1840 Damascus blood libel: restoration of Turkish rule in Erez
     Israel

1852 Confirmation of "Status Quo" in Holy Places

1870 Mikveh Israel founded

1878 Petaḥ Tikvah founded; d. of Judah Alkalai

1881 Ben-Yehuda arrives in Erez Israel

1882 Beginning of First Aliyah (Bilu); Rishon le-Zion founded

GLOSSARY

Adar, twelfth month of the Jewish religious year, sixth of the civil, approximating to February–March.

Aggadah, name given to those sections of Talmud and Midrash containing homiletic expositions of the Bible, stories, legends, folklore, anecdotes, or maxims. In contradistinction to *halakhah.*

Aḥaronim, later rabbinic authorities. In contradistinction to *rishonim* ("early ones").

Aliyah, (1) being called to Reading of the Law in synagogue; (2) immigration to Ereẓ Israel; (3) one of the waves of immigration to Ereẓ Israel from the early 1880s.

Amidah, main prayer recited at all services; also known as *Shemoneh Esreh* and *Tefillah.*

Amora (pl. **amoraim**), title given to the Jewish scholars in Ereẓ Israel and Babylonia in the third to sixth centuries who were responsible for the *Gemara.*

Aravah (Arabah), rift valley between Dead Sea and Gulf of Elath.

Aravah, the willow; one of the "four species" used on Sukkot ("festival of Tabernacles") together with the *etrog, hadas,* and *lulav.*

Asarah be-Tevet, fast on the 10th of Tevet commemorating the commencement of the siege of Jerusalem by Nebuchadnezzar.

Ashkenazi (pl. **Ashkenazim**), German or West-, Central-, or East-European (Jew(s), as contrasted with Sephardi(m).

Av, fifth month of the Jewish religious year, eleventh of the civil, approximating to July–August.

Av bet din, vice-president of the supreme court *(bet din ha-gadol)* in Jerusalem during the Second Temple period; later, title given to communal rabbis as heads of the religious courts.

Bar, "son of . . ."; frequently appearing in personal names.

Battei Din, plural of Bet din.

Battei Midrash(ot), plural of Bet midrash.

Ben, "son of . . ."; frequently appearing in personal names.

Berakhah (pl. **berakhot**), benediction, blessing; formula of praise and thanksgiving.

Bet din, rabbinic court of law.

Bet ha-midrash, school for higher rabbinic learning; often attached to or serving as a synagogue.

Dayyan, member of rabbinic court.

Diaspora, Jews living in the "dispersion" outside Erez Israel; area of Jewish settlement outside Erez Israel.

Dunam, unit of land area (1,000 sq. m., c. $\frac{1}{4}$ acre), used in Israel.

Elul, sixth month of the Jewish religious calendar, 12th of the civil, precedes the High Holiday season in the fall.

Erez Israel, Land of Israel; Palestine.

Etrog, citron; one of the "four species" used on Sukkot together with the *lulav, hadas,* and *aravah.*

Exilarch, lay head of Jewish community in Babylonia and elsewhere.

Galut, "exile"; the condition of the Jewish people in dispersion.

Gaon (pl. **geonim**), head of academy in post-talmudic period, especially in Babylonia.

Gaonate, office of gaon.

Gemara, traditions, discussions, and rulings of the *amoraim,* commenting on and supplementing the Mishnah, and forming part of the Babylonian and Palestinian Talmuds.

Genizah, depository for sacred books. The best known was discovered in the synagogue of Fostat (old Cairo).

Hadas, myrtle; one of the "four species" used on Sukkot together with the *etrog, lulav,* and *aravah.*

Hakham, title of rabbi of Sephardi congregation.

Hakham bashi, title in the 15th century and modern times of the chief rabbi in the Ottoman Empire, residing in Constantinople (Istanbul), also applied to principal rabbis in provincial towns.

Halakhah (pl. **halakhot**), an accepted decision in rabbinic law. Also refers to those parts of the Talmud concerned with legal matters. In contradistinction to *aggadah.*

Halukkah, system of financing the maintenance of Jewish communities in the holy cities of Erez Israel by collections made abroad, mainly in the pre-Zionist era.

Hanukkah, eight-day celebration commemorating the victory of Judah Maccabee over the Syrian king Antiochus Epiphanes and the subsequent rededication of the Temple.

258 **Hasid,** adherent of Hasidism.

Ḥasidism, (1) religious revivalist movement of popular mysticism among Jews of Germany in the Middle Ages; (2) religious movement founded by Israel ben Eliezer Ba'al Shem Tov in the first half of the 18th century.

Haskalah, "Enlightenment"; movement for spreading modern European culture among Jews c. 1750–1880. An adherent was termed *maskil*.

Ḥazzan, precentor who intones the liturgy and leads the prayers in synagogue; in earlier times a synagogue official.

Ḥerem, excommunication, imposed by rabbinical authorities for purposes of religious and/or communal discipline; originally, in biblical times, that which is separated from common use either because it was an abomination or because it was consecrated to God.

Ḥeshvan, see Marḥeshvan.

Ḥibbat Zion, see Ḥovevei Zion.

Ḥovevei Zion, federation of Ḥibbat Zion, early (pre-Herzl) Zionist movement in Russia.

Iyyar, eighth month of the Jewish religious year, second of the civil, approximating to April–May.

Kabbalah, the Jewish mystical tradition.

Kabbalist, student of Kabbalah.

Kahal, Jewish congregation; among Ashkenazim, *kehillah*.

Karaite, member of a Jewish sect originating in the eighth century which rejected rabbinic (Rabbanite) Judaism and accepted only Scripture as authoritative.

Kasher, ritually permissible food.

Kashrut, Jewish dietary laws.

Kefar, village; first part of name of many settlements in Israel.

Kiddush ha-Shem, term connoting martyrdom or act of strict integrity in support of Judaic principles.

Kislev, third month of the Jewish religious year, ninth of the civil, approximating to November–December.

Kolel, (1) community in Ereẓ Israel of persons from a particular country or locality, often supported by their fellow countrymen in the Diaspora; (2) institution for higher Torah study.

Lulav, palm branch; one of the "four species" used on Sukkot together with the *etrog, hadas,* and *aravah.*

Marḥeshvan, popularly called Ḥeshvan; second month of the Jewish religious year, eighth of the civil, approximating to October–November.

Marrano(s), descendant(s) of Jew(s) in Spain and Portugal whose ancestors had been converted to Christianity under pressure but who secretly observed Jewish rituals.

Masorah, body of traditions regarding the correct spelling, writing, and reading of the Hebrew Bible.

Masorete, scholar of the masoretic tradition.

Masoretic, in accordance with the masorah.

Menorah, candelabrum; seven-branched oil lamp used in the Tabernacle and Temple; also eight-branched candelabrum used on Ḥanukkah.

Meshullaḥ, emissary sent to conduct propaganda or raise funds for rabbinical academies or charitable institutions.

Midrash, method of interpreting Scripture to elucidate legal points *(Midrash Halakhah)* or to bring out lessons by stories or homiletics *(Midrash Aggadah)*. Also the name for a collection of such rabbinic interpretations.

Mishnah, earliest codification of Jewish Oral Law.

Mitzvah, biblical or rabbinic injunction; applied also to good or charitable deeds.

Nagid (pl. **negidim**), title applied in Muslim (and some Christian) countries in the Middle Ages to a leader recognized by the state as head of the Jewish community.

Nasi (pl. **nesi'im**), talmudic term for president of the Sanhedrin, who was also the spiritual head and, later, political representative of the Jewish people; from second century a descendant of Hillel recognized by the Roman authorities as patriarch of the Jews. Now applied to the president of the State of Israel.

Negev, the southern, mostly arid, area of Israel.

Nisan, first month of the Jewish religious year, seventh of the civil, approximating to March–April.

Rabban, honorific title higher than that of rabbi, applied to heads of the Sanhedrin in mishnaic times.

Rabbanite, adherent of rabbinic Judaism. In contradistinction to Karaite.

Rishonim, older rabbinical authorities. Distinguished from later authorities *(aḥaronim)*.

Sanhedrin, the assembly of ordained scholars which functioned both as a supreme court and as a legislature before 70 C.E.

Semikhah, ordination conferring the title "rabbi" and permission to give decisions in matters of ritual and law.

Sephardi (pl. **Sephardim**), Jew(s) of Spain and Portugal and their descendants, wherever resident; contrasted with Ashkenazi(m).

Shabbatean, adherent of the pseudo-messiah Shabbetai Zevi (17th century).

Shali'ah (pl. **shelihim**), in Jewish law, messenger, agent; in modern times, an emissary from Erez Israel to Jewish communities or organizations abroad for the purpose of fund-raising, organizing pioneer immigrants, education, etc.

Shavuot, Pentecost; Festival of Weeks; second of the three annual pilgrim festivals, commemorating the receiving of the Torah at Mt. Sinai.

Shehitah, ritual slaughtering of animals.

Shekhinah, Divine Presence.

Sheluhei Erez Israel (or **shadarim**), emissaries from Erez Israel.

Shemittah, Sabbatical year.

Shephelah, southern part of the coastal plain of Erez Israel.

Shevat, eleventh month of the Jewish religious year, fifth of the civil, approximating to January–February.

Shofar, horn of the ram (or any other ritually clean animal excepting the cow) sounded for the memorial blowing on Rosh Ha-Shanah, and other occasions.

Shulhan Arukh, Joseph Caro's code of Jewish law in four parts:
> *Orah Hayyim,* laws relating to prayers, Sabbath, festivals, and fasts;
> *Yoreh De'ah,* dietary laws, etc;
> *Even ha-Ezer,* laws dealing with women, marriage, etc;
> *Hoshen Mishpat,* civil, criminal law, court procedure, etc.

Sivan, third month of the Jewish religious year, ninth of the civil, approximating to June–July.

Sukkah, booth or tabernacle erected for Sukkot when, for seven days, religious Jews "dwell" or at least eat in the *sukkah* (Lev. 23:42).

Sukkot, festival of Tabernacles; last of the three pilgrim festivals, beginning on the 15th of Tishri.

Takkanah (pl. **takkanot**), regulation supplementing the Law of the Torah; regulations governing the internal life of communities and congregations.

Talmud, "teaching"; compendium of discussions on the Mishnah by generations of scholars and jurists in many academies over a period of several centuries. The Jerusalem (or Palestinian) Talmud mainly contained the discussions of the Palestinian sages. The Babylonian Talmud incorporates the parallel discussion in the Babylonian academies.

Tammuz, fourth month of the Jewish religious year, tenth of the 261 civil, approximating to June–July.

Tanna (pl. **tannaim**), rabbinic teacher of mishnaic period.

Tevet, tenth month of the Jewish religious year, fourth of the civil, approximating to December–January.

Tishah be-Av, Ninth of Av, fast day commemorating the destruction of the First and Second Temples.

Tishri, seventh month of the Jewish religious year, first of the civil, approximating to September–October.

Torah, Pentateuch or the Pentateuchal scroll for reading in synagogue; entire body of traditional Jewish teaching and literature.

Tosafist, talmudic glossator, mainly French (12th–14th centuries), bringing additions to the commentary by Rashi.

Waqf (Ar.), (1) a Muslim charitable pious foundation; (2) state lands and other property passed to the Muslim community for public welfare.

ABBREVIATIONS

Abramson, Merkazim	S. Abramson, *Ba-Merkazim u-va-Tefuẓot bi-Tekufat ha-Ge'onim* (1965).
Ar.	*Arakhin* (talmudic tractate)
Avot	*Avot* (talmudic tractate)
Av. Zar.	*Avodah Zarah* (talmudic tractate)
BB	*Bava Batra* (talmudic tractate)
B.C.E.	Before Common Era (B.C.)
Bek.	*Bekhorot* (talmudic tractate)
Ber.	*Berakhot* (talmudic tractate)
Beẓah	*Beẓah* (talmudic tractate)
Bik.	*Bikkurim* (talmudic tractate)
C.E.	Common Era (A.D.)
I (or II) Chron.	Chronicles, book I and II (Bible)
Cowley, Aramaic	A. Cowley, *Aramaic Papyri of the Fifth Century B.C.* (1923)
Dan.	Daniel (Bible)
Dem.	*Demai* (talmudic tractate)
Deut.	Deuteronomy (Bible)
Deut. R.	*Deuteronomy Rabbah* (Midrash)
Eccles.	Ecclesiastes (Bible)
Eccles. R.	*Ecclesiastes Rabbah* (Midrash)
Er.	*Eruvin* (talmudic tractate)
Esth.	Esther (Bible)
Est. R.	*Esther Rabbah* (Midrash)
Ex.	Exodus (Bible)
Ex. R.	*Exodus Rabbah* (Midrash)
Ezek.	Ezekiel (Bible)
Ezra	Ezra (Bible)
Gen.	Genesis (Bible)
Gen. R.	*Genesis Rabbah* (Midrash)
Ger.	*Gerim* (post-talmudic tractate)
Git.	*Gittin* (talmudic tractate)

Hab.	Habakkuk (Bible)
Ḥag.	*Ḥagigah* (talmudic tractate)
Haggai	Haggai (Bible)
Ḥal.	*Ḥallah* (talmud tractate)
Hor.	*Horayot* (talmudic tractate)
Hos.	Hosea (Bible)
Ḥul.	*Ḥullin* (talmudic tractate)
Isa.	Isaiah (Bible)
Jer.	Jeremiah (Bible)
Job	Job (Bible)
Joel	Joel (Bible)
Jos., Ant.	Josephus, *Jewish Antiquities* (Loeb Classics ed.)
Jos., Apion	Josephus, *Against Apion* (Loeb Classics ed.)
Josh.	Joshua (Bible)
Jos., Wars	Josephus, *The Jewish Wars* (Loeb Classics ed.)
Judg.	Judges (Bible)
Ker.	*Keritot* (talmudic tractate)
Ket.	*Ketubbot* (talmudic tractate)
Kid.	*Kiddushin* (talmudic tractate)
Kil.	*Kilayim* (talmudic tractate (TJ))
Lam.	Lamentations (Bible)
Lam. R.	*Lamentations Rabbah* (Midrash)
Lev.	Leviticus (Bible)
Lev. R.	*Leviticus Rabbah* (Midrash)
Ma'as	*Ma'aserot* (talmudic tractate)
Ma'as. Sh.	*Ma'aser Sheni* (talmudic tractate)
Mak.	*Makkot* (talmudic tractate)
Mal.	Malachi (Bible)
Mann, Egypt	J. Mann, *Jews in Egypt and in Palestine under the Fatimid Caliphs,* 2 vols. (1920–22)
Mann, Texts	J. Mann, *Texts and Studies,* 2 vols. (1931–35)
Meg.	*Megillah* (talmudic tractate)
Men.	*Menahot* (talmudic tractate)
Mid. Tan.	*Midrash Tanna'im* on Deuteronomy
MK	*Mo'ed Katan* (talmudic tractate)
Nah.	Nahum (Bible)
Naz.	*Nazir* (talmudic tractate)
Ned.	*Nedarim* (talmudic tractate)
Neh.	Nehemiah (Bible)
Nid.	*Niddah* (talmudic tractate)
Num.	Numbers (Bible)

Num. R.	*Numbers Rabbah* (Midrash)
Obad.	Obadiah (Bible)
Or.	*Orlah* (talmudic tractate)
Or. Sibyll	Sibylline Oracles (Pseudepigrapha)
Pe'ah	*Pe'ah* (talmudic tractate)
Pes.	*Pesaḥim* (talmudic tractate)
Prov.	Proverbs (Bible)
Ps.	Psalms (Bible)
RH	*Rosh Ha-Shanah* (talmudic tractate)
Ruth	Ruth (Bible)
Ruth R.	*Ruth Rabbah* (Midrash)
I and II Sam.	Samuel, books I and II (Bible)
Sanh.	*Sanhedrin* (talmudic tractate)
Shab.	*Shabbat* (talmudic tractate)
Shek.	*Shekalim* (talmudic tractate)
Shev.	*Shevi'it* (talmudic tractate)
Shevu.	*Shevu'ot* (talmudic tractate)
Sifra	*Sifra* on Leviticus
Song	Song of Songs (Bible)
Song. R.	*Song of Songs Rabbah* (Midrash)
Sot.	*Sotah* (talmudic tractate)
Suk.	*Sukkah* (talmudic tractate)
Ta'an.	*Ta'anit* (talmudic tractate)
TB	Babylonian Talmud or Talmud Bavli
Ter.	*Terumah* (talmudic tractate)
TJ	Jerusalem Talmud or Talmud Yerushalmi
Yev.	*Yevamot* (talmudic tractate)
Yoma	*Yoma* (talmudic tractate)
Zech.	Zechariah (Bible)
Zeph.	Zephaniah (Bible)
Zev.	*Zevaḥim* (talmudic tractate)

BIBLIOGRAPHY

Z. Frankel, *Mevo ha-Yerushalmi* (1870; repr. 1967).

W. Bacher, *Agada der Palaestinensischen Amoraeer* (Heb. ed. *Aggadat Amora'ei Erez Yisrael*), 2 vols. (1892–99).

idem, *Agada der Tannaiten* (Heb. ed. *Aggadot ha-Tanna'im*), vol. 1, pt. 1 and 2 (1903); vol. 2 (1890).

E. Schuerer, *Geschichte des juedischen Volkes im Zeitalter Jesu Christi*, 3 vols. and index vol. (1901–11[4]).

I. H. Weiss, *Dor, Dor ve-Doreshav*, 2–3 (1904[4]).

H. Graetz, *Geschichte der Juden*, 4 (1908[4]).

J. Juster, *Les Juifs dans l'Empire Romain*, 2 vols. (1914).

R. Hartmann, *Palaestina unter den Arabern*, 632–1516 (1915).

N. Sokolow, *History of Zionism* (1918).

J. Mann, *Jews in Egypt and in Palestine under the Fatimid Caliphs*, 2 vols. (1920–22).

R. Kittel, *Geschichte des Volkes Israel*, 3 vols. (1922–28).

Z. Frankel, *Darkhei ha-Mishnah* (1923[2]; repr. 1959[2]).

M. Gaudefroy-Demombynes, *La Syrie à l'époque des Mamlouks d'après les auteurs arabes* (1923).

B. Z. Dinur, in: *Zion (Me'asef)*, 2 (1927), 38–66.

M. Noth, *Das System der zwoelf Staemme Israels* (1930).

H. T. Olmstead, *History of Palestine and Syria* (1931; repr. 1965).

J. de Haas, *History of Palestine . . . .* (1934).

M. Assaf, *Toledot ah-Aravim be-Erez Yisrael*, 1 (1935), Arab period; 2 (1941), Mamluk period.

S. Klein, *Toledot ha-Yishuv ha-Yehudi be-Erez Yisrael* (1935).

idem, *Erez Yehudah* (1939), 108ff.

idem, *Erez ha-Galil* (1946), 41ff.

A. Revusky, *Jews in Palestine* (1936).

Y. Kaufmann, *Toledot ha-Emunah ha-Yisre'elit*, 4 vols. (1937–57).

S. Assaf and L. A. Meyer, *Sefer ha-Yishuv*, 2 (1942).

E. Ashtor (Strauss), *Toledot ha-Yehudim be-Mizrayim ve-Suryah Tahat Shilton ha-Mamlukim*, 3 vols. (1944–70).

S. Lieberman, in: *Jewish Quarterly Review*, 3 (1945/46), 329–79.

J. Prawer, *Mamlekhet Yerushalayyim ha-Zalvanit* (1946).

idem, in: *Zion*, 11 (1946), 38–82..

M. Avi-Yonah, *Bi-Ymei Roma u-Bizantiyyon* (1946).

S. Yevin, *Milḥemet Bar Kokhba* (1946).

J. W. Parkes, *A History of Palestine from 135 A.D. to Modern Times* (1949).

B. Klar, in: S. Yeivin and H. Z. Hirschberg (eds.), *Erez Kinnarot* (1951), 90–117.

F. M. Abel, *Histoire de la Palestine*, 2 (1952).

S. W. Baron, *Social and Religious History of the Jews*, (1952).

idem, in: *Jewish Social Studies*, 2 (1940), 179–208.

idem, in: *Jewish Studies in Memory of George A. Kohut* (1935), 72–85.

H. Orlinsky, *Ancient Israel* (1954).

M. Noth, *History of Israel* (1958).

Y. Guttmann, *ha-Sifrut ha-Yehudit ha-Hellenistit*, 2 vols. (1958–63).

G. Alon, *Toledot ha-Yehudim be-Erez Yisrael bi-Tekufat ha-Mishnah ve-ha-Talmud*, 1 (1958³), 2 (1961²).

idem, *Meḥkarim be-Toledot Yisrael bi-Ymei Bayit Sheni u-vi-Tekufat ha-Mishnah ve-ha-Talmud*, 1 (1958³), 2 (1961²).

B. Dinur (Dinaburg), *Yisrael ba-Golah*, 2 vols. in 7 (1959–68).

Z. Ankori, *Karaites in Byzantium* (1959), 3–25.

J. Pedersen, *Israel, Its Life and Culture*, 4 vols. (1959²).

J. Bright, *A History of Israel* (1959).

V. Tcherikover, *Hellenistic Civilization and the Jews* (1959).

Y. Kaufmann, *The Religion of Israel* (1960).

I. Ben-Zvi, *Eretz Israel under Ottoman Rule* (1960; offprint from L. Finkelstein (ed.), *The Jews*, vol. 1).

R. de Vaux, *Ancient Israel; its Life and Institutions* (1961, paperback 1965).

S. Safrai, in: *Zion*, 27 (1962), 216–22.

M. Avi-Yonah, *Geschichte der Juden im Zeitalter des Talmuds* (1962).

idem, *The Holy Land from the Persian to the Arab Conquest* (1966).

J. Prawer, *Toledot Mamlekhet ha-Zalbanim be-Erez Yisrael*, 2 vols. (1963).

Y. Yadin, *Ha-Mimẓa'im mi-Ymei Bar Kokhba bi-Me'arat ha-Iggerot* (1963).

B. Z. Gat, *Ha-Yishuv ha-Yehudi be-Erez Yisrael* . . . (1963).

267

H. W. Robinson, *The History of Israel, Its Facts and Factors* (1964²).

World History of the Jewish People (1964ff).

S. Abramson, *Ba-Merkazim u-va-Tefuẓot bi-Tekufat ha-Ge'onim* (1965), 25–33.

J. Neusner, *History of the Jews in Babylonia,* 5 vols. (1965–70).

D. Ben-Gurion, *The Jews in their Land* (1966).

Historiyah shel Am Yisrael, ser. 1, vol. 2, *Ha-Avot ve-ha-Shofetim* (1967).

H. H. Ben-Sasson (ed.), *Toledot Am Yisrael* (1969).

G. Kressel (ed.), *Netivot Ẓion vi-Yrushalayyim, Mivhar Maamarei A. M. Luncz* (1970).

INDEX

270

273